DON SPEARS

IN SEARCH OF GOODPUSSY
Living Without Love

Illustrated by Keith Douglas

Published by:
Spears Publishing
New Orleans, LA
(504) 723-9716
donspears@cox.net

Distributed by:
Professional Publishing House
1425 W. Manchester Ave. Ste B
Los Angeles, California 90047
323-750-3592
Email: professionalpublishinghouse@yahoo.com
www.Professionalpublishinghouse.com

Cover design: Donald Spears
Illustrator: Keith Douglas
Photography by: Peggy Stewart
Fiftieth printing April 2013
ISBN:978-0-9641496-0-1

"In Search of Goodpussy"
Is Everything
You Need To Know
About Today's Black Man,
And It Is
One Of The Most
Compelling and Important
Books You Will Ever Read

ACKNOWLEDGEMENTS

Many thanks to Earnestine Liggians for her research assistance, to Carla Baker for her production assistance, to Keith Douglas for his inspiring illustrations and to Elorial Monette for her technical assistance. My gratitude also to Juanita Spears, Julius Spears, Arnold Spears, Mary Castillo, Raymond Lewis, James Borders, Claire Creppel, C.J. Blache, Julie Sardie, W.J. and Gertrude LeBlanc, Fran Lawless, Cynthia Gaudin, Noah and Karin Hopkins, Brenda and Harry Williams, Kathleen Howard, Debra Roche, Kurt Pellerin, Peggy Stewart, Patrice Bordenave, Beverly Robinson, Sandra Gunner, Adillah Dawan, Ricky Searcy, Barry Mayeux, Velma Benjamin and to my son Patrick Shannon Spears.

Thanks also to Norbert Simmons, Carol Balthazar and to the hundreds of people whose cooperation and assistance was invaluable in providing information through interviews and surveys. Without their help this book would not have become a reality.

Don Spears

Love God, Believe in Yourself, Adapt

This book is dedicated to all the women in my life, those who have wrecked it, and those who have helped to rebuild it, but most especially to my loving mother Ruth, my grandmother Creasia, and my deceased father Julius.

Society would have us believe that black men's brains are in our penises and that we have no minds or hearts.

CONTENTS

PREFACE

Now that I've got your attention, why this book? In fact, why yet another book about men and women? One more would just be one too many. Well, maybe not. The reason for this particular book is rather easy to understand. I, for one, am tired of turning on Oprah, Geraldo, and Donahue only to come face-to-face with some middle class white housewife who has been married to the same middle-aged white man for the past 27 years promoting herself as an authority on sex. Now black women are writing books, too, talking about how black men feel and what we need. A woman, any woman, no matter how smart she is, or how astute she may be, is no better qualified to tell me or any other man who we are than we are capable of telling her how it feels to give birth. A man is a man. A woman is a woman, and that is the simple long and short of it. This is a book for the brothers and the sisters, all of them, black, white, red, yellow or brown, with the hope that it will help them to better understand some of the things that make men men, especially those things that make black men men. Black women and even well meaning white men and white women do not really understand because they are not black males living in this country. "In Search of Goodpussy," is the story of today's black man and his struggle to live the elusive All-American Dream of life, liberty and the pursuit of happiness; the story of overwhelming adversity and undying hope.

In creating Goodpussy I was searching for an idea, a word, a special word that would be universally understood by everyone, especially men, hoping that even those men who do not read other books, will read this one. This is a book that I hope will work for men and women, from a man's point of view. A book with a title like, "Looking For Happiness," would probably be too soft for most men to even consider picking up. I'm sure most men and most women know what sex is. Similarly, both men and women know what pu--y is.

1

JUST ABOUT EVERY MAN WHO HAS EXPERIENCED AN ORGASM
KNOWS WHAT "GOOD SEX" OR WHAT "GOOD PU--Y" IS, AND
WHAT THAT VERY SPECIAL FEELING IS LIKE. It is important,
however, that you ladies remember this is a man's book, so do
read it with patience, understanding and an open mind. It is
absolutely not intended to be chauvinistic, insulting or a
callous put down of women. I am a man who cares about the
well-being of both women and men, so I established an
unconditional reference to ensure that we are all thinking and
talking about the same things at the same time. THE WORD
"GOODPUSSY" AS IT IS USED IN THIS BOOK IS A UNISEXUAL TERM.
It is neither sexist nor demeaning. Goodpussy is a metaphor
and a socio-political term which is intended to be neither
sexist nor demeaning. For in today's society women too are
in search of Goodpussy, chasing that illusionary rainbow. It is
a "new age" word that reflects and engenders a higher level of
awareness.

More importantly, Goodpussy is a candid and
descriptive reference to that ultimate nut that each of us longs
for in life. It is an original and legitimate concept that creates
a bold new image in our minds. Before the word Goodpussy,
there was no way to accurately describe this deliriously
delicious high we all hunger for.

There is still another reason why I have chosen to
write this book and to entitle it as I have. First, I am a black
man so I added a little symbolism, because overall, society
believes that good pu--y is the only thing black men are
interested in anyway.

While this may in fact be true of some black men, it
absolutely does not apply to all of them. In all honesty, good
pu--y is the only thing some black men may be interested in
because it is the only thing they believe they have access to.
Having good pu--y, and some money if they can get their hand
on it, is their Goodpussy. In America it is all but impossible
to separate the Black male from images of sex, mostly
negative. For that reason as well as others, it would be very

2

difficult to write a credible book about him without using a sexual frame of reference. If two women are walking down the street at night and come upon a group of young black males, their first paranoid thought is probably that they will be raped and robbed as they nervously clutch their purses. If you hear about a 14-year-old girl getting pregnant you quickly assume that she is black and that a young black male who couldn't control his penis is the irresponsible father. Women and children on welfare -- it is the black man's fault for leaving babies everywhere he goes. The only universal identity that men of African American decent do have is sexual. William, a close friend, thought that he would field the title of this book for me. While having lunch with several professional black women, he asked them what their thoughts would be of a book called "In Search of Goodpussy." Predictably they were stunned and appalled. Such a book would most certainly be obscene. Furthermore, they would not even look at it...It is truly pitiful that educated black women, or men, who have been judged all their lives by the color of their skin (their covering) would likewise be guilty of judging a book simply by looking at its cover. In fact, with the historical deprivation blacks have suffered they should be eager to read anything that offers new ideas. And if their sensibilities are so acute that they cannot admit, not even to themselves, that they know what pu--y is, then, they should not be reading this book anyway. As a matter of fact, with minds as closed as theirs must be, they should not even have taken the time to learn how to read. This is a book for real people, not for pseudo-intellectuals or moral hypocrites. We begin to develop thought patterns and word associations during infancy. Surely, if we were to be honest with ourselves, whether we like it or not, or whether we want to admit it or not, every 8-year-old in America has probably heard the word pu--y somewhere from somebody. Again, this is an honest book that is based on just plain common sense. Remember, society defines and reduces black men by their sexuality when

3

it really has so little knowledge or understanding of that sexuality or of the black man.

Also, when I hear statistics saying that 3 to 4 out of every 10 married men have had an extra-marital affair, or that the average age for children having sex for the first time is 16 or 17, I wonder just who these so-called experts are getting their information from, certainly not from anyone I know. Those are nice numbers for white people who insist on feeding themselves large portions of moral optimism, but they don't work well in most of the black neighborhoods I have seen. Black Americans are eager to know the truth for themselves, the good and the bad, and it is time we started getting our own information about ourselves for ourselves.

Looking around, I saw that many good black men seemed to be having some of the same problems. Relationships with black women were falling apart, families were dysfunctional, children were in trouble and society treated them like second-class citizens. A slow agonizing death seemed imminent...I wanted to know why.

Lastly, what qualifies me to write this particular book? Well, I have yet another simple answer for you. If women can write books about men, surely I can too. Women may be genuinely interested in understanding and discovering what makes a man tick. They may sympathize and even empathize, but they are not men.

I am a reasonably attractive, reasonably intelligent black man who has dated thousands of women -- black, white, older, younger, Oriental, Hispanic, poor and well-to-do. Over the years, as a result of my affiliations with some of the most exciting night clubs in naughty old New Orleans, if I haven't seen it all, I've probably seen most of it, and surely more than you have. Once and for all, many of the erroneous myths and misconceptions about today's black man must be dispelled.

So I'm going to share with you some of the priceless lessons I have learned from a man's point of view.

4

WHAT IS GOODPUSSY?

Goodpussy is whatever absolutely makes your day. It is that feeling or that thing which gives you undeniable euphoria and brings true rapture. Just think of the best thing that has ever happened to you. That was Goodpussy. But again, you really did not know how to associate it with anything else in your life. It was just a feeling.

GOODPUSSY IS THAT WHICH GIVES YOU THE RICHEST, MOST HEART-THROBBING, TEAR-TEASING FULFILLMENT IMAGINABLE. It is the stuff dreams are made of, not just any dream, but your very own inner most personal dream.

Goodpussy may be the most perfect woman who has ever walked out from the pages of a magazine and into your fantasies, that shiny new car you drool over on the showroom floor, the perspiration covered, rock-hard body you envision pressed firmly next to yours. Whatever really strokes your soul, that is Goodpussy.

WE HAVE ALL FELT IT, WE JUST DID NOT KNOW WHAT TO CALL IT. A family seeing their healthy new-born baby for the first time, the utter contentment of a loving mother breast feeding her tiny infant, an Olympic contestant who has just won the Gold Medal, your wedding day -- that is Goodpussy, too.

For those of you who still may be just a little bit unclear, I will cite a few more examples of Goodpussy. It is your doctor saying to you, "No, you do not have cancer," or that exhilarating feeling you get when the basketball goes through the hoop during the last two seconds of the game and your team wins. Even more universally, it is the letter that comes in the mail announcing you the winner in your state's lottery, with your name on a check for ten million dollars ($10,000,000.00). Now, that is Goodpussy. Excellent, brilliant, and even wonderful are good descriptions, but they are somehow still not quite enough to explain how you really feel. That marvelous, ecstatic, supreme state of being is Goodpussy.

James Bond, Agent 007, had his Octapussy and his Pussy Galore, which in the cinematic tradition was the ultimate Goodpussy. But exactly who was James Bond, this mastermind of allure who each year drew millions of anxious viewers to the box offices of over-stuffed theaters? He was handsome, charming, sexy, intelligent, well-to-do, and he tended to have that which all the ladies desired and could not do without. And once they got some they had to have more. Mansions, exotic sports cars, sexy lovers -- James Bond lived it all, all the mystical things Ian Fleming imagined for us. Hollywood understood long ago that "the good life" was the one common fantasy we all shared -- our Goodpussy -- and we lived our lives vicariously through the fascinating characters they created for us.

Often we reserve our feelings because we, ourselves, do not understand them and fear ridicule from others. We feel good, and we know it. In fact, we feel even better than good, but because we do not know how to tell ourselves what we feel, we hesitate to openly share so much emotion with others, even those close to us. When you know what you are feeling, however, and you are comfortable with it, you can freely open the doors to yourself and let others in.

As an example, in my own case, if I were in love, I would pick the busiest street in my city, Canal Street in New Orleans, stand in the median and kiss my lady's behind at high noon, waiting 15 minutes to draw a crowd. The whole world could know that I loved her and that I would do anything, anything, for her. That is Goodpussy.

Again, if you can remember the happiest and most touching moment in your life, then you already know what Goodpussy is. IT IS A FEELING THAT IS TOTAL, COMPLETE, AND ALL THAT IT CAN BE. Goodpussy is that wondrous magic that leaves your very heart alive and tingling with delight.

If I were your friend, and I loved you, the most and best that I could wish for you would be that you have a beautiful Goodpussy life, and that you "HAVE A WONDERFUL GOODPUSSY DAY."

IN THE BEGINNING. . .
AMERICAN GOODPUSSY

"THOSE WHO DO NOT KNOW THEIR HISTORY ARE DOOMED TO REPEAT IT." This simple quotation, by George Santayana, when applied to the black experience becomes absolute. Because the black man in America has never had any real control of the press, he naturally has little knowledge of his history, of his place in society, or of the contributions he has made to civilization. Young black men who have no heroes or role models are inventing their own by making heroes and role models of themselves. In child-like desperation they are making connections, linking with the only history they do know, that of the slave. Although they have traditionally had or read few books, they and their friends did watch and indeed identify with author Alex Haley's historic accounts in "Roots". From then until now they are filling in

8

their own blanks. Lines in the hair, names (brands) on their clothes, and chains around their necks, they are going backwards when they should be moving forward. Rap music, drum beats and images of hearty Africans chanting as they worked tirelessly in the scorching fields, today's black youth are trying to create their own language. Common cliches like "What's happening?" or "He just don't know how to act," are compellingly revealing because many young black men really do not know what is happening or how to act, because no one has ever told them or shown them just "how to act." Unlike others who try to tell us what a black man is or is not, I intend to help you understand who he is. To better understand today's black man, I believe it is crucial that you first of all understand the undeniable significance of his beginnings.

In his native homeland, Africa, he lived in families with hundreds of common ancestors. Africans generally had wooly hair, thick lips, broad features, and were almost true black in color. The Nilotics averaged 6 feet in height and the Pygmies were less than 5 feet tall, all speaking distinct languages.

The coastal dwellers were predominantly fisherman and boat makers while those in the grasslands herded goats, sheep and cattle. Individuals owned crops and not land and they believed in plural marriages. If the groom could afford it, payment to the bride's family was made in livestock.

The European slave trade began in 1441 when Prince Henry the Navigator sent men to the west coast of Africa for skins and oils, but instead found gold, elephant tusks, pepper and slaves. For their black brothers the chiefs received rum, brandy, trinkets, looking glasses, beads and bracelets.

The first landing was to establish the trading station. One of the first buildings erected was the baracoon, where the slaves were to be housed. The whites did not go into the interior but did business with chiefs whose tribes raided each other. Granny Judith, an African slave, said that she had never seen red cloth before. Following pieces of red flannel that had been dropped on the ground, she and others followed a trail leading right up to the slave ship.

After the slaves were taken they were examined or inspected, their eyes, chest, belly, teeth, genitals and butt, then sometimes branded like animals with red palm oil. Others might be branded later on with their master's initials, like any other horse or cow that belonged to him.

Slave ships carried about 250 slaves and the trip to the Middle Passage or West Indies took about 50 days. And once the Africans were brought to the ship they did not immediately sail off into the sunset. Terrified, they waited and waited and waited until the ship was full. Wearing leg irons, slaves were placed in different compartments in "the slave galley," according to sex, where they remained throughout the voyage. Weak and sickened, they lived among rats, in their own vomit, bowel movements and urine, developing diseases like scurvy, smallpox and the flu. Some captains were "loose packers," while others were "tight packers" who believed that a larger cargo would offset their losses. Slaves were wedged in and given only the amount of space needed to lie down, barely enough for a man in a coffin. With the intense heat and no air, many suffocated and were found dead the next day.

The meal, usually consisting of coarse bananas, yams and coconuts was thrown down among them. Both food and water sometimes ran out.

Refusing to remain captives, some of the slaves committed suicide. Others refused to eat. When this happened the captain gave the command that mouth openers or live coals be forced into their mouths. Sometimes small children were brought on board. In one especially cruel instance three babies too small to eat alone or walk were pulled from their mothers' arms and thrown overboard. Two women drowned trying to save their young. The third, chained to another woman broke her arm struggling to get free and died several days later. Man-eating sharks often followed the ships.

As far back as a year before the Mayflower, a pirate ship dropped anchor off the coast of Jamestown, Virginia in 1619, after robbing a Spanish ship of her cargo, including 20 Negroes who were exchanged for food. Those first twenty Negroes were not slaves but indentured servants and in 1623 or 1624 Antoney and Isabella gave birth to William, the first black child born in America. (Incidentally, Africans who were expert navigators and seamen, had already traveled to the Americas on trading expeditions centuries earlier, guided by the extraordinary genius of a black man called Imhotep.) By that time, 1619, the African slave trade (internationally) was already over 100 years old and less than a century later slavery had become a way of life in America. In less than 100 years the African had emerged from a man who was simply a different color with a different culture to a full fledged slave.

Many whites believed that if a Negro was not hanged he could live forever, and he seemed to have a greater resistance to diseases like measles, yellow fever and malaria. It was also believed that blacks adjusted better to the plantation system than did the Indian, whom they had first tried to enslave. A Negro could do the work of four Indians, the Indians were hard to work with, and they did indeed die from the white man's diseases. Often captured Indians who had friends nearby and who were not agricultural were shipped to the West Indies and traded for blacks who were ideally suited for slavery. It was also very dangerous to capture and hold Indians, plus they knew the country. Although both the Indian and the black man were savages different from the white man, the Indian proudly knew his place and was willing to fight to keep it. Blacks who were already under control were relatively helpless. And although the Indian was different, he still was not quite so different as the African.

11

From the moment the first white Europeans had come face-to-face with the first black Africans their differences were compelling. Negroes were immediately viewed as "strangers" or as the "others." This perception in fact about the Negro being different became one of the key pro-slavery arguments for maintaining his enslavement. The African's skin color and the way he lived automatically made him a savage heathen. Before the 16th century the Oxford English Dictionary defined black as "deeply stained with dirt, soiled, foul...Having dark or deadly purposes, malignant, pertaining to or involving death, deadly; baneful, disastrous, sinister...Foul, iniquitous, atrocious, horrible, wicked." Black was dangerous and disgusting while white was just the opposite. White was directly related to innocence and God. Whiteness was desired while blackness was condemned, and the black man's evil nature was undeniable and unmistakable because of his hideous color. Historically, even on English stages, as far back as the 1500's, the souls of those who were damned had been represented by actors painted black or wearing black costumes. Christians were white while heathens were non-white, especially Negroes...Blackness was a curse. In Africa, however, the opposite was true. The devil was white.

Many believed also that the Negro was a "distinct order of being," the connecting link between men and monkeys. There was supposedly some logical relationship between the lowest man and the highest animal. The African was that connection or missing link, with the only difference between him and the ape being that the African could speak. Ironically, both the black man and the anthropoid ape had been discovered at the same time and in the same place. The fact that men who resembled apes and apes without tails who resembled men existed hinted that there may have been a sexual connection as well. Negroes were also considered to be just as wild and equally as lustful as the Orangutan. What they were really comparing them to was the chimpanzee. Apes and men who had low, flat nostrils and comparably shaped skulls were too much alike for their similarities to be overlooked. Some, in fact, even argued that the ape was the offspring of the Negro and some unknown African beast. Still, others believed that the Negro and the ape were having intercourse, specifically that the apes were having sex in the jungle with hot, passionate Negro women.

Because the ape was beastly and lustful, the Negro was also considered beastly and lustful. An early English writer, Samuel Purchas, in a segment of his writings wrote, "They are very greedie eaters, and no less drinkers, and very lecherous, and theevish, and much addicted to uncleanness: one man hath as many wives as hee is able to keepe and maintiane." During the early 1500's Leo Africanus, a Spanish Moor, wrote of Negroes that "there is no nation under heaven more prone to venery, principally addicted to Treason, Treacherie, Murther, Thaft and Robberie." Africanus further stated that "the Negroes likewise lead a beastly kind of life being utterly destitute of the use of reason, of dexterity of wit, and of all arts. Yea, they so behave themselves as if they had continually lived in a forest among wild beasts. They have great swarms of harlots among them; whereupon a man may easily conjure their manner of living." One 17th century traveler reported that the Negroes sported "large propagators" and another stated that Mandingo men were "furnisht with such members as are after a sort Burdensome unto them." The implications were clear. The Negro was a well endowed wild savage who was beastly and who had no control over his carnivorous sexual appetite.

Again, many of the first Negroes were not slaves however, but indentured servants, some sold by their captains. They voted, accumulated land and some owned other Negro servants. Realizing however that negroes were strong, inexpensive and couldn't be protected by the law, they soon became indentured servants for life, and their supply was inexhaustible. Originally some slave merchants sold negroes and whites as well as liquor, clothing and other goods, with no racial implications. Poor whites, prisoners and debtors were sent to the colonies, and men, women and children were often kidnapped. Free blacks were kidnapped as well. But whites could run away and change their names while the African could not. He might run but he could not hide. Because of his conspicuous visibility, slavery and the black man seemed to be made for each other. Many whites believed that slavery was the black man's salvation.

A slave was not a human being but a thing like a horse or a pair of pants, somebody else's property. But slaves were human beings, not things, and they did know what was going on around them. Solomon Northup, a former slave once wrote "They are deceived who flatter themselves that the ignorant and debased slave has no conception of the magnitude of his wrongs. They are deceived who imagine that he arises from his knees with back lacerated and bleeding, cherishing only a spirit of meekness and forgiveness. A day may come -- it will come, if his prayer is heard - a terrible day of vengeance, when the master in his turn will cry in vain for mercy."

On the plantation the slaves replaced themselves by breeding and the offspring belonged to the master, not to their own parents. ("IN OTHER WORDS, THE CHILDREN HE WAS MAKING WERE NOT THE SLAVE'S FAMILY NOR HIS RESPONSIBILITY.") Other masters thought it was cheaper to buy new slaves than breed the old ones. They believed it was less expensive to get every ounce of work out of them for 4 to 7 years, and that the babies were worthless because of the costs of rearing them. Many women were commanded to have children and sold if they could not. For their services they were rewarded with new dresses, pigs, and sometimes their freedom after a certain number were born. Even though they were encouraged and compensated for having children, slave women who were pregnant were accused of not being worth their salt because they always found excuses for not working. There was a 3-year period for breaking in a new slave and

14

during that time he was taught pidgin English, or French or Spanish and given a new name. Slaves were given new names to destroy their minds and lose their identity, to forget who they were. He was always Mr. So and So's nigger. During the early days drivers (other black slaves) broke in the new arrivals, and at the end of 1 year the master or overseer took over the tamed Negro.

In Louisiana, where I am from, Negroes were also destined to be the beast of burden and even the Indians learned to enslave their captives, both blacks and whites. The colonists used slave offspring to sell, often enslaving their own children. White women sometimes favored black men and white indentured servants often married free Negro women. Frenchmen and Spaniards often married black Creole women, sometimes keeping them as second wives with fine homes and carriages and beautiful horses, clothes and jewelry.

Obviously, slavery in Louisiana was not as brutal as it was in the American colonies. The Code Noir (black code) instituted by the French required master's to feed, clothe and house their slaves adequately, even when sickness or old age prevented them from working, and they were not to be worked on Sundays or holy days. Under Spanish rule many slaves had been freed as well. A number of Black Creole families gained huge fortunes. They held almost 2,500 of their own slaves with over $15,000,000 in cash, real estate and other valuables.

In most of the other colonies slavery was indeed a very cruel institution. Slaves toiled in the scorching fields (sometimes naked) from sun up till sun down with 10 or 15 minutes for cold bacon, working long into the night if there was a full moon. If he fell short during picking time he would be whipped, sometimes receiving as much as 100 lashes for standing idle in the field. Masters were poisoned, crushed glass was put into milk, tools were destroyed and many slaves ran away. White men lived in as much fear as the black man, because at any moment slaves might try to kill them.

15

The strategy of breaking tools and slowing down work was called "out dumbing" and slaves did just that, played dumb. They pretended to be the stupid animals their masters thought they were. The more ignorant the slave was the less work he would have to do. And slaves always wanted to do as little work as possible getting as few beatings as possible. Dr. Samuel W. Cartwright was actually convinced that the Negro suffered from a disease of stupidity which he called Dysesthesia Aetiopica. Others who knew better called it Rascality. But what Dr. Cartwright had misdiagnosed as a disease was actually nothing more than sabotage. It was alright to steal from the master, too, because the slaves felt that they had already worked for whatever they took. The only crime was to steal from another slave. Blacks indeed remained human under the most inhumane conditions. One of their favorite songs was "Got One Mind for the Boss to See: Got Another Mind for What I Know is Me." The slave's body may have belonged to the master but his mind was clearly his own. He refused to be the white man's puppet.

Dr. Cartwright believed that the Negro suffered from another disease as well, "Drapetomia," the disease of running away. He also argued that the Negro and the Indian were created before Adam and Eve and that they were part of the dominion over which Adam was to rule. He suggested as well, that the serpent who tempted Eve in the garden was actually a Negro gardener. Many white people believed Dr. Cartwright, including Jefferson Davis, President of the Confederacy.

Generally, slave quarters were more fit for animals than human beings. As many as a dozen men, women and children might live like cattle in one small room with no windows and a dirt floor. In the winter the wind would blow through the cracks and whenever it rained the slaves lived in slop like pigs. They were given old clothes to wear and sometimes children were barely clothed or not clothed at all. Stiff Negro brogans were given out when it was time to work in the fields and sometimes in the winter they wrapped their feet in burlap or had toes freeze off. (Whenever they would sneak off to dance, the women would always kick their shoes off, complaining that they hurt their feet and kept them from moving the way they wanted to.) Slaves who did not have to work on Sundays were sometimes allowed to have a good time on Saturday nights. Thomas Jefferson once wrote of the Negro that "They seem to require less sleep. A black after hard labor through the day, will be induced by the slightest amusements to sit up till midnight, or later, though knowing he must be out with the first dawn of the morning."

On larger plantations with more specialization there were field Negroes, house servants, artisans, nurses, a black driver and a white overseer to make sure the slaves worked and did not run away. Overseers also whipped the slaves, along with the master, the black driver and even the master's wife. While a wealthy plantation owner might have over 1,000 slaves, most masters owned less than four Negroes, often working side-by-side and even eating together.

Slaves and poor whites did not work well together. White males usually got the easier jobs and better wages, working in the fields while their women and children waited in wagons. Black women and children hoed, chopped cotton, weeded and helped clear swamps. The whites worked during the summer and begged in winter. And slaves frequently complained that the whites were lazy. Black men were also leased to the railroad. Some even hired out their own time by the day, week, month or year for as much as $600, even though they were supposed to be ignorant.

On many plantations house servants who tried to make things easier for themselves were hated by the field slaves. Expecting rewards or possibly gratitude, house servants had often exposed planned insurrections. Wearing uniforms or the master's old clothes they sometimes felt superior and close to the master looking out for the slave owner's interests as well. Uncle Tom's, as they were called, were trained to be that way

17

as children, often sleeping on a pallet on the floor beside the master's bed and eating his left over food. As long as they stayed close to the white man they would be alright. All house servants did not feel that way, however, and some actually spied on the master instead.

Field slaves who were not as close to the master were also not overwhelmed by his ideas. Also, because the master was up in the big house they could get away with more, and some liked it that way. By discouraging the two classes from associating with each other the master was teaching the slaves to discriminate against themselves, but that plan did not always work either.

There were several factors that had led to the alleged inferiority of all blacks. Slave traders in Africa had always handled Negroes the same way they handled any other animal. The slave owner had even profaned the Portuguese word for Black -- "Negro" -- and made it "nigger." Men who ate like animals and grunted like animals were clearly inferior and sub-human. Some believed that the Negro's blood, skull, brains and even semen were black. Negroes had even been catalogued into five classes according to intellect, 1st Negroes, 2nd Orangutans, 3rd Apes, 4th Baboons and 5th Monkeys. The original color of man was also white like Adam his creator, and every other color was a degenerate mutant. Because the Negro was an inferior savage he was naturally meant to be a slave. Blacks were meant to obey. Whites were meant to rule. Negroes were ignorant, stupid and barbaric. Slavery would civilize them and make them better men, if in fact they were men at all. Besides, slavery was the only thing Negroes were fit for anyway. That is what many American colonists believed.

During this time, however, it was the slave owners who seemed to be sub-human, perpetrating all kinds of vicious atrocities against the Negro. They deprived the black man of his freedom, destroyed his family, whipped him, branded him, castrated him, cut off ears and feet, lynched him and even

18

burned him. Some crimes were even more gruesome and horrendous. Slaves were sometimes boiled and at least one man was cooked over a slow fire for 8 to 10 hours. If a slave rebelled he might be hanged in chains with his severed head on a pole as a reminder to other blacks never to raise their hands against their masters. A former slave, Ben Simpson, left a written account of his own mother's death. When his master died, he, his sister and his mother were left to a son who had to leave the area quickly because he was in trouble. Chained and walking from Georgia to Texas, it snowed and they had to sleep on the ground. When his mother's feet became raw and swollen and started bleeding the new master took out his gun and shot her, leaving her to die in the middle of the road. "Damn a nigger what can't stand nothing," he said, as he kicked her two or three times.

Many slaves felt that their only hope was to run away, traveling northward in search of freedom. Others had simply had their fill of being treated badly by their masters. They wanted to make their own choices as to how they should live. The "Underground Railroad" or secret roads on the Ohio River became the escape route for fugitive slaves looking for a new life. Field agents directed them to a "conductor." The conductor was usually a sympathetic white or free black person who would hide the fleeing slave in places such as barns and attics during the day while a message was sent to the next station. Slave holders, sheriffs, bounty hunters and even some blacks would chase the fugitives trying to catch them, even if they had already reached the north. Sometimes slaves would run away, get past paddyrollers who patrolled the roads and hide out in the woods, sometimes starting their own secluded settlements where they would raise families.

And slaves never knew when they might be sold. A white man just might ride up and say "You my nigger now. Get in the wagon." And that would be the last anyone would see of him. No goodbyes, no farewells, nothing. And he would be gone. So a slave might have lived on several plantations.

Free Negroes were a real problem. Too often they had served as bad examples for Negro slaves. They were potential trouble makers who had been accused of helping runaways, selling liquor to slaves and receiving stolen property. They were said to be "degraded and vicious" and "given to idleness, frolicking, drunkenness, and in some cases dishonest." They were also said to be dangerous and burdensome, which may well have been the case because of cruel mistreatment and the fact that they could not find jobs. Even Thomas Jefferson, who believed that the Negro was both mentally and physically inferior, felt that blacks and whites would never be able to live together harmoniously because "deep routed prejudices entertained by the whites; 10,000 recollections by the blacks of the injuries they have sustained; the real distinctions nature has made; and many other circumstances, will divide us into parties and produce convulsions which will probably never end but in the extermination of one or the other race." Although free blacks were in trouble up to their necks, many whites believed that this too was due to their unfortunate circumstance. During that time there was also a disproportionate number of blacks in jail and the fact that blacks were walking around unsupervised made the whites believe that there would be even more problems.

And there were more problems between white men and black men, both free and slave, and between white men from the north and white men from the south. There were planned insurrections by men like 24-year-old Gabriel, against his cruel master Thomas Prosser; by Denmark Vesey, a free black man who spoke several languages; by a slave preacher named Nat Turner and by John Brown, a white abolitionist whose plan was to capture an arsenal at Harper's Ferry and give the weapons to the slaves.

But even though there was mass paranoia and hysteria, white men, women and children still managed to enjoy themselves. America during the 1850's was a thriving and booming country with men bragging about everything -- mountains, cities and even the size of the country. By the last half of the century people were having fun at amusement parks, horse races, learning the latest dances and playing a new game called baseball. They were indeed great times for all but the black man.

Slaves were still articles of property, not human beings. But Americans were beginning to fight each other more and more everyday over the same issue with words, fists and with weapons. In fact, things had become so intense that many members of Congress had come to session armed with knives and pistols.

In 1857 the Supreme Court ruled that Dred Scott, who was a slave in Missouri, was still a slave when he returned after traveling with his master to the state of Illinois which was free and later to the free northern part of the Louisiana Purchase. Most of the judges had held that since he was not a citizen of Missouri he did not have the right to sue in its courts. Slaves could be taken anywhere. They were still slaves. The Dred Scott decision firmly established that Negroes were not citizens, confirming what many whites had believed all along, that even the Declaration of Independence did not include the Negro because he was not considered a man.

When Abraham Lincoln took office in 1860 the United States was already involved in a bitter struggle. Lincoln, a brilliant politician with a humorous way of getting his point across, was against the expansion of slavery. He did not intend to free the slaves. He simply felt that "a house divided against itself cannot stand." Southerners, however, believed that any state could leave the Union if it wished to do so and many pro-slavery southern states seceded. In 1861 the Confederate forces fired on Fort Sumpter which was occupied by the Union and the Civil War began.

Again, the North did not want to destroy slavery, only to preserve the Union. Approximately 500,000 slaves joined the Union lines working as laborers and soldiers. Hoping for better treatment, well-to-do Negroes from New Orleans, not one worth less than $25,000, had formed the Native Guard in support of the Confederacy to show their patriotism. But when the Union Army captured the city they switched sides. Contraband slaves also flooded the streets, living on half-rations handed out by the soldiers and jammed into huts in filthy camps. Negroes in the Confederacy were often drafted but most of the slaves were left to raise food and fiber so that the men would be free to fight. But when the master and his overseer did leave the plantation the Negroes who were still there often ate up everything in sight. Southern Negroes also helped escaped northern troops, providing food and guiding them.

In the beginning -- when they thought it would be easy -- everyone wanted to go to war, especially white aristocrats who would be officers. Reality, however, changed many things, including Abraham Lincoln's mind about giving Negroes guns. But even then the black man was discriminated against for the Union was not legally required to pay them the same thing white soldiers were paid. Black soldiers received $10 a month, not enough to feed a family, minus $300 for uniforms, while white privates received $13 a month and a clothing allowance of $3.50 a month. Many black soldiers felt good because they were learning to read and write, but whenever they marched into a town, the whites would stay inside.

The Emancipation Proclamation was designed to weaken the South's hold on the slave and it did. Thousands of slaves left crops and hoes in the fields and guns and ammunition in the factories to get to the "Moses" in the north, Abe Lincoln. The North had the manpower and resources it so desperately needed while the South suffered from deprivation and disease. In 1865 the Confederacy collapsed.

After the war many rag-tag poor blacks followed Union troops into the cities and the whites found themselves facing yet another obstacle. How would they protect themselves from contamination while the pitiful blacks reverted to savagery which would make them extinct? The older slaves had been loyal and cooperative but the new generation was anything but that. Prejudice had become worse when slavery was abolished. Many in fact believed that the Negroes were incapable of being assimilated politically, socially or physically into a white society. They also believed that blacks with a slave past were typically ignorant and would not frequent hotels and restaurants even if they knew where they were and could afford them. And they absolutely did not believe that the Negro would work since it was no longer compulsory. Whites were still afraid, however, that there might be a payback for all that they had done to the black man.

Experts agree that the Jim Crow system of racial separation was full-fledged immediately after the Civil War. Negroes who had gained rights when whites disagreed lost them when they (the whites) made up. Once again the Negro was accused of being shiftless and hopeless and unfit for the white man's civilization. Many blacks and whites who had been friends found themselves drifting apart as well. Whites, of course, who were disgusted at seeing black and white friends eating and working together, and blacks going just about everywhere they wanted to go, could not be any more pleased with the turn of events. In the name of White Supremacy the Negro became the scapegoat in bringing the North and South together. Wherever the black man went he was reminded of white superiority and supremacy and black inferiority and subordination. Like the slave, he was made to know his place. There were Negro pews in church. Negroes were given the Lord's Supper after the white members of the congregation and there was even a Jim Crow bible for Negro witnesses to kiss. Blacks also passed on the outside of whites, even stepping in the road if it became necessary.

Abraham Lincoln once said "A universal feeling whether well or ill-founded, can not be safely disregarded. We can not, then, make them equals." Jim Crow laws applied to not some Negroes but to all Negroes. One Alabama representative said "No Negro in the world is equal to the least, poorest, lowest-down white man I ever knew." And any responsibility the whites may have felt for the black man before the Civil War they soon lost. Instead, they feared revenge.

Segregation was also leading to an alienation of sympathies and a decline in white influence over blacks and more racial friction. Because whites were no longer near the Negro they could not watch him. And because they were losing their control they believed that the blacks would become more aggressive. Being politically and economically powerless blacks would become socially dangerous. Depravity would make them more depraved, retrogressing once more to savagery. But the black man was already degraded, he might as well stay where he was. That is what the whites thought. He did not need to get a good education either because he would not learn anything anyway. There was more determination than ever to do the Negro in and to keep him away from decent white folks. "They are niggers" who cannot be helped so why waste the time. Leave them in the gutter where they belong.

Some cities had all white blocks and all black blocks, while others had separate districts. In New Orleans, potential residents, whether white or black, had to get the consent of the majority of the people living in the neighborhood before moving in. Negro prostitutes and white prostitutes even worked in separate districts. Small towns sometimes prohibited Negroes from living there. And other cities like Mobile had curfew laws requiring blacks to be off the streets by 10 p.m.

"Whites Only" and "Colored" signs were popping up everywhere - at water fountains, rest rooms, stairways and even entrances and exits. In some states there were Negro nurses for Negro patients, and Alabama prohibited white nurses from taking care of male Negro patients. Oklahoma had separate telephone booths and in Florida blacks and whites used textbooks that were kept separated, even when they were in storage.

Jim Crow laws were like smoking, non-smoking restrictions today but the punishment was acutely more severe. Many Negroes became victims of mob violence. In a colored district in Wilmington, North Carolina 400 white men set fires, chased hundreds of Negroes out of town and killed and wounded others. There were similar riots in cities like St. Louis and Memphis as well, where 46 black men, women and children were murdered, and in New Orleans an uncontrolled mob murdered, robbed and assaulted Negroes for three days. A Negro postmaster in Lake City, South Carolina was burned to death in his own house and his family shot down while trying to escape. This is the violent legacy of the black man in America, before the year 1900, almost a century ago. The Jewish people were admittedly the victims of a despicable crime when they lost six million of their people, but from the time slavery began the African continent brutally lost between forty and fifty million of her youngest and strongest sons and daughters to the most insidious and horrendous crime perpetrated in the history of mankind. SOCIETY HAS INDEED WHITE-WASHED SLAVERY, BUT AN EVEN MORE TRAGIC SITUATION PREVAILS AS IT NOW BLACKBALLS TODAY'S BLACK MAN.

GOODPUSSY FROM BOYHOOD
TO MANHOOD

So now that you know what Goodpussy is, let's see how it works. Let us briefly consider a few phases of the Goodpussy philosophy as it relates to the development of young men in America. This is an important issue because before we can understand why things happen as they do, we must first understand the nature of the factors or elements involved. And since this is a book about men, we are going to start out by taking a leisurely walk through the hypothetical life of a man socialized in the good old U.S.A.

Even before you were thought of, you were already building up steam for your journey. The fantasies, the passion and the lust your father had for your mother were a very real fact of life before you became an embryo. Your very own personalized link was being forged on the Goodpussy Chain, actually commencing at that precise moment your father fertilized your mother's eggs deep down in her womb. As he exhaled in utter ecstasy, you had already been on your way, through kissing and courting, perhaps petting. But in that instant alone, you happened. You became you.

And isn't it still interesting that even though you were there, they couldn't be sure, not until the doctor confirmed it. But, you were there all the time, just waiting for the right moment to spring out. AS YOU PASSED FROM YOUR MOTHER'S WARM BODY AND INTO THE OPEN ATMOSPHERE, USING YOUR OWN LUNGS TO BREATHE INDEPENDENTLY FOR THE FIRST TIME, YOU YOURSELF, FOR THE SECOND TIME, BECAME THE GOODPUSSY PRIZE FOR THE LOVING PARENTS WHO HAD CREATED YOU, AND WHO WERE NOW PROUDLY DISPLAYING YOU. They had received their first prize when they found out that your mother was pregnant.

Even the attending medical staff was all smiles because they had picked up extra Goodpussy points for another successful delivery. Your father passed out cigars while everyone else patted themselves on the back, and since you were a boy, your parents received bonus Goodpussy perks for bringing yet another man-child into the world. Little biddy you had validated all of them. You had shown all of them that they could do it. You had survived because your parents were good and deserving and because the medical team was competent. And you did it all by yourself, just by taking the time to show up. YOU WERE THEIR LITTLE MAN, THEIR VERY OWN LITTLE HERO, THEIR DREAM COME TRUE....THEIR GOODPUSSY.

And so fortunately, or unfortunately, as the case may be, began your life's run with society. You are born of expectations, and live the rest of your life that way. If you are a boy, born with a bat (no matter how many they have seen), anxious crowds will be waiting in the bleachers to see how well you use it. From the moment you were wrapped in your own soft blue blanket the seed is planted that a penis is more valuable than a vagina.

THE NEXT MAJOR CONCERN, OF COURSE, WOULD BE THE SIZE OF YOUR BAT, BECAUSE AS EVERYBODY KNEW, BIGGER WAS (SUPPOSEDLY) BETTER. The mere fact that you had a healthy bat was hardly important, as everyone gawked at your ding-a-ling and flipped out their rulers.

But then, that never really worked either, because those who did not have big bats made sure those who had big bats could not use them. And as bats, both big and little, became scarce, technology, and necessity -- the mother of invention -- popped up with an ultra lite, ultra durable, ultra lasting bat, so that those who did not have their own bats could simply run down to their nearest adult novelty shop and buy one. Now they too could know the pride of ownership in having their own bat, offered in various sizes, shapes and colors with a variety of deluxe features. This, of course, proved quite disarming for those who had for so long coveted their own prized phalluses.

From "poking tits" and "shooting squirrel" it's up and on to the little league to see how well he swings his bat, or to the basketball court or to the football field. Goodpussy at this stage is winning. After all, it really isn't just how well you play the game, but if you won it, because the winner gets the trophy, and to kiss the pretty girl. That was 20 years ago. Today, the winner still gets to kiss the pretty girl, but all over if he wishes to, and she will do the same thing for him if that's what he wants. Today, the girl, or more specifically sex, is the prize. Losers only get to watch.

Scotty, one of those "dirty young men" said that as a child he always liked being picked up by women because he enjoyed squeezing and poking their breasts. Greg, his buddy, smiled too as he talked about his youth. He said that when he was about six or seven years old, if he was watching TV and a pretty lady was sitting in a chair, he would walk up close to the screen to try to look under her dress. He did it even though it was only television and you couldn't see anything that wasn't already on the screen.

At any rate, let us now consider the next link in our neat little chain: feeding, or rather breast feeding. As infants, either male or female, the love affair with these milk bearing fatty glands is begun. Little boys grow up to be carnivorous breast hunters, willing to do or say almost anything to "see that tit." Little girls too, soon discover that having "mouth watering tits" is half the battle in the mating game. Today, however, just as men gain pleasure by suckling female breasts, females now feel free to titillatingly nibble on their man's nipples, too.

So, it becomes a compulsion for the loser as well to validate himself, to get his prize, his Goodpussy. Even at this early stage in his development, sex has become a benefit of achievement.

Now you are in your twenties, ready to "show your stuff" and challenge the world, but how do you go about doing that?... Again, the answer is simple. Way, way back when, when your dad climbed on your mom it all started, remember? That's the answer. To get your own Goodpussy, get yourself some pu--y... any pu--y. After all, if you've got some sex, you're obviously a winner because you've already been awarded the prize. And what could possibly be any better than having your own trophy? That's right, having many trophies. Sex itself has become Goodpussy, independent of any personalization or feelings. The other person, the woman, becomes incidental and unimportant except in her role as a servicing agent with a vaginal prize for your accomplishments. She is simply your servant and your "ego booster."

Being a man is to be a member of a potentially lonely lot. During teens and twenties you are busy swinging your bat and winning prizes. In your thirties, life just isn't working out the way you thought it would, and at forty you are divorced and on your back. What have you built? What do you have that is really yours? If you had anything, your ex-wife has it

29

by now. If you are fortunate enough to have a relationship that is still working, you are indeed one of the lucky ones. If you're single, the few friends who are still around don't open up anyway, so it's you against the world. But alas, all is not lost. There is yet hope on the horizon.

Coming to your aid, that's right, is some good and loving woman. She helps you to pick yourself up and brush yourself off. She cleans you up, finds you some decent clothes, feeds you and nurses you back to health, helps to restore your self-confidence, then sets you back on the straight and narrow.

So, this is your life Mr. _____. What happened? Why did everything go wrong? And what about all your hopes and dreams? The answer is painfully simple. "IT'S A MAN THANG." Now that you are tired, lonely, alienated and isolated with no affection or intimacy you begin to realize something. ALL THAT MACHO GARBAGE YOU'VE BEEN FED THROUGHOUT YOUR LIFE ISN'T WORTH A POT TO P_ _ S IN. Being cool and independent, hiding and suppressing emotions and believing that you didn't need anyone doesn't feel good right now.

You have always been in control and in charge, but now there is nothing to control or take charge of. IN ESSENCE, THERE IS NOTHING YOU ARE GOOD AT ANYMORE OR GOOD FOR ANYMORE. You are no better than a faded rag or a worn old piece of furniture unless someone recognizes your worth as a decent human being. You've got a real dilemma on your hands but it's too late now. There's not much you can do about it.

At this point in your life you realize that your Goodpussy has somehow slipped past you. ALL THAT IS LEFT ARE GOD AND EACH DAY OF THE REST OF YOUR LIFE. Your youth is gone, your security is gone, the power and the sex prizes you have courted all your life are gone...LOVE HAS ALWAYS MEANT SEX TO YOU AND NOW THAT THE SEX IS GONE, THAT MEANS THAT LOVE IS GONE TOO...YOU ARE ALONE... You didn't let anyone get close to you so now there is no one close to you. You have become a lonely old man whose only Goodpussy is the one hot meal delivered to you daily at noon by the "Council on The Aging," and those few visitors who occasionally drop by. Goodpussy then, becomes your final reward as you are placed in a solitary coffin in a lonely cemetery, lowered into dear mother earth and covered with dirt, hopefully to once again share communion with your maker.

WHAT BLACK MEN WANT AND NEED

LOVE, DEVOTION AND RESPECT, that's what black men need, along with a little KINDNESS from SOMEONE WHO CARES FOR THEM AND BELIEVES IN THEM. Black men also need to be touched and held and played with affectionately. What their fathers had with their mothers is what they want. And just what was that? Love, devotion, respect and kindness from someone who cared about him and believed in him. Black men need and want the security and unconditional love they knew as a child. They also want to feel that same sense of companionship and of feeling needed.

What they also need and want is to be thought of as human beings rather than things. EVERYBODY ELSE SEEMS TO BE A PART OF THE HUMAN RACE EXCEPT THE BLACK MAN. It is almost like he is a species all unto himself. Hardly anyone understands him, and typically where there is the unknown, there is fear. NOBODY KNOWS HIM, SO NOBODY TRUSTS HIM. Needless to say, a racist white male dominated society has done its fair share to perpetuate as well as traumatize that perception.

Today's black man also needs to have society's expectations of him reassessed. Instead of being criticized for what he is not doing, he needs to be praised for all that he has done, in spite of the overwhelming obstacles he has had to overcome. For example, black men are blamed for not working, when they are not the ones doing the hiring. Black men are accused of being lazy, worthless no accounts, when their blood and sweat built this country. Those who wanted no parts of work said that he was trifling and the label stuck.

Today sociologists and psychologists caution us about putting our children down, ridiculing them because of the possible adverse effects. Black men in America have been put down for over 300 years, by almost everyone. Even his own ally, the black woman, has bought into this myth. That person with whom he once shared love, devotion, and respect is all too often his enemy too. If you tell a child, "You're nothing but a trouble maker" or "You're never goin' to amount to anything," he may not. These are the messages black men have always gotten.

The blame for the black man's failure has always rested on the black man himself. Because he was not there to take care of the children he had made, he was especially suspect. Although he did make these children, he was not creating a family. Let me draw an interesting little parallel for you. A rancher in Arizona wants to build up his herd so he mates a stallion with five of his mares every year. At the end of five years this stallion has had 25 mates and at least 25 offspring. How could he possibly be the head of all 25 families at once? After all, he was only one horse. And how could he possibly keep up with the offspring of his offspring? Was the fact that he was bred really his fault at all, except for being properly equipped and good at what he did?

33

Some black men had similar experiences during slavery. Like the stallion, he produced many offspring, and also like the stallion he could not be in 25 places at one time. Not only could he not keep up with his 25 families, he could not clone himself so that he could even catch up. So theoretically we have at least 24 families with no head, but it is the slave's fault for not being there. "BULL SHIT!" I think it's somebody else's greedy fault for using him like a prized horse or bull in the first place. What black men really need is not to be blamed for problems they didn't create. They didn't load themselves in shackles onto filthy slave ships so that they could take a cruise to America where they would become wealthy land barons. Are we really so ignorant that we do not realize that the black man is the VICTIM not the PERPETRATOR?

Again, like the stallion, the black man cannot fix everything or be expected to. Both he and the black woman must come to grips with that. Of course he has always believed that if he can't fix it he's not in control, that he's less than a man, but there are some things that just cannot be fixed. Feeling responsible is just another "man thang." He is just going to have to learn to let it go. The black woman must also understand that she too may be compounding the problem by expecting something he cannot possibly deliver, then getting an attitude when he doesn't. Or maybe he can pull it off, but he just can't do it alone. He needs cooperation instead of antagonism. BOTH THE BLACK MAN AND THE BLACK WOMAN MUST REMEMBER THAT IN SPITE OF ALL HIS MACHOISM HE REALLY IS NOT SUPERMAN.

Sure, at times he may be confused, short tempered, uncommunicative, bitter, stressed out, insecure, unsure of what he wants and even be in denial. But, again, it's a "man thang" and he doesn't even know why. With all that pressure on him, frustration and resentment are predictable, especially in a society where men are expected to be men.

The black woman must be patient and try to understand that his moodiness is not intentional. The black man is not against her. In fact, he is actually doing more harm to himself, but he knows no other way. So, to that love, devotion, respect and kindness add a little COMPASSION, UNDERSTANDING AND APPRECIATION.

Another thing that black men want and need is to be able to open up and actually be who they are. But before they can accomplish this, they need to be able to get in touch with their own deepest feelings. Relationships with other men are often competitive, and that man you share your insecurities with or tell what a "great lover your girlfriend is" may try to find out for himself.

I have my own rule that I live by. I don't hang around friends' houses talking to wives or girlfriends when they are not there, and I don't carry on long telephone conversations with them. Whenever "mad day" comes for them, I want to make sure my shoulder is not the one she wants to cry on. If I get too close to her and begin to see her as a close friend, that closeness will ultimately transcend the limitations of my friendship with my original friend, her husband or boyfriend.

Conversely, because women do listen when men want an understanding ear -- and men do need someone to communicate with -- attraction to her warmth and understanding may also lead me to be sexually attracted as well. So the bottom line for me is that I don't want to be friends with any of my friends' women. When a man finds a woman he is comfortable with, it is easy to open up and reveal his gentleness and sensitivity. With that kind of companionship too, he may feel that he has indeed found his Goodpussy.

Just as there are things that a black man wants and needs from a woman, there are things that he doesn't want or need. One of the most obvious things is a woman who feels superior to him, or a woman who tries to make him feel small. Another thing black men don't need or want is a woman who is always letting her friends do her thinking for her. His relationship with her may already be fragile at best, so the very last thing they need is any outside interference.

A black man also doesn't want or need women who cannot cope, women who are put-ons, women who cannot function when they have problems, or a woman who rejects him or leaves him when the going gets tough.

The number one thing black men don't need, however, is a woman who is disloyal. Cold, conceited and stuck-up women are also a problem, as well as nagging, domineering, unsupportive, selfish women. Bossy women are a very special problem too. One of the worse things that any woman can do to a "real" black man is try to push him around. Remember, one of the "man thangs" he has been taught not to do is take orders from you. He's the one who is supposed to be in charge.

Many black women, like black men, are know-it-alls who really do not know anything at all. Some black women want to show how self-sufficient they are. They don't need anyone else, especially you. They have forgotten what it means to be gentle, honest, nurturing, and a caring friend and confidant. Many black women are beginning to exhibit masculine traits, adapting to society's ideas of what winners are. Assuming masculine roles, they are at odds with and competing against black men. Some black women may, in fact, be angry that they were born black females (in this man's world), and since they cannot change themselves, the logical thing they can do is to change the world, and you.

Some others are electing to be Cinderella or Little Red Riding Hood. And to be sure, the black man does not want or need any of these women who have become I's rather than We's. A black man needs and wants a real woman who is devoted and committed, and who believes as he does that a good relationship is worth the effort.

In whatever form, one more thing black men want and need is companionship, a partner. They need someone to do things with, someone they can take trips with, wine and dine, share dreams with, or just sit around and watch television. They want and need a loyal friend with whom they can share that satisfying relationship. Goodpussy, for me, were those wonderful moments when I found myself cradled in my lady's arms, with her leg draped over mine, falling asleep together. I'm sure that is what some other black men may want and need, too. And, women, if you aren't in a position to give that, still show him that you care and let him show you that he cares. "GIVE A BLACK MAN A GREAT BIG HUG TODAY!"

WHAT BLACK MEN THINK
BLACK WOMEN WANT AND NEED

Someone once wrote that what black women need is the truth -- the whole truth, including the truth about themselves. Most women are looking for **MR. RIGHT**, even though they are not interested in being **Ms. RIGHT**. Sure women want someone to love and protect them, someone who is understanding, caring and supportive. In essence, they want a "**GOOD MAN**," a faultless knight in shining armor.

Now that we've gotten that out of the way, let's consider some of the other things black women seem to want. Just as men want a decent woman, SOMETIMES women seem to want a decent man. SOMETIMES. Men seem to be drawn to women other men want while women seem to admire men they know are screwing around. At parties women seem to come alive when a lady's man enters the room. Though they often try to conceal it, they really do get excited, and if he makes a move on them it actually appears to validate them. And speaking of validation, if these same women can maneuver it, they will literally place themselves in this same lecherous man's path to volley with him. On that list are some of those girl friends who got out without their husbands and boyfriends, sitting around a table to see who will be hit on first, how many times, and who will be doing the batting (using his bat). Why do so many good girls find themselves in such lascivious settings? And why are they wearing their sexiest dresses and faces, without their men? If they really "just wanted to look nice," they could have done that with their mates.

What many black women want is to do whatever they want to do. What some of them need is to be slowed down a little bit.

Far too many black women need to be reminded of where they come from and how they got where they are. There is a saying, "Don't forget the bridge that brought you over," and many black women seem to have forgotten just that. They see the world as their very own great big giant juicy oyster, and they're going to get out there and suck every delicious drop of it up, kind of like a female vampire with warm red blood still dripping from her mouth and fangs. What she seems to have forgotten, however, is that for every vampire there is somebody running around with a wooden stake to drive through its heart.

Some black women do need to be taken down a couple of notches. Those who have a biblical background do generally tend to remember that the man is important, while those who are more secular tend to be more independent thinking -- more "I," less "We."

And speaking of "The Man," all too often the white man is referred to as just that. Well, if the white man is "The Man," where does that leave the black man? This idea, too, is one that black women seem to have bought into as they form coalitions with white men, feeling somehow more validated. If "The Man" thinks I'm great, then I must be. Who cares about what some black man thinks? Or even other black women? As the comic book philosopher Pogo once said, "We have seen the enemy and the enemy is us."

Black women have always been the black man's best friend and his most prized possession. During the days of slavery she faced the same hardships he did, plus the abuses imposed upon her as a woman, confronting both sexism and racism. Not only was she worked and whipped, she was brutally raped as well -- often as a mere child.

And breeding (sex abuse), was typically cold and unfeeling, without today's luxury of artificial insemination. Imagine the dehumanizing horrors of being raped to produce children, over and over and over again. Or try to see women being publicly stripped and fondled anywhere, by anybody, or imagine being forced to lie on your back and have intercourse at the whim of someone who owns you.

Black women need love, devotion, respect, compassion, support, understanding, kindness and appreciation just as the black man does. Moreover, they need to be able to return those same sentiments after they realize that "WE'RE ALL IN THIS TOGETHER!"

DO BLACK MEN KNOW WHAT LOVE IS?

Of course they do. Everyone does. There are many, however, who believe that if the black man knows any love at all it is the love he practices for himself only. It is this stereotypical mischaracterization that has once again made the black man both the victim and the target at the same time. Society cruelly treats him like a wild animal then casually expects him to behave like a country gentleman. He is abused and accused of not being capable of love and then is not loved because he has been accused of not knowing how.

Historically, black men have always been some of the most gentle and loving creatures on the face of the earth. In fact, black men were so docile that many whites, who were aggressive by nature, even considered them womanish.

And during the days of slavery it was the overwhelming love that the black man had in his heart that kept him from taking off, leaving everyone else behind, and simply saying "I'm outta' here." Black men have always known what love is.

While it may be true that the ability or willingness to express love may have been sucked out of the hearts of some black men, we must remember that those hearts are not well and that indeed some of them no longer function normally. We must also remember who broke them and why. For whatever reason, some unconscionable black men really have become products of their environment who show no mercy and who feed upon anything that crosses their path. They are heartless predators who will devour everything in sight. The only thing that matters to them is the "kill." Because they have been so victimized, aggression, or rather destruction, is the only thing they know. They do not want to make anything. They do not want to build anything either, especially something based on sensitivity. And they absolutely will not risk being thought of as weak or vulnerable.

These black men are afraid to trust or to open themselves up to any more pain. To be in love is to be

41

dependent and to have someone else dependent on you, to share and to have that sharing returned. That is too big a gamble for some black men to take when they have been stepped on too many times already. They do not need to hurt anymore for anybody, or for any reason. Nobody should be able to make them go against their own will or have power over their own better judgement. HOW CAN THEY BE EXPECTED TO RETURN LOVING SENTIMENTS LIKE RESPECT, UNDERSTANDING, SACRIFICE AND CARING WHEN NONE HAS BEEN GIVEN TO THEM. The only Goodpussy they know is themselves.

In spite of the fact that some black men are hard and unfeeling, they still know what honesty is, even if they do not practice it. It is simply an investment they cannot afford to make. Suppose he is willing to do all the right things by his lady, what proof does he have that it will not be one sided or that he can trust her? He has learned the hard way, "if you're weak you're beat." He knows who he is, but how can he be sure about her? His life is hard enough already. He does not need any more misery. (That is one of the reasons why some black men resort to violence, to maintain control and thereby avoid their own suffering.) Nobody is going to use him.

Again, for many black men love means sex. Because they are socially, economically and politically powerless, the only happiness these men may know is having their way with a woman, or women. Even as boys one of the first things they learned, one of their "rights of passage," was that having sex makes you a man. A woman is the only thing these black men have ever conquered. Having women made them men, even though they felt no responsibility for them. That was all the love they needed for both their chest and their penis to be pushed out. And getting some money out of it or anything else valuable and they really felt that they "got over."

Being aggressive will also keep others from getting close enough to see who he really is. And since he is not willing to risk vulnerability, he opts instead to continue to exploit his sexual prowess. But again, while some black men

42

intentionally travel this path to keep from getting hurt, others do so because it is the only course they know. Many of these black men have turned their emotions off, choosing instead to use manipulation and their bodies from the waist down.

Other black men, however, do believe in a love that is genuine. Mark, a 27-year-old real estate developer, says that for him it was love at first sight. From the very first moment that he saw Tanya he knew she was the one. Because of their inexplicable attraction from the very beginning, he wanted to be with her all the time. But the real reason why he said he was ready for her was that he already loved himself first. Mark explained that before Tanya he had always thought that love just started as a good feeling that matured as time passed, and developed into something special. It was based upon mutual trust, devotion, commitment, closeness and a feeling of security, but the euphoria he felt with Tanya had instantly given him a new point of view. Mark said he knew that he was taking a chance, but he believed that true love only comes along once in a lifetime.

Certainly trusting a stranger so completely is risky, but Mark believes in unconditional love and what could possibly be any more unconditional. He could sense deep feelings of admiration and respect and felt that Tanya could easily become the center of his life. How could he possibly live without her?

Brandon, on the other hand, is a widower who believes in love, too. But unlike Mark, Brandon believes that love, especially true love, takes time to grow and blossom. He believes in the old axiom that "haste makes waste." Brandon, like many other black men, feels that leaving yourself open and vulnerable to someone before you really know them is a foolish move.

He admitted loving several women, some of them at the same time, but said that he had only known true love once, with his wife Linda. While he explained that love is something that must be worked at as it continues to survive the test of time, he too mentioned the same kinds of unconditional elements Mark had. He and Linda were friends, a team who were honest and committed to each other. And this trust was even more important to them than physical attraction or the intense sexual intimacy they shared. Making her happy made him happy, and it was so easy. "There is nothing better than giving and receiving love," he said. "And there is no greater gift than living a life filled with love."

Many black men feel as Mark and Brandon do. They may differ on the time it takes to find love (whether you have to work at it or if it just happens), but their feelings are generally the same. Love requires trust, friendship, caring, real intimacy, commitment and acceptance. Most black men would also do almost anything for the woman they love, agreeing that love itself may have little to do with sex. In fact, if there is true love or real intimacy, there may be no interest at all in casual sex. And while black men may be divided on beliefs about whether real love lasts forever, they do agree that you must work at it to keep it alive.

Other black men did not share their enthusiasm. They felt that being vulnerable (in the name of love) is not worth the risk. Many of them believe that love is only an illusion, an illusion that can be quickly dispelled by reality. Sure, everybody loves a winner, but he is a black man, and black men are seldom winners. Is he to believe that he will be one of the lucky ones? Is his happiness in fact based on luck? Does he take a chance -- open up and put his woman on a pedestal only to have her crush him? Can he deal with the pain and the rejection if it fails?

Scott, 33, had been divorced from his wife Jerry for six months. They were both paralegals who had met in school. After graduation they were married. For the first two years everything was perfect. There were no defensive masks, and he and Jerry shared everything together. They were ecstatic and infatuated as they made sacrifices for each other and supported each other. He was so happy that God had brought her into his life and was always finding things to do for her or surprising her with little gifts and cards. But then she changed. As they became more comfortable with each other and routine sat in, Jerry became bored and love just wasn't enough anymore.

Today, Scott is angry and still trying to pick up the broken pieces of his life. His hands shake and his imagination runs wild as he wonders where Jerry is and who she is with. Bitterness and loneliness cause many sleepless nights, and he often sits on the side of his bed with a loaded .38 nearby. Frequently, he has cried himself to sleep, and he still finds functioning at work extremely difficult.

Like so many other black men, when Scott fell in love he surrendered his own independence. He had been seduced by what Jerry appeared to be. Like Scott, many black men find themselves out of control when they are blinded by love. Far too often we see what we want to see, only realizing that our vision was blurred after it is too late.

Real love is sometimes described as being a profoundly tender or passionately affectionate feeling of warm personal attachment. It is a deep and emotional regard which is free from fear and selflessness. Many black men realize that the value of loving is in giving it so that it will come back to them. Goodpussy would be getting that opportunity!

WHY MEN CHEAT

Men don't cheat. They simply need more than one woman sometimes. Remember, men are dogs, right. Wrong. They are little boys who grew up hearing that they were different from little girls. And as men one of their differences from women is sex. As little boys they remembered lessons like "Big boys don't cry." But when they were hurt they did cry, privately, if not publicly. A little girl could fall on the playground, scratching her arm, and she was expected to shed a few tears, but not little boys. He was supposed to pick himself up, brush himself off, and pretend that nothing had happened.

As he grows older he still remembers those rules. When he is hurt in a relationship, again he cannot cry, not publicly, no matter how deep his hurt may be. He vows to himself that it will never happen again, and buffers himself with, that's right, more women.

In the beginning, as a young man, the prize was scoring and sex, but as recent surveys indicate, men are now more interested in companionship. They are no longer interested in purely sexual gymnastics, but they still do not want to be alone. As friends say time and time again, "When things go wrong, as they will, if I've got four or five women, I'll just move on to the next one. I'm not going to be hurt anymore." Because men avoid emotions they are especially hard hit when a relationship goes sour, and cheating keeps them from getting too involved with one woman.

And if men are dogs, what can be any more evil and menacing than a black dog? That's an easy one, too. The only thing that can be worse than a simple black dog is a big black mean dog. He is certainly the worst of all creatures, and of all the cheaters. As a matter of fact, he is an unconscionable cheater possessing absolutely no morals at all. Well, if white men aren't cheating, only protecting themselves from hurt, how could any black man possibly be cheating?

Harry, a state trooper, said that the chase turns him on, and the thrill of conquest when he seduces another unsuspecting woman. Harry loves the challenge of seeing which of his programs will work on each new woman. He said that he had learned his codes and programs by watching his father who was a cheater, too. Harry really believes that he loves his wife Jinx, but says that his ego makes him do it. It is his right as a man. Other men expect it, too, and so do women.

Jason, 21, said that he just wanted to have a good time. Since women outnumbered men, he was only doing his duty when he "tightened them up." And it was so easy because the women he met often wanted it just as much as he did. Jason admitted that he had been in love once, but when she cheated on him it nearly killed him. (But women cheat too, and many black women seem to have a revolving door in

47

and out of different men's lives.) Cheating was alright for a man, but a woman was supposed to be better, stronger. "Screwing around" was Jason's way of avoiding commitment.

Cheating is an act of dishonesty, but as history will remind us, the black man was delivered to the shores of the North American continent to work and to replenish his own kind. With a little encouragement from the plantation owner and the overseer, he did a wonderful job of developing this country's raw resources, and of populating it.

The white man in all his glory and wisdom had successfully created a low maintenance machine that worked magnificently and reproduced itself. How splendid, how marvelous, until Abraham Lincoln's Emancipation Proclamation and the end of the wealthy plantation owner's free ride.

The black man had indeed proven to be a prolific breeder. But the old saying, "If it ain't broke don't fix it" became "Break the damned thing, break it." And they have been breaking the black man (and woman) ever since. The difference is that he was first being broken to be maintained as valuable property, and now he is being broken to be eliminated.

Historically, servicing more than one woman was not only expected, it was demanded of many black men. Some plantation owners believed that it was more cost-effective to breed and build up their inventory and assets, or to have children to sell. With sexual indoctrination so heavily tilted toward studding, part of the black man's problem is that he was never taught or has never taken it upon himself to learn anything else or any other way of doing things.

So the black man was loosed upon the world, and now the A.S.P.C.A. wants him taken out, because he has made one even more grave mistake. Not only has he bred successfully with the prime stock, he has bred with the private stock as well. If he had some chance before he has none now. Miscegenation -- not failing to rise above welfare roles -- is his

48

real crime. He was only a distasteful nuisance until he began to spoil and make worthless that which was so highly valued by "the man," his white woman. And now he faces condemnation by both "the man" and his black female counterpart as well.

Cheating was inbred in the black man before it was called cheating -- even though in Africa it is still customary to have more than one woman. The black man in America has become a trained professional, and it is hard to break old habits, especially when there is so little help.

Today black men still maintain a long list of reasons for having more than one woman. Primarily it is that things are just not right at home. Many of them say that sex with their wives or girl friends is not what it should be, that there is no passion and that the relationships are just not satisfying anymore. Some say their mates are too inhibited and that they add spice to their lives by learning some of the tricks a new lover may offer, and perform a few tricks of their own that they can't do at home. Since some wives or girlfriends do not like certain positions or allow things like oral sex or anal sex, they simply get those favors somewhere else. Other black men said that sometimes people just don't have the same needs, desires or sexual appetites, and that going outside of a relationship may indeed have helped to save it. Still, it helped some of them over the frustrations and hard times of being in relationships where the excitement was gone.

Stewart, 43, a social studies teacher, said that his marriage to Claudette is a classic blunder. Claudette, a special education teacher, is just a pretty shell who validates him. From the outside everything seems perfect, but behind closed doors they sleep in separate bedrooms and haven't touched each other in almost a year. Before that she had taken him for granted for months while she chased rainbows. All the trappings were there, but their marriage was empty. He was absolutely miserable at home.

49

During an "open house" at school he had met Belva, the mother of one of his students, and they had started seeing each other. Stewart said that Belva was more of a real wife than Claudette, the woman he was married to. He felt complete with Belva and sex was a bonus.

Stewart said that he was tired of Claudette's constant bitching and that a ship could have only one captain. Someone has to make the final decisions and he said that he had "no time for the pain." Claudette was so bossy he said, that even if he tried to do his job as a protector and good provider, she would want to tell him how he should do it. Instead, he felt more fulfilled becoming Belva's protector and provider. The only time he could be himself and feel like a man was when he was with the other woman. Stewart said that he felt more at home when he was away from home.

As in Stewart's case with Claudette, many 80's and 90's women who consider themselves liberated will not let a man be a man. You cannot tell them anything. Their minds are blocked and locked. These women will throw away everything before they will allow themselves to be "controlled," as they see it. Because of this uncompromising attitude, the situation becomes hopeless. Because of her adamant posture, which is beyond his capacity, the man must either repulse her or forfeit his manhood. This type of black woman is herself controlling and out of control as well. Even if the man wants to make a commitment, he cannot. TODAY MANY BLACK MEN ARE STARVING FOR LOVE.

B.J., an attorney, says because of this attitude that he finds in so many so-called "successful" black women, who falsely think that they are in control, all he wants them for is sex. Many black men are forced into other relationships.

Parker, a bartender and confirmed bachelor, said that he is just having too much fun, and that some people simply aren't meant to be married. "Being good looking or being successful, even if you're married, people expect you to fool around." He said that they almost make you do it. And

50

definitely if you're single, Parker added, women know that you've got to have it. That's why you're not married. So they're standing in line just waiting for their turn. Finally, Parker, smiling mischievously, said, "If women don't respect themselves why should I? If they're old enough to bleed they're old enough to butcher."

Many black men just frankly admitted that having only one woman can be too confining, monotonous and restrictive, and that having more than one woman boosted their egos and made them feel more manly.

Still others felt that spending time with more than one woman or developing more than one relationship helped them to better understand themselves, that they were learning more about life and growing.

A few said that they had felt insecurity, guilt and anxiety that they had tried to ignore or rationalize after they had gotten caught. But what could they do? What could they say when the truth was staring them squarely in the face? They had not been honest with themselves, in anticipating how bitter and helpless they would feel if she found out.

Generally, they agreed, however, that monogamy was more stable and helped couples be more honest with each other. But most of them did not feel guilty about having more than one woman, especially those who said they purely enjoyed the excitement of the chase and were doing it to their mates before it was done to them.

Personal reasons like these, and the every day pressures of life are undermining stable, loving, meaningful relationships. But those who do have healthy relationships had better protect, cherish, and not take them for granted, before they find out the realities of having to live without them.

Men do make excuses. But if you try harder to give her what she needs, she may try harder to give you what you need. And above all else, know the truth because what you don't know may very well hurt you.

51

INCOMPATIBILITY
AND UNREALISTIC EXPECTATIONS

From the beginning we both knew that we were different. I was single and college educated, an educator myself as well as a business person and a socialite. She was a high school graduate with no further training or skills, and three children she was raising alone.

I lived in the abstract world of ideas and concepts. She lived in a world of how am I going to pay the rent this month, buy the new bra my oldest daughter needs, and how much am I going to be able to get from the grocery store this week? Insurance was a luxury for her, as was spending a weekend out of town.

I became fully aware of our incompatibility only after serious, heart-wrenching, soul-searching when we separated. I knew I loved her, that I was, in fact, in love with her. I had loved other women before, some more than others, but this was the first time my heart had actually poured out of my body and slipped into the dirt. I had lived each and every day of my life living my love for her. But somehow that still wasn't enough.

The answer was reasonably simple and had been before me all the while. A couple of my mentors had always said to me that there were two reasons why things generally went wrong. Those two things were incompatibility and unrealistic expectations. INCOMPATIBILITY is quite recognizably the lack of being reconcilable. UNREALISTIC EXPECTATIONS means anticipating something that just will not be. In either case, however, it is important to remember, "IF IT DON'T FIT, DON'T FORCE IT." The Goodpussy of my life had gone up in a puff of smoke, because I had fallen in love with someone I was incompatible with.

A book had recently been published by a female author who suggested that black women were out of control and needed to be brought back into the ranks. On several points I agreed, having become a divorce statistic myself. My best friend and the most wonderful woman I had ever known changed before my very eyes after getting a promotion, an expense account, and a new attache case.

Generally, I do not believe that even after nearly 150 years many black women have learned how to be free. Before you go off half-cocked, however, let me say that I do not believe most black men have learned how to be free either.

"IN AMERICA TODAY BLACK MEN AND BLACK WOMEN ARE NOT FREE." We are encouraged to believe that we are, and permitted certain liberties. Our freedom and our Goodpussy are an illusion. White America wisely appeases and pacifies us capitalizing on our gullibility and egocentrism by leading us to believe that we are making progress. The pseudo black middle class excitedly embraces this ridiculous farce because they are the ones who falsely believe that they are "making it" in America. How foolish! If we make sacrifices we can buy that new house, as long as we buy it in a mixed or black neighborhood. If we work very, very hard we can get that promotion. We might even get an invitation to the boss' house, but we won't be going to the executive locker room at the country club.

WHAT BLACK WOMEN AND BLACK MEN DO NOT UNDERSTAND IS THAT WE ARE ALL WE'VE GOT. We are our own Goodpussy. We are our only Goodpussy.

There is still hope however. A popular television evangelist is quoted as saying that "Attitude is more important than fact," and he is right. For example, if your rent is due, the landlord comes over, and you tell him to kiss your ass, there is a good chance that your furniture will be out on the street when you get back. Same landlord, same situation, but you say to Mr. Smith that you are trying to get the money together, and that you should have something by the end of the week. You'll probably get a reprieve. The same principle applies to saving your relationship. The right attitude can even overcome both incompatibility and unrealistic expectations.

We all have ideas of what we want that very special person in our lives to be like, but it is just that, only an idea. The reality, however, is that factors like age, attitude and background should never be taken for granted. Although similar backgrounds may make a relationship easier, there are exceptions. Some people chose complements (opposites) hoping to find a balance they do not have.

Another reason why black men and black women may be drifting apart is that some black males are succumbing to their own egotistical desire to be pumped up. This kind of man wants to be placed on a pedestal and worshiped like an Adonis, while leaving some black woman alone, with his children, to deal with the harsh realities of her world. While she cries out for help, he tells himself how beautiful he is. Like Narcissus, he has seen his reflection while polishing his car, and has fallen in love with himself. It is indeed men like these who do not listen to women, because they do not believe that women have anything worthwhile to say. Only their thoughts and feelings are important. These men and their women definitely do not understand each other because whatever communication there is is meaningless, and they see each other as separately as "in" and "out." They do not feel that there is anything at all that they can learn from a woman, and their women often feel the same way about them.

Not all, but some of those same black men want to be praised and edified because they still have their penises, and because their masculinity now exists only in their own shallow egos, rather than in the well defined muscles of their backs. These black men mistakenly believe that the world revolves around the invincible team of them and their phalluses. If they were to lose their prizes, however, what would they have left besides a nub? In fact, lower-class black men are often singled out because of the habit of grabbing their crotches in public, and I have often wondered myself why they do it. Is it to draw attention to their prize, to protect it, or to make sure it is still there? I've come to the conclusion that the former is true. They do it because it's all they've got. No money. No new car to proudly show off. All they've got is their d_ _ks, and using their hands to cradle it, they make sure you don't miss it. Not being successful at anything else, his penis really is his only "tool." One of the sisters once remarked that that is why black men are always saying, "Hey man, what's happening?" Because they really do not know what is happening. For many of them nothing is happening.

Again, historically the black male has been deprived of his dignity, self-respect, and love. His powerful body worked hard in the fields while the slave owners had their way with his daughters, mothers, sisters, and wives. The black man could not say anything for fear of being sold, beaten, or even worse, killed. He has never had possession of the black woman and to this day that condition generally remains true. He doesn't know how to possess her. And he is confused.

55

The term "Black Man" once held a certain proud, majestic connotation, a majesty that is now being held by the black woman because so many black men have been broken, become losers. What was once an image has become no more than a physical description. Black men, not all black men, have been so watered down until all that remains are a few real men. MANY BLACK MEN ARE SIMPLY COLORED, AMERICANIZED MALES.

Just as you turn on a television set and see an Oriental person whose only identifying ethnic trait is the way he or she looks, the same thing has happened to the black man. BLACK MEN WHO ACT WHITE AND TALK WHITE, YES, AND WHO EVEN LOOK WHITE IF THEY CAN FIND THEM, ARE WHAT WE SEE ON TELEVISION, CONSTANTLY REINFORCING THE IDEA THAT THIS IS WHAT SUCCESS IS, A WHITE BLACK PERSON. Even sitcoms, and other programming may feature black characters, but their roles are usually just as white. ONLY THEIR COLOR HAS CHANGED TO ADD A LITTLE COLOR AND TO BOOST THEIR RATING. We have allowed white people who are always defining and redefining themselves, to define and redefine us, to tell us what being black is. Success has itself become synonymous with being like the white man. That means being in control and taking care of himself and his family. Historically, that is what his woman wanted, it is what many of our women want too. But white men are not better than black men, they are just in a better position.

There is still a man of color, however, who resists these contemporary stereotypes. He seems to be in a constant state of survival with his outrageous haircuts, excessive jewelry and loud music. Like the field slave, he has never gotten close enough to be changed. He is still playing the old OUTDUMBING GAME, and appears to be saying "I'm not going to let you use me, to break me to be more of your hired help." This contemporary warrior, who is in his prime, is strong, aggressive and eager for a challenge. With no direction, however, he keeps spinning in the same sinking spot, going nowhere. Unfortunately, he may be one of the few real black men remaining. He has been replaced by the African-American man, or rather the American-African man. His skin may still be dark, but he is just as soft and as Europeanized as anyone else.

Italians, Greeks and Hispanics are all white Americans. Even Asian Americans are white Americans. The only Americans who are not white are African-Americans. It is fascinating that African-Americans are so despised, in spite of the fact that world renown paleoanthropologists have traced man's origins all the way back to "Lucy" (the oldest human fossil) - discovered in dear old mother Africa.

What that means is that even though African-Americans are supposedly not real Americans, Americans are all of African descent. Eighteen thousand years ago African descendants occupied caves in southern Europe. The Magdalineans who had migrated to France were wonderful artists, story tellers and sophisticated hunters. Walking erect freed their hands to create tools such as those used in hunting. Hunting allowed the males to spread socialization like developing language, while the women took care of domestic responsibilities. Even on the evolutionary chain, however, the last or most civilized link is always white.

I had often wondered why applications for employment listed race, until I realized that it was one way a potential employer could immediately determine who was not white, and act accordingly. When a black person filled in the space marked black, it might as well have been marked convict.

Race		Race	
White	[ ]	White	[ ]
Black	[ ]	Convict	[ ]
Hispanic	[ ]	Hispanic	[ ]
Asian	[ ]	Asian	[ ]
Other	[ ]	Other	[ ]

Again, black men and black women are being destroyed by incompatibility and unrealistic expectations of each other. As we drift apart however, we need to remember that no matter how important we are, we are still part of the same problem. Black men complain that they cannot find a good women, while black women complain that they cannot find a good man. I believe that both groups are wrong. I think that there are good men and good women, decent people all over the place. THE REAL PROBLEM IS NOT FINDING A GOOD PERSON, BUT FINDING A GOOD PERSON ·YOU ARE COMPATIBLE WITH, USING REALISTIC EXPECTATIONS. That is the real key. To be sure, one thing that you both have in common is that you are black.

Admittedly, it may be very difficult for a real black man who is successful and who knows who he is to find a compatible black woman. When you have worked hard to learn to understand things and to make a difference, it is difficult to be compatible with someone who has not expended a similar amount of energy to understand things and to make a difference. It is not a matter of "you" being better than they are or "them" being any better than you are, you are just in different places. Communication and intelligence are essential to a successful relationship, and it is very difficult to talk to someone on the first floor when you are on the tenth floor yelling.

Likewise, a woman who has experienced growth herself, many times may be carrying around her own old baggage, and is resentful. She has become hardened, and reasonably so, but a healthy relationship with such a woman might still be difficult. Then there are those women who have made it, who are looking for a C.E.O., not a mate. It is indeed a tough proposition, and a black man who has become successful professionally may never find that same success in a loving relationship with a black woman.

THE BLACK WOMAN SAYS THAT SHE WANTS A "REAL MAN," BUT WHAT SHE THINKS THAT IS AND WHAT HE THINKS THAT IS

MAY BE TWO ENTIRE DIFFERENT THINGS. If he grew up in the 60's before Women's Liberation, the black man was definitely the "man of the house." He was a strong and dependable protector and provider with feelings like anyone else. His self-esteem was intact because he was working and doing what a man was expected to do. He wasn't a white man with power but he was still respected as a man and nobody looked down on him. MAMA MAY HAVE DONE HERE FAIR SHARE BUT THERE WAS ONLY ONE "DADDY."

In the 60's, with the passage of Civil Rights Legislation, it finally seemed that black folk might finally have a real shot at that 40 acres and the mule. In the 70's, however, came the seemingly unimposing but catastrophic "White Women's Liberation Movement." BLACK MEN WERE MEN BECAUSE THEY HAD ALWAYS BEEN ABLE TO FIND WORK (NOT AS WELL PAID AS WHITE MEN), BUT SUDDENLY WHITE WOMEN WERE GETTING MANY OF THOSE JOBS AND BLACK MEN BECAME EXPENDABLE.

BECAUSE BLACK MEN HAVE ALWAYS BEEN SEEN AS AN EVER PRESENT THREAT TO WHITE MEN, HIRING WHITE WOMEN WAS A WONDERFUL OPTION. It was also an opportunity, because now that the white woman was working too, she could help the white man pay for that house out in the suburbs, and those two new cars in the double garage. MORE BLACK WOMEN WERE GETTING JOBS TOO, AND EVERYBODY SEEMED HAPPY, EXCEPT FOR THE BLACK MAN WHO WAS NOW HANGING OUT ON STREET CORNERS BECAUSE HE DIDN'T HAVE A JOB TO GO TO. In 1960 less than 4% of women with children were working, but todaay that number has risen to 60%. Making matters worse is the fact that black men and black women who are working must fight for the few jobs that remain. Today, a couple of decades later, it is easy to see why black women and children, but especially black men, were the real "losers" and "casualties" of the Women's Liberation Movement.

AGAIN, AS A MAN HE IS EXPECTED TO FIX THINGS, AND MANY BLACK WOMEN ARE DISAPPOINTED AND ANGRY BECAUSE

EVERYTHING IS FALLING APART. It must be remembered, however, that he didn't break anything, and that he cannot fix everything by himself. When black women say "what have you done for me and my children lately," he blows up. Does anyone really believe this is where he wants to be?

Unknowingly, many black women want to be like white women. IN AMERICA A BLACK WOMAN CAN COME NO CLOSER TO BEING LIKE A WHITE WOMAN THAN A BLACK MAN CAN COME TO BEING LIKE A WHITE MAN. When a black woman tells a black man that she wants respect and equality she fails to realize that they are already equal. Both the black woman and the black man are already powerless as a result of discrimination, prejudice and racism. We cannot afford to be at odds in relationships, and incompatible because our expectations of our mates are unrealistic fantasies.

Buster, 33, had found a very real way to deal with his ex-wife, Paula. The courts demanded that he pay child support, but when he tried to comply his low income job would not leave him with enough to live on. Buster said "What the hell," and decided to stop working. He knew that he would be routinely picked up about every six months for failure to pay child support, so he had it worked out so that, since he was homeless, he would end up in jail during the winter months. Once during an especially severe cold spell his time was up and he was put out. Buster pleaded with the authorities to let him stay but they put him out anyway. He immediately picked up a brick and shattered the windshield of a nearby police car. People said that Buster was crazy, but he knew that he would have shelter and three hot meals a day. Black men and black women often end up divorced enemies who hate each other. Society, with its unrealistic expectations, helps to make black men and black women incompatible.

Incompatibility and unrealistic expectations among black men and black women appears to be a problem that may never be solved. FOR HIM A REAL MAN IS A STRONG INDIVIDUAL WHO IS IN CONTROL. FOR MANY BLACK WOMEN A REAL MAN IS

A COOPERATIVE, COEXISTENT, INTERDEPENDENT MALE PARTNER WHO SHARES CONTROL. Romantically, she idolizes the former, but when it's time to clean the house or pick up the children, she wants the latter. Culture and society are making them incompatible by creating and perpetuating diametrically conflicting expectations.

Other black women identify with successful black men. If this black man meets the model of the successful white man he too can have his pick. All too often, however, he makes the same mistakes that the greedy woman does. He doesn't chose the woman by the content of her character either, but by the way she looks. In either case the implications are clear. LOVE IS GREEN.

CLASS DIFFERENCES TOO, ARE A MAJOR REASON WHY BLACK RELATIONSHIPS ARE NOT WORKING OUT. Not "stuffed shirt" class, but simple every day actions and priorities. For example, being educated versus being uneducated, being talented versus being untalented, being a thinker versus being ignorant, having correct behavior versus being common, having self-respect and respect for other versus being ill mannered, being generous versus being selfish or being successful versus being unsuccessful. These are but a few of the reasons why differences in behavior and attitude often lead to incompatibility and failed relationships. If you know that you and your mate are very different, do not have unrealistic expectations about your relationship. Denial is telling yourself that she will change, but suppose she cannot. You cannot afford to fool yourself. IF YOUR RELATIONSHIP IS FALLING APART YOU MAY SURELY ALREADY KNOW WHY.

Goodpussy is us, who we really are as opposed to who others may be leading us to believe that we are. We need to remember that as we strive to overcome petty differences that threaten our relationships. And how we resolve a problem may be even more important than the problem itself. Compromise, communication and mutual respect are essential. Black men and black women must be willing to work together to work things out. In a subsequent chapter I will deal with a concept called a Frontal Relationship and its connection to compatibility and the theory of Goodpussy.

RIDING FINE, DRESSING FINE
AND TALKING FINE

If you are a black man in America and not riding fine, dressing fine and talking fine, with lots of money in your pockets, you can hang it up -- the fat lady will never sing for you anyway. Many black women think these material things tell them who you are. So without them you are obviously nobody, or at least nobody worth knowing. It's almost axiomatic. If you do not look like a winner, you must be a loser. Because of course as everyone knows, anyone who is successful wants everybody else to know it. This just shows how shallow many people are, however, because anybody can buy clothes or take on an expensive car note. That doesn't mean that they are about anything, and some of the most well spoken men I know are also the biggest bull shitters I know. They are Goodpussy pros.

Black people, who have never had much, distinguished themselves from other blacks, not with the mansions they didn't have, or the Rolls Royces they didn't have, but by the gaudy or trite name-brand clothing or shoes that they wore. So while white America wore Thom McCann and rode, black America wore Stacy Adams and walked. Today, we are still trying to out-do each other to be the biggest nigger on the American plantation.

White people are still manipulating and out-thinking black people. Years ago no woman wanted to be seen at a function wearing the same dress as someone else. But realizing how demanding it was to create original clothing for millions of people, white America once again came through with another stroke of genius -- mass-producing originals or designer labels. Now they make a fortune mass-producing the same item and selling it for more rather than for less. And black people especially, who wear their wealth on their backs, keep on buying.

Today we spend $300 for a pair of tennis shoes that cost only $15 to make, simply because they have some famous name on them, and say that we are somebody. What they really say is "SUCKER," because if you really were somebody who knew who you were, you wouldn't need a pair of tennis shoes to tell you who you were. You would have spent the first $20 on a good pair of tennis shoes and put the remaining $280 in your bank account.

But again, many black people wear their wealth on their backs -- at least they used to. Today many of them are wearing rings on every finger, seven or eight bracelets at one time, and big, ugly, heavy slave chains (SLAVE CHAINS) around their necks that weigh 30 pounds or more. These are the riding fine, dressing fine and talking (rapping) fine young, cool brothers (and sisters). Their cars and their music are always nearby, as are their trusty home boys.

These slave chain-wearing brothers (who do not know their history or who they are), do not seem to realize that the

64

world over, they are the only idiots on this planet choosing to wear shackles on their minds. White boys whose families own the gold mines and the jewelry stores are not wearing chains, but they are making phenomenal profits by selling them to misinformed and uninformed fools. Young black boys in college, those who do want to become somebody, are weighed down with books, not jewelry. Another one of my friends (and as you can probably see by now I have many), once said that "INTELLIGENCE IS NO MATCH FOR STUPIDITY." And he was right, it is not. Foolish people will do stupid things and make asses of themselves, no mater how hard you try to make them understand.

> "As he stepped from his brand new 751-BMW, his white teeth glistened as he spoke with the smooth savvy of a romance ballardiere. His Hugo Boss suit was 100% worsted wool and his Giorgio Armani tie was nothing but the finest silk. His grey Bally boots glistened under the noonday sun almost as much as his 18 carat Cartier chains and the two carat diamond rings that he wore on three fingers of each hand, as finely dressed women eagerly approached him, swooning with adoration and grabbing his hand as they awaited his instructions. . .Yes, that was Reverend Smith, who like so many other ministers, is wrecking black relationships by holding black women captive, turning them against their men and alienating the men."

Black women have historically revered black ministers as their leaders. They have grown up relying on their spiritual leaders (daddy) to guide them. SOME BLACK WOMEN HAVE OBEYED THEIR MINISTERS WITH CHILDLIKE ABANDON, FEEDING THEM, RUNNING ERRANDS FOR THEM, AND SOMETIMES EVEN

SLEEPING WITH THEM. Historically he was the leader, or the only man of power, wisdom, knowledge or learning in the black community, except for an occasional doctor or a lawyer.

WHAT MANY BLACK WOMEN DO NOT SEEM TO REALIZE IS THAT EVEN THOUGH HE IS A MINISTER, HE IS STILL A MAN. When men, who know him better than she ever could, do not attend his church, naive women write them off as hopeless sinners, not realizing that they are the ones who are hopeless hypocrites. When they took their wedding vows they promised to love, honor and obey their husbands, not their preachers. (ALSO, A MAN, ANY MAN, WHO PLACES TOO MUCH CREDENCE ON MATERIAL GAINS IS BY VERY DEFINITION MATERIALISTIC HIMSELF, WHETHER HE IS A DOCTOR, AN OIL TYCOON, A DRUG DEALER OR A MINISTER.) And what these women should realize next is that she herself represents something materialistic too, if no more than one more faithful body with a purse on her arm.

Anthony, a forty year-old seaman, said that his wife's minister "can pimp the rest of the women in that church if he wants to, but if he steps inside my house I'm gonna kick his a--." Not only is the minister riding fine, dressing fine and talking fine, the sisters are often the ones keeping it that way. LIKE THE OLD DAYS OF SLAVERY, THESE WOMEN STILL WANT TO BELONG TO THE WEALTHIEST MASTER AND TO BE PART OF THE BIGGEST PLANTATION, EVEN THOUGH THEY CANNOT SEE IT. Often women who cannot gain power in their every day lives jockey for position within the church, frequently forgetting other responsibilities at home.

We must all remember, especially our black women, that "CLOTHES DO NOT MAKE THE MAN." They are not your knight in shining armor, your Goodpussy. They are only clothes, and no more. His fine car is simply that -- his fine car, not yours.

Black people, even as slaves, had often carried everything they owned on their backs. So having more than the next slave had was what validated the black man. Today that is still true, whether it be expensive starter jackets, flashy street clothing, diamond studded gold teeth or 50 pound radios. Black people who really have nothing else going for themselves gain a false sense of control by validating themselves with junk.

There is an old saying "No money - no honey," and black men understand that only too well. You've got to be riding fine, talking fine and dressing fine or your options will be limited. With money and power you get to pick and chose. Socialization and culturalization have made black people materialistic and greedy too. A man is no longer judged by the content of his character but rather by the content of his wallet. Because of their concessions to materialism (if you've got some money I'll give you some pu_ _ y), many black men are losing respect for some black women. Thelma, 47, wearing diamonds and rubies, says that she never gives a man any pu_ _ y unless he pays for it.

This type of attitude reflects the old saying, "You've got to pay to play." Jaison, 29, said he realized that this was the drill even when he decided to get married.

We must learn to look at the inner person and stop placing so much value on material things. White people can dress anyway they want, and you can never tell who has the money and the power and who does not. Black women who think a black man has to ride fine, dress fine and talk fine are the ones who are really confused. They are the ones who have the real problem because they do not yet know who they are.

THE AUTOMOBILE:
AMERICAN GOODPUSSY

Why do we love cars so much? Why do American teenagers live for the day they get that almighty driver's license? Why are Americans, in fact, automobile addicts? The answer is another easy one: Freedom, or rather independence. THE AUTOMOBILE HAS GIVEN MOBILITY TO AMERICA, MOBILITY WHICH HAS BEEN ONE OF THE GREATEST DISRUPTIVE ELEMENTS IN BLACK FAMILY LIFE SINCE SLAVERY.

Again, we need to remember that freedom is always accompanied by certain unanticipated consequences. While the automobile favorably brought the two coasts -- east and west -- closer together, it has driven humankind further apart. BECAUSE OF THIS NEW-FOUND MOBILITY (INDEPENDENCE), PARENTS CANNOT FIND THEIR TEENAGERS, WIVES CANNOT FIND THEIR HUSBANDS, AND HUSBANDS CANNOT FIND THEIR WIVES, BOYFRIENDS CANNOT FIND THEIR GIRLFRIENDS, AND GIRLFRIENDS CANNOT FIND THEIR BOYFRIENDS.

The automobile has meant that people are no longer restricted to their own communities. CARS HAVE FIGURATIVELY ALLOWED PEOPLE TO DISAPPEAR AT WILL. Men, women and teenagers feel that since I can go anywhere I want to, I will.

Jokes once made about the housewife and the mailman or the milkman are almost never made anymore because we all realize that today's housewife has her own wheels, and the mobility to go wherever or whenever she wishes -- while her husband is at work, when she is supposed to be at the shopping center or just plain whenever.

On a popular syndicated talk show, husbands -- and wives who had cheated on them -- complained about their wives coming in at 3 or 4 o'clock in the morning. WHERE COULD YOUR WIFE OR GIRLFRIEND POSSIBLY BE UNTIL 3 OR 4 O'CLOCK IN THE MORNING? AND MOREOVER, WHAT CAN SHE BE DOING ALL THAT TIME WITHOUT YOU?

In the past, the good ole boys could always go down to the neighborhood watering hole for a few stiff ones. Today, because they have rights too, and because they have their own keys to their own cars, women are going out, either with the girls or by themselves, while dad babysits. BECAUSE OF THIS NEW-FOUND INDEPENDENCE AND ITS ABUSE, MEN AND WOMEN NO LONGER TRUST EACH OTHER. The automobile that we love so much has truly helped to improve the quality of our lives, but it has also helped to erode that quality.

Another bad thing about cars is that everybody has one. Dwayne, a dentist, was in his car on the expressway when he glanced to the right and saw his wife Rosalyn in the next car with another man. Well, he ran them off the road and into a ditch and he repeatedly chased the man around the car with a tire tool, in broad daylight on the expressway, even though he said he no longer loved his wife.

This same dentist was out one night while his own wife was out of town. He met Charlene, another housewife who was out on the town with her girl friends. While driving to his house they had a blowout and rode 15 miles on a flat tire because he said he refused to let an opportunity like that slip past him. And as I listened to him I realized that he, too, seemed to have forgotten the axiom "what goes around comes around."

The automobile and your woman. Is there any solution? Well, maybe. Keep her barefoot and pregnant and take away her driver's license. (Just kidding, folks.)

As a matter of fact, the automobile has always been one of America's most popular bedrooms. Many of us got our first kiss and our first thrill in the back seat of a Ford or Chevy. But even before that, boys who did not play football or basketball or participate in any other sport could use their transportation to capture their own Goodpussy.

During the 60's and the 70's the emphasis was on "Muscle Cars," with big engines and extra horsepower. The interesting thing is the connection between muscles and power

69

in reference to cars. If you had the right kind of car you could have muscles even though you were not an athlete.

In the old days the good ole boys raced for pink slips in cars that really did go fast, and they got the girls. Today, even in advertising, where there is a powerful car, or what looks like a powerful car, there is either a pretty girl or a sexy man. Are we to interpret that as meaning that a sexy muscle car is an extension of a sexy muscle? Since the law has now imposed strict restrictions on speed, auto makers have come up with add-ons that make slow cars look like they go fast, or have muscle. These add-on appearance packages sometimes add thousands of dollars to the sticker price of a car that does not perform any better.

Considering the cost of cars today, it would be much cheaper just to generously stuff a sock, put on a tight pair of designer jeans, and stand on a street corner...And what about the poor sap who has to catch the bus? No Goodpussy for him.

ARE BLACK WOMEN OUT OF CONTROL?

This is a very broad question, but I would certainly agree that some black women are indeed very much out of control. This is not to say that they are not in control of themselves -- that is, their own bodies, their own careers and even their own bank accounts. But what of their sons, daughters, homes and families? Is the same order and organization there?

In the real world husbands are being left stupefied, scratching their heads; homes are falling apart and children are running wild. Many men are resentful and frustrated, and feel they have nowhere to turn. Confusion is running rampant while no one seems to have any answers. The only way many of us can see any type of normalcy is to turn on old episodes of "Ozzie and Harriet," "Father Knows Best," or "Leave It to

Beaver." To find an intact family today you need a television set.

JUST AS AMERICA EXPERIENCED PROBLEMS AFTER THE SLAVES WERE FREED, UNFORESEEN PROBLEMS DEVELOPED AS WELL WHEN WOMEN'S RIGHTS BECAME A REALITY. This is not to say that women were not deserving of their liberties, just as the slave was, but like the slave no consideration was given to the overall possible consequences. The Civil War was fought to preserve the Union, not to free the slaves. Nobody had any idea of what was happening. Yes, the slaves were freed, but they had nowhere to go, nothing to eat, no clothing or medical supplies. In fact, many of them elected to remain on the plantation. The 40 acres and the mule never materialized.

The same thing is true of White Women's Liberation. There was no thought of consequences or contingencies. There was no plan, especially among black women who bought into something that was not intended for them in the first place. Black men have never had any real control over black women anyway, so what did black women need to be liberated from? Working together is one of the reasons why black women and black men have managed to survive. But today black women who want to be the boss seem to have forgotten that "In America the white man is the boss."

A freed people reject authority and are demanding of that which they believe is rightfully theirs. They are not conciliatory. TODAY, WOMEN ARE CONFUSED AND ANGRY, FAMILIES ARE CONFUSED AND ANGRY, AND SOCIETY IS DYSFUNCTIONAL. For every cause there is a corresponding consequence. But this time the consequence is that many black relationships are no longer working either.

In the 80's and 90's latch key kids go home to empty houses. There is no one there to feed them, to help them with homework or to discuss the enormous challenge of growing up in today's world. Boys needing love often turn to mischief while girls find it in sexual relationships with boys or older men, and sometimes drugs or both.

72

MANY WOMEN, DEMANDING THEIR RIGHT TO NOW PURSUE THEIR DREAMS, HAVE FORGOTTEN THAT SOMEONE HAS TO MIND THE STORE. As equal citizens they believe that they are due equal participation, and they certainly are, but someone still has to maintain the family.

In a war that has been raging for almost 200 years, black women who have just been given guns now consider themselves Generals. But because someone gives you a gun, that doesn't mean you know how to shoot it or that you even know who you should be shooting at.

Today, black women who mistakingly consider themselves free want to exercise their options. Feeling that black men have not done a very good job, they are eager to step forward and clean up the mess they believe we have made. Because of their new-found freedom, many black women are unnecessarily argumentative. You cannot tell them anything, especially if you are a black man. They have all the "right" answers already. They know everything they need to know. It's kind of like a relay race where the last man to get the baton thinks he has won the race all by himself. MANY BLACK WOMEN HAVE FORGOTTEN HOW FAR THEY HAVE COME AND THAT THEY DID NOT MAKE THE TRIP ALONE.

Good black men have done their best, and given their all, to get us where we are today. Notable men and the common man as well -- fathers, uncles and brothers who made a difference, many times for some of these same women.

If black women think their hearts have been broken, consider the man who loves his mate dearly, only to have her turn on him. WOMEN WHO WANT MORE AND BELIEVE THEY CAN GET IT ARE GOING FOR IT, NO MATTER WHO THEY HAVE TO LEAVE BEHIND. Some black women actually seem to think that it is a disgrace to care for a man.

Again, many black men want the same thing their fathers had with their mothers, a loving, nurturing, faithful, supportive woman. Women, who want what they want, reply "F--k you and your mama." Many women resent their mothers-in-law and other older women who take pride in caring for a man, because they see them as shuffling, condescending traitors. They see them as throwbacks to the old attitudes like "keep 'em barefoot and pregnant," and "when you say jump" she should say "how high?" For today's liberated black woman that will never do.

In turning from the black man many black women are turning to the white man. Some women feel that they aren't doing any less than the black man did when he turned to the white woman. Many black women who are making it today will have nothing to do with a black man unless he is riding fine, dressing fine, and talking fine with a good job and lots of money in his pockets. They've forgotten about the 60's and 70's when the black man was making $100.00 a week and still managing to take them out to movies and restaurants. These days a black woman will come straight out and tell you, "Oh no, I don't go there." Some of these "important" black women are so impressed with their own "specialness" that they no longer want to have anything to do with a black man. Some publicly advertise that they are seeking a white male.

Some black women fail to realize that while they are allowed to move up, a racist society holds the black man back. When they reach the top there will be no friendly face waiting there to greet them. Sure, white America will reward them, but it will take something back too, by controlling and restricting her personal options. Rodney, 27, was disgusted as he bitterly joked about his relationships with women. Rodney said, "Half the black women I meet are over qualified." Gerald, an army captain, says that when he goes downtown all he sees are black women in business suits and black men making deliveries.

As I listened to them I laughed too, until I thought more deeply about what they were saying. Are black women over qualified, or is it more accurate to say that they are equally qualified? Are black women out of control or are

74

some of them simply trying to gain some sense of security and stability?

IS AN AMERICAN PATRIARCHAL SOCIETY BASED ON WHITE MALE SUPREMACY DISTORTING OUR THINKING BY TELLING US THAT WOMEN ARE THE WEAKER SEX? And is that why black women who behave uncustomarily are frequently considered bitches? After all, American culture is based on tough individualism, competition, and an almost obsessive compulsion to excel. ARE SOME BLACK WOMEN SIMPLY ADAPTING TO WESTERN CULTURAL IDEAS, AND TO AN ENVIRONMENT WHERE THEY BELIEVE THEY HAVE ACCESS AS COMPETENT CITIZENS? But while black women are deserving of an opportunity to live fulfilled lives, it is critical that they keep things in their proper perspective, especially their families and their surroundings. DO THESE BLACK WOMEN REALIZE, HOWEVER, THAT AMERICA DOES NOT AND HAS NEVER CONSIDERED THEM EQUAL CITIZENS? That is why, as slaves, they had to work in the fields with the men while white women did not. America has never even considered black women equal women, that is, equal to white women.

SOME BLACK WOMEN ARE <u>APPARENTLY</u> BECOMING MORE INDEPENDENT, AND A TOO HASTILY LIBERATED SEGMENT OF ANY POPULATION WILL ALWAYS RESULT IN CONFUSION AND PROBLEMS OF ADJUSTMENT. Whenever there is rapid change some people will move ahead while others predictably fall behind. The old rules no longer work. This is especially important in black relationships because the old rules (our own rules about supporting each other) were the ones that worked for us.

ONE THING THAT BLACK MEN ABSOLUTELY MUST DO IS STOP SEEING WOMEN AS THE WEAKER SEX. That is one of the reasons why black women can so easily "depersonalize" seemingly ineffective black males when they (the women) become stronger. The old rules socialized black men and black women to be caring and protective, but today's 80's and 90's black women want to be a tough, independent developer or industralist. BUT HER HEART IS NO BIGGER, NO SOFTER, NO

75

MORE FEELING AND NO KINDER THAN YOURS IS...Don't forget that.

Another tragedy is that these same women are so consumed with themselves that they do not understand why they are getting those good paying jobs. CONTRARY TO PUBLIC OPINION, NOT EVERY BLACK MAN IS A HIGH SCHOOL DROPOUT. Many black men are well-qualified for those same jobs black women are getting, but she is less threatening -- individually or collectively. Also, quite contrary to her egotistical thinking, and predictably, the white man knew that once she started making money she would leave the black man, and many have. Without access black men can never become successful.

I am reminded of a company picnic a friend told me about. He said company policy prohibited management from mixing with labor, but on this occasion one of the black women all the black men admired at a distance was making moves on a white manager. He said that he saw the two of them in the parking lot and the guy was all under her clothes. Later that night the white manager approached him saying, "I can get the best ya'll have, and you can't even sniff it."

The ultimate example of a woman being out of control recently occurred in New Orleans when a world-class entertainer failed to appear for a sold-out concert. Even before leaving the airport she was enraged because her limo was white instead of black. The marquis at the theater listed someone else besides her; that had to be changed. Specified in writing, in her contract, was a clause that stated no stage help could speak to her or have eye contact with her. On stage, during a sound check, she suddenly stopped to ask, "What city are we in?" Dissatisfied with the theater, she said that she was not feeling well and had the show cancelled. While anxious fans were lining up for the show, her jet was flying over their heads. "No Eye Contact," in writing. Now that's out of control.

JUST AS BLACK WOMEN WANT BLACK MEN TO REMEMBER WHAT IT IS TO BE A MAN, THEY MUST REMEMBER WHAT IT IS TO

BE A WOMAN. Are black women out of control? If they are not loving, respecting and supporting themselves, their men, and their families, yes they are. EVEN BACK ON THE PLANTATION YEARS AGO, THE WHITE SLAVE MASTER REALIZED THAT HER STRENGTH AND CHARACTER MADE THE BLACK WOMAN THE REAL GOODPUSSY. AND ONLY SHE CAN DESTROY HERSELF.

TOO MANY GIRL FRIENDS

A black man's and a black woman's biggest enemy is often too many girlfriends. Not his, but hers. According to a male friend of mine, "Women are dangerous." THEY CAN MEET EACH OTHER IN THE LADIES ROOM, EXCHANGE TELEPHONE NUMBERS, BECOME THE BEST OF FRIENDS, AND BEFORE YOU KNOW IT THEY KNOW ALL YOUR BUSINESS AND EVERYBODY ELSE'S TOO. They become their own Goodpussy.

And girlfriends do know each other's business. After all, they are constantly interacting. THEY KNOW EACH OTHER'S SECRETS AND INFLUENCE EACH OTHER'S DECISIONS. Girl friends also tend to be jealous and possessive. They want you with them, literally, and their "sisterhood" set must never be broken up. "MISERY LOVES COMPANY AND WOMEN WHO DO NOT HAVE A GOOD RELATIONSHIP WILL MAKE SURE YOU DO NOT HAVE ONE EITHER BEFORE IT'S OVER."

GIRL FRIENDS, EAGER FOR INTRIGUE AND MORE HOT TOPICS TO TALK ABOUT, WILL ENCOURAGE YOU TO TAKE ON A NEW RELATIONSHIP, AND SWEEP YOUR OLD ONE UNDER THE CARPET. Hearing you talk about how wonderful your man is, or how sweet he is is boring, old business. But talking about a new man is exciting and filled with expectations. They would rather say, "Girl, I wouldn't take that" rather than "I wish I had a man like yours." They use you to fill the pot holes in their otherwise uneventful lives.

A great lady, Miss Pearl Bailey, once said, "Whenever people try to give me all kinds of accolades and introduce me as Miss Pearl Bailey, I always tell them I'm just plain Pearl." She said, "WHENEVER SOMEBODY PUTS YOU UP ON A PEDESTAL JUST WATCH OUT THAT THEY'RE NOT UP ON THAT PEDESTAL AND YOU'RE LEFT HOLDING THE STEM."

That's like the good-looking woman who has a nice man in her life, but her girlfriends are always pumping her up and keeping her around because she draws the men. Her ego and conceit allow these so-called friends to use her. They end up getting the attention they want, but she loses her boyfriend.

AND MOTHERS CAN ALSO BE ONE OF THOSE GIRLFRIENDS WHO SPEND TOO MUCH TIME WITH HER NOSE BURIED IN YOUR BUSINESS. After all, those ugly mother-in-law jokes had to come from somewhere. In some cultures the mother-in-law and the son-in-law are supposed to stay clear of each other, and he can't go near her home, even if she's not there.

Alton, 27, a newly-wed, said that Rose, his new bride was in the kitchen humming as she prepared some of his favorite dishes when his mother-in-law, Rita scolded her, saying "I know you're not fixing all that just for him." Alton said he could see right then and there that the handwriting was on the wall and that he would have to erase it before it was too late. Rose was his wife. And if she felt good about doing something for him -- well why not?

Too many girl friends can wreck your life, and his.
KNOW WHO YOUR FRIENDS ARE, YOUR REAL FRIENDS.

MILKTOAST (HONEY-DO) MEN

Before men can get themselves together, they've got to get themselves together.

SURE, HE MAY WASH HIS HOT-LOOKING CAR EVERY SATURDAY, SIT RELIGIOUSLY GLUED TO MONDAY NIGHT FOOTBALL ON TELEVISION WEEK AFTER WEEK, FISH IN THE SPRING, HUNT IN THE WINTER, AND EVEN PLAY BASKETBALL WITH THE FELLOWS ON THURSDAY NIGHTS, BUT HE MAY STILL BE JUST ONE MORE SOFT AND MUSHY, HONEY-DO "MILKTOAST MAN." His voice is deep and his tone commanding as he orders his five year old daughter to put her toys away, but he barely raises an eyebrow when his wife casually says that she and her girl friends are going out of town for the weekend. For her he has neither bark nor bite, and he is just one more dull and boring "apple pie kind of guy." ON THE OUTSIDE HE IS NORMAL ENOUGH, BUT

81

THE PERSON ON THE INSIDE IS LESS ASSERTIVE THAN A TWO-DAY-OLD LAMB.

"Nobody owns anybody else," he explains. She (his wife) is a grown woman. She can come and go as she pleases, and she does just that. In fact, it is almost as if she has switched places with him. HE BABY SITS, COOKS, WASHES THE DISHES, MOPS THE FLOOR AND SUPERVISES THE HOMEWORK WHILE SHE IS OUT TAKING CARE OF MORE IMPORTANT PERSONAL BUSINESS, HERS. He has no problem with her constant male companion (friend) sitting at his kitchen table when he comes home from work, or relaxing in front of the television set while he leaves to run down to the supermarket. It is almost as if his wife's friend is the man in their house. Even when close friends and associates begin to ask questions about seeing his wife out with the other man, he still sees no problem.

Bull shit! WOMEN DO NOT RESPECT MEN WHO ARE PU--YS. If you are that easy going and unconcerned about her comings and goings, you might as well be one of the girls, and that's exactly how she begins to see you more or less. Instead of setting a strong example that the family may follow, she overtakes you and begins to set the tone of your relationship. As far as she is concerned you are hopeless and helpless and you might as well be invisible. SOMETIMES MEN TEND TO FORGET THAT IF YOU MAKE A DOOR MAT OF YOURSELF, SOMEONE WILL WALK ON YOU.

One of the most obvious signs that something is seriously wrong is that the two of you are no longer making love, or even having sex, but you still remain both publicly and privately unmoved. In fact, she couldn't care less whether you are sleeping with another woman, or even another man. You have become that unimportant and insignificant. She is now wearing the pants, not just a second pair of pants. She is wearing your pants and your next birthday present will probably be an apron and a feather duster.

IS VIOLENCE EVER JUSTIFIABLE?

Is violence ever justifiable? I'm not really sure. Do you believe in capital punishment? For the answers to this one I'm afraid you are going to have to search your own conscience, because it is such a personal matter. SOCIETY IMPERSONALLY AND INSENSITIVELY SIMPLIFIES THINGS SO MUCH, ESPECIALLY SOMEONE ELSE'S PAIN AND SUFFERING. When a criminal kills somebody else's son, we dispassionately say, "Oh, give him five years." But suppose it was your son or daughter who was killed? Would you still be so casual?

I have heard people say over and over again that there is never any reason for a man to hit a woman. Well, I'm not so sure about that either. IF SHE FORGETS HOW A REAL WOMAN IS SUPPOSED TO ACT, THEN I GUESS SOMETIMES TWO WRONGS DO MAKE A RIGHT, AND HE CAN FORGET HOW A REAL MAN IS SUPPOSED TO ACT.

Let me tell you another little true story. There was once a bus driver, Sam, who loved his wife very much. He was also a good provider. Sam and his family lived in a nice house in a clean community and enjoyed many of the comforts of life. He worked while she was a homemaker. Well, one day Sam left for work as usual, but became ill and had to go home early. (Remember that this is a real person living in the real world.)

When he opened the door to their home, his home, the one that he was working hard every day to pay for, on the living room sofa, in his own home, was a gut wrenching sight. HE FOUND ANOTHER MAN LYING ON HIS COUCH, BUCK NAKED, IN THE PRONE POSITION, WITH HIS WIFE ALSO NAKED AS A JAY BIRD KNEELING BESIDE THIS STRANGER, WITH SEVEN INCHES OF THE OTHER MAN'S PENIS JAMMED IN HER MOUTH AND SEMEN DRIPPING FROM HER LIPS.

Seeing a sight like that has to be the next worst thing to losing a loved one, because obviously your wife on her knees, in your home, making love to another man, is the loss of a loved one. IT WAS AS UNEXPECTED AS FIRST DEGREE MURDER AND EQUALLY AS DEVASTATING.

Well, you know it. He beat his wife's a--, and put her out. Instinctively, he did not touch the man, because after all, the fellow had not done any more than Sam's wife allowed him to do.

Many men have been conditioned to see things that way, but that is only one way of looking at it. This man was disrespecting Sam, both by being in his home and by being in his wife's mouth. So maybe he did deserve a little something, too, for his trouble. In fact, he should have gotten something for all the pain he was now causing the bus driver, with his wife's help. He knew he was violating this man's home and the sanctity of his marriage. That's why he waited until Sam had gone to work to sneak over. He was as responsible for his actions as she was for hers. If he had gone into a bank to rob it but was caught in the act, he would be punished, and being found with this man's wife was surely a more severe crime. For Sam this sight could not have been any worse than helplessly watching as his wife was being raped.

For anyone this would have been a shocking ordeal. This one incident, in that single instant, forever altered the course of this man's relationship with his wife and changed the rest of his life. Maybe trust can be born again, but it will never be the same.

Society would have us believe that in a situation like that Sam should have walked in, excused himself, allowed them to finish, and then talked about it like reasonable adults, over coffee, which he prepared. "Be real." People should try putting themselves in the other guy's shoes sometimes.

The story doesn't end there however. Sam beat his wife, threw her out, cried and told all the neighbors what she had done, and then he took the little lady back, forgiving her I suppose because he couldn't live without his Goodpussy.

EVERY 15 SECONDS IN AMERICA, A HUSBAND OR A BOYFRIEND BATTERS A WOMAN. Surely, black men and black women represent a significant portion of that number. Unlike Sam's situation, however, many of these women did not provoke the aggression.

Angry black men who have been battered and abused by society and rendered socially impotent try to project control and manliness by striking out against those least prepared to defend themselves, their women. "I'm hitting her so whatever is wrong it must be her fault..." No, try accepting some responsibility yourself.

These men are cowards who are running away from shadows of their own frightful hopelessness. They are weaklings who have forgotten that black women were abused, too, perhaps even more than he was. So now he is beating up on the best friend he has ever had rather than the person he is really afraid of, the one who still has his foot on the black man's neck. (Let's not forget those old slavery lessons about never raising your hand to a white man either.)

85

In Africa the woman is the "queen mother" and her main protector is the brother who will always be part of the family. If the husband abuses his wife he answers to her family. In America, with its emphasis on individualism, if the husband beats his wife, and sometimes even his children, it's nobody else's business.

Historically, white men called the black woman a bitch and a whore while they knocked her up and knocked her around. Now some pitiful black men are doing the same thing. CONTRARY TO WHAT HE MIGHT BELIEVE, THE MORE HE BEATS HER THE SMALLER HE BECOMES. And everybody seems to know it but him.

Angry black men who are powerless, frustrated, bitter and insecure batter and abuse helpless women and children because they do not know who they are. But beating others up will not help them find themselves. Perhaps they should try beating their own behinds for a while for being so stupid.

WHAT IS A FRONTAL RELATIONSHIP?

WELL, A FRONTAL RELATIONSHIP IS ONE THAT IS JUST THAT, UP-FRONT. In a frontal relationship the two people involved are figuratively juxtaposed and facing each other. They are sealed together, air tight, water tight and vacuum packed, from head to toe, in loving harmony. IN A FRONTAL RELATIONSHIP THE COUPLE IS ESSENTIALLY ONE AND THEIR ONENESS IS NOT CONTRIVED OR IMPOSED. It is a feeling that comes as easily and as freely as breathing or sleeping, and it needs no motivation. A frontal relationship is the ultimate security. In a frontal relationship the partners fit together as naturally as a hand in a warm, well seasoned glove. It is peaches and cream, colors in nature, mother's milk or an autumn breeze. It is both true and truth.

The existing alternative to a frontal relationship is a Lateral Relationship. IN A LATERAL RELATIONSHIP THE PAIR ARE SIDE BY SIDE OR IN SOME OTHER SIMILAR CONFIGURATION THAT IS ANYTHING BUT FRONTAL. A lateral relationship is one that is capable of working, but with concessions or compromises, because it is not as intrinsically balanced as a frontal relationship. Like a frontal relationship, it is not a matter of liking or of disliking or of wanting or not wanting. It simply is what it is. A lateral relationship however may sometimes infer blame or guilt, and require decision-making or trade-offs. YOU MAY FIND YOURSELF ASKING, IS A LATERAL RELATIONSHIP WORTH IT?

A figurative example of a lateral relationship may be a man and a woman standing side by side or lying side by side. Even though they are close, their vision may be focused somewhere else, and not on each other, specifically. Generally they are not each other's single most important interest. Not being immersed in each other, they are hardly absorbed by each other. They are distracted and their interests are varied. Another way of putting it is that two lateral people would probably not be in love with each other. They may well love each other, or love certain things about each other, but they are not in love with each other. A man who spends all of his time gambling and drinking with the boys or a woman who spends all of her free time going out with her girlfriends are not focusing on each other and are not in love with each other.

IN A FRONTAL RELATIONSHIP, THAT OTHER PERSON IS THE MOST IMPORTANT THING IN YOUR LIFE. Others may matter and be important, but this one person gives purpose to your being. He or she brings out that real person in each of us, personally.

Sometimes people say when someone commits suicide over someone else that they must have been crazy, that nobody is worth dying for, and this is what they believe. The answer may in part be due to the fact that they have never been fortunate enough to have experienced a true frontal relationship with another adult. Parents in frontal relationships with their children are prepared to die for them. Are they crazy? Sometimes an elderly person dies and a short time later their mate dies also, of natural causes. Is that crazy? A frontal relationship is real Goodpussy. TO KNOW A FRONTAL RELATIONSHIP, OR GOODPUSSY, IS TRULY TO HAVE LIVED AND TO HAVE KNOWN LOVE. It is the delicious icing on your favorite cake or that single juicy red cherry that tops your ice cream sundae. I may attempt to try to help you understand what a frontal relationship is, but the only way to really know it is to be in it, to feel it, to live it.

I BELIEVE TOO, THAT THERE ARE COMBINATIONS OF FRONTAL AND LATERAL RELATIONSHIPS AS WELL AND THAT A FRONTAL RELATIONSHIP MAY ALSO BE CONFRONTATIONAL. Sometimes two people's feelings for each other may be so intense, so passionate, that their situation cannot be considered anything but frontal, but because of their innate differences, their relationship is also antagonistic. This is one of those Love/Hate relationships that really do exist. You know, the ones people joke about all the time, "I can't live with her and I can't live without her." And their feelings are quite genuine. Their life is miserable with that person and equally as miserable without them. It is probably the same for people on drugs. They love the euphoric high and hate the abysmal low, but they just cannot leave it alone.

ANOTHER TYPE OF FRONTAL-LATERAL RELATIONSHIP IS THE ONE WHERE ONE PERSON GIVES HIS ALL AND THE OTHER PERSON'S INTERESTS ARE ELSEWHERE. In a relationship like this that lasts, the absolute commitment from the primary party somehow compensates for the insensibility of the latter partner. It's like the woman who works, keeps house, raises the children, pays the bills and deals with broken pipes while her husband hangs out. She gives so much that things still somehow have a way of working out. The same thing may be true in a situation where the man works two or three jobs, comes home to a dirty house, and has to feed himself because his wife has been watching the soaps all day or talking on the telephone to girlfriends, or boyfriends. A Frontal Relationship (Goodpussy) is a pairing. Anything else is a trade-off.

A PERSON MAY ALSO HAVE A FRONTAL RELATIONSHIP WITH AN INANIMATE OBJECT. Athletes may have it with a particular sport just as a sailor may have it with boating.

SOMETIMES MEN WHO HAVE DIFFICULTIES WITH COMMITTING TO A SINGLE WOMAN FORM FRONTAL RELATIONSHIPS WITH SEX. I have an uncle (89 years old and counting), my Uncle Johnny, who has a Frontal Relationship with fishing, his Goodpussy. My Uncle Johnny fishes on the lake with his friends every day, and everybody knows "Cigar" (he keeps one in his mouth but never lights it). I'm sure this keeps him and his friends going. Even the day his wife, my Aunt Mildred, died, he had to go to the lake to see his friends. Over the years, old white fishing buddies have also died, willing to Cigar, money, cars, trucks and even a house, because this long-standing camaraderie was their Goodpussy too. Again, Goodpussy is whatever makes you, you.

IT IS IMPORTANT TO REMEMBER HOWEVER THAT BEFORE YOU CAN HAVE A TRULY HEALTHY AND LASTING FRONTAL RELATIONSHIP WITH SOMEONE ELSE, YOU MUST FIRST HAVE A HEALTHY FRONTAL RELATIONSHIP WITH YOURSELF.

Like the quick home pregnancy test today, understanding Frontal and Lateral Relationships can immediately help to give you a better understanding of your own relationships. If your relationship is Frontal there is rapture, love, and your mate will not cheat on you because you are as important to her as she is to herself. In a Lateral Relationship many things may be just as important or more important than you are.

In today's competitive world, many people are electing to form Frontal Relationships with their jobs and turning their backs on loved ones. In dealing with Frontal Relationships with things, it is still important to remember that it is just that, a thing. It may give you many things, but it is still not another human being.

90

In concluding this chapter I would like to say that I believe "the ultimate frontal relationship lies with God." It is wisdom and truth whereby God is with and in each of us.

THAT ONE WOMAN

THERE IS ALWAYS THAT ONE WOMAN WHO CAN MAKE YOU FEEL EVERYTHING THAT YOU HAVE DREAMED OF BUT NEVER REALLY BELIEVED POSSIBLE: HEART THROBBING PASSION, WEAKNESS, LUST, DEPENDENCY, EXHILARATION, LOVE, AND EVEN ONENESS. She can lift you higher than ether or make you feel even more worthless than dust. With her you are complete. Without her you are nothing, worth less than a sheet of paper.

YOU LOVE EVERY SQUARE INCH OF HER, FROM THE VERY TIP-TOP OF THE LONGEST HAIR ON HER HEAD TO THE VERY EDGE OF HER LITTLE TOE AND THE BOTTOM OF HER FOOT. You love being near her, the smell of her, the way her skin feels. In fact, you actually love her skin, and if you could eat her she would be the most delicious meal you ever had. Making love to her is the most absolutely euphoric, passionate experience. With her you discover there is more to making love than just making love and that just having sex is not enough anymore. She is your Goodpussy.

Her breath is your breath, her body your body, even to the extent that as she quietly sleeps, if a drop of saliva sneaks from the side of her mouth, you will move nearer to her and delicately catch it with your own tongue. If she rests her head on your chest, you feel it in your soul. EVERYTHING THAT YOU CAN DO FOR HER IS NOT NEARLY ENOUGH. PROTECTING HER FROM COLD OR BAD WEATHER, CARING FOR HER WHEN SHE IS ILL, YOU LOVINGLY LAY YOUR HEART AND YOUR LIFE AT HER FEET. Her self is all and more than you feel you need in life. No mansions, no Mercedes, no partying every night, no other woman, taking trips together and visions of you rocking together side by side in your old age. She is truly all that you feel you need. More important, life without her would not be worth living. But it only works when she feels the same way, too.

When Mickey, 33, saw Joan for the first time he was struck, as if by a bolt of lightning. After work, during rush hour traffic, there she was holding a long stemmed red rose in her hand. Cutting illegally across traffic Mickey pulled up beside what he called the sexiest woman he had ever seen. He said, "Excuse me. I really don't mean to be intrusive. But, are you married?"

Joan's bright dancing eyes and her sparkling smile almost melted Mickey in his convertible when she playfully responded, "Hey, are you married?" They had snowballs together and went to a baseball game that same afternoon.

As he quietly reflected, Mickey said that Joan was truly unforgettable. She wasn't just one thing in particular but many things at one time. She was serious, funny, intelligent, independent, giving, loving, sexy, charming, witty and self-confident. But above all else, Joan was trusting and honest. She knew how to talk to Mickey. But she also knew how to listen to him. Joan knew how to care for Mickey too, and she couldn't care less what anybody else thought about it.

"That one woman" is the indescribable woman who touches a warm, soft spot in your heart that no one else can ever reach. She is the sexual and emotional live wire to your very soul. "That one women" alone is truly exciting, vibrant and at the same time she is intriguing and mysterious. She is vital...She is real...And her beauty is both external and internal. SHE IS THE MOST COMPLETE WOMAN YOU WILL EVER KNOW.

HOW TO SURVIVE A BREAK-UP

REMEMBER, SHE CAN BE A BITCH, LIKE A ROTTWEILER, A DOBERMAN OR A PIT BULL. That cute little doggie you saw in the pet store window (sweet little Goodpussy) is fully capable of biting your heads off, both of them, if she feels she has been provoked. THIS IS A DOG-EAT-DOG WORLD, AND IF SHE HAS TASTED YOUR BLOOD ONCE, SHE MAY BE BACK FOR MORE. After all, hell hath no fury like a woman scorned. Yes, she cooks and cleans and sings like an angel, but she scratches too, and she can be very dangerous.

This little scenario may or may not be true because certainly not all women are so vicious and destructive. It is important, however, that you be honest with yourself, and that you do not cause yourself any further grief by romanticizing who she is. DO NOT MAKE EXCUSES FOR HER ANYMORE.... TELL YOURSELF THE TRUTH.

Be sincere with yourself about what you really feel, no matter how much it hurts. Try to remember who you are and what you really want. If there are loving friends and relatives who care about you, do not shut them out, because part of the problem may be that you already feel that you have been shut out, abandoned. REMEMBER THAT YOU ARE A MAN.

During the 70's and 80's black men, like white men, were told to be more caring, more sensitive and more sympathetic to the needs of their women. The only problem with this was that nobody remembered to remind the women to be caring, sympathetic and sensitive to the needs of their men also. In essence, the roles have been reversed, and many men have become passive while their women have become aggressive. It's almost like the mouse coming to a screeching halt and saying to the cat, "Let's talk more" and when the cat kneels to listen, the "man-eating rat" jumps him.

REMEMBER, THIS NEW-FOUND FREEDOM IS NEW TO ALL OF US, ESPECIALLY TO WOMEN. Like the teenager who takes the family sedan out alone for the first time, she has not yet mastered either the car or the road. She is bound, and even entitled, to make a few mistakes. The problem, however, is that these particular mistakes are adversely and severely affecting all of us, and our lives are coming apart.

Again, not all women are predators. Some women do realize that we are running on red, and they are sincerely doing their best to make things work, too. A female author has sparked heated debate by suggesting that the only way black men can regain control of their women is by slapping them back into submission. While I do not necessarily agree with her solution, I do believe if some white women are out of control, then surely some black women are too, and that the problem began with the white women's liberation movement as I previously stated.

White men have always been held in high esteem, so no one was going to walk over them. Black men have never been respected as much or been as free as white men, white women and even black women. If something is bad for white people it is critical for black people. If white families and relationships are falling apart, then black families and relationships are disintegrating.

Those black men and women who are familiar with biblical teachings know that the man is the head, and is to be respected. The only thing the black man ever had any semblance of control of from time to time was his family, but as the family became more socialized, secular and educated, or uneducated, values changed and respect was lost. Once his word was the last word, if not the only word. As the number of black males declined and their role as head of the family shifted, black women, of necessity, picked up the torch, leading to further alienation between black men and women. AS BLACK MEN CONTINUED TO BE CUT DOWN AND BLACK WOMEN PICKED UP MOMENTUM AND THE TWO SEXES BECAME MORE ESTRANGED, THEY WERE STILL NOT ABLE TO RESOLVE THEIR DIFFERENCES, NOT EVEN FOR THEIR OWN SURVIVAL. The old adage of divide and conquer was working only too well, and we were all losing. The love was gone, and so was the trust.

As one man I know said, "The only way that a man can make it is to keep 100% for himself." Many black men that I know who have tried to be fair to women and who have been hurt by them have vowed never to leave themselves open again. Men do suffer and they do hurt; from the pits of their twisted guts to their chronic headaches and bleeding hearts. They feel hopeless, helpless and worthless, like nothing. Black men are not omnipotent and nobody expects them to really be that way, except themselves. Because they are perceived as the stronger of the sexes, however, their feelings are often ignored, feelings that they do their best to hide anyway. AND UNLIKE WOMEN, MOST BLACK MEN LACK THE TIES AND SUPPORT MECHANISMS THAT WOMEN ENJOY, SUCH AS CHILDREN, PARENTS THEY ARE CLOSE TO, AND OTHER GIRL FRIENDS.

97

Any man can be hurt, as many men I know have been hurt. One friend of mine, Raynard, had an agreement with his wife. She told him, "If you ever see me fooling around with another man, put your hands on me." Well, while she was on vacation in Detroit, he flew up and surprised her. Wearing his diamonds and a full-length mink coat, Raynard found his wife in a lounge, in another man's arms. This 230-pound black man placed both of his hands firmly on both of his wife's arms saying, "Bitch, you told me to put my hands on you and that's what I'm doing!" She passed out.

He said he flew back home to New Orleans and that two months later when she returned he had already filed for legal separation. He told me that he had lost all respect for her and that he just could not trust her anymore. He said that he was really f--ked up, and that her unfaithfulness had devastated him.

The irony about this particular little story is that Raynard had been a pimp for most of the years I had known him, and as he said, "Man, I was selling that pu--y." But his own wife was unfaithful. Raynard, like many of us, had somehow forgotten to "do unto others as you would have them do unto you" and that "what goes around comes around."

You cannot do bad and expect good to come from it. If he was not doing the right thing by her, how could he possibly expect her to do the right thing by him? And as he vowed, with a bible in his hand, that he would never let another woman get that close to him, I recalled my own late father's words to me. He said, "DON'T LOVE ANY SUCKER MORE THAN THEY LOVE YOU." A young man at the time, I remember thinking that he was being crude, but I realize now that he understood far more than I gave him credit for. He loved me and he was only trying to protect me. He wanted me to understand too, how deep the hurt may be when you trust and care too much.

Like Raynard, you may want to kill your unfaithful woman, too. But don't. He said the one thing that stopped

98

him from doing just that was the thought of spending the rest of his life behind bars. Prisons are not known for their pleasant accommodations and your new companions could be even worse than she was, although you do not think about that at the time. Besides, no matter how pretty she is or how fine she is, she isn't worth it anyway. And it probably wasn't all her fault either. Sure, you may blame her, but what did you do while you were there? Hatred is a stronger motivation than love and even economics, but is it worth losing everything for?

Sometimes our pride does us in too, like the man who has a woman that he just cannot walk away from, even though she may already have left him sick, literally, and standing in his own smelly puke. He has this big, fine healthy woman and refuses to let anyone know that she is getting the best of him. She is kicking his a-- but what can he do? He is like the cowboy in the corral surrounded by the rest of the hands, who tries to ride a horse that keeps bucking him off, too stupid to realize that nobody else can ride that particular horse either. Some black women are like that, too. Nobody else can ride them either.

One of the most difficult battles you may have to fight is your own ego, or more specifically, rejection. Breaking up may be alright. But the fact that she left you is another story, a nightmare.

Troy, 34, a waiter, said that he had fallen in love with Shana, so he was ready to leave Opel anyway. But Opel beat him to the punch. Troy said that he wanted the breakup to be his idea. He refused to believe that Opel no longer wanted him. In fact, Troy said he spent so much time running after Opel so he could be the one to call the relationship off that he ended up losing Shana, too. When he would call, her mother would say that she wasn't home. If he called her job, Opel would hang up on him, and threaten to call the police. Finally, Troy just couldn't take anymore. At 2:00 a.m. he drove to her house, and when her car was gone, he frantically drove everywhere he thought she might be. When he found her car parked in front of her cousin's house he poured gasoline on it, and striking a match, set it on fire. To this day Troy believes that insecurity and foolish pride cost him the love of his life when he lost Shana as well.

REMEMBER, YOU CANNOT GET YOUR ACT TOGETHER UNTIL YOU GET YOUR ACT TOGETHER, AND THE LONGEST JOURNEY STARTS WITH THE FIRST STEP. Just pray and remember to keep God in your life. And keep getting up, taking life one day at a time, one step at a time. You can be in love with her and still never be able to be happy together.

A wise man is one who knows that life is a delicate balance of mind over matter, and again, IF YOU WANT DIFFERENT RESULTS, DO THINGS DIFFERENTLY. Do not depend on defense mechanisms and crutches like drugs, alcohol or loose sex, and above all else DO NOT TAKE YOURSELF TOO SERIOUSLY.

It's time to find yourself and your own Goodpussy. Black men have always had to dig deep to survive. Just believe in you. I am reminded of a wonderful song by Gale Garnette that goes...

My daddy he once told me
Hey don't you love you any man
Just take what they may give you
And give but what you can
And you can sing in the sunshine
You'll laugh every day
You'll sing in the sunshine
Then be on your way.

Some will tell you the best way to survive is to keep your distance in the first place. When you let people get too close, they can do just that, they can get too close to you and to your heart. But the question is, "If you never get that

close, do you ever really sing in the sunshine or truly know
Goodpussy?"

DO BLACK MEN CRY?

Do black men get sick? Do they use bathrooms? Of course they cry. They just do so quietly and privately.

IN SOCIETY'S MIND BLACK MEN ARE GENERALLY INCAPABLE OF ANY EMOTION EXCEPT ANGER. What could possibly affect him so much that he could be moved to tears? After all, he didn't cry as a slave, the movies have shown us that. He may have complained a lot, because he wasn't supposed to be good for anything, but he never cried. He was too dumb to cry. He didn't even weep, so crying was unforgivably and absolutely out of the question.

WHEN A BLACK MAN HURTS, HE HURTS VERY DEEPLY, BUT IN KEEPING WITH SOCIETY'S EXPECTATIONS OF HIM, HE WOULD RATHER NOT LET YOU SEE HIS PAIN. After all, society sees a man who cries as a weak man, as someone who is not in control, and that is tantamount to castration for a black man. He has learned early on in life, "If you're weak, you're beat," and that the weak are pounced upon and taken advantage of. MAINTAIN THAT INDIFFERENT TOUGH GUY FACADE AT ALL COSTS.

AND WHEN BLACK MEN DO CRY THEY DO NOT TALK ABOUT IT. It is ironic, though, that when a reasonable black man does admit to another reasonable man that he hurts and that he has cried too, both men seem to breathe a sigh of relief, realizing that they are not alone. That is one of the few times when black men can open up to each other and relax their defenses.

ONCE A BLACK MAN HAS OPENED UP, HE BEGINS TO FEEL A FREENESS THAT HAS ELUDED HIM THROUGHOUT HIS LIFE. He finds out there is still honor after tears, and honor after hurt or even heartbreak. He learns that he himself is valuable and not just that "He-Man" front he has so diligently protected. Yes, he is a black man, but he is also a human being, and it is alright to act like one.

BLACK MEN DO HAVE HEARTS, AND THEY DO BLEED AND CRY WHEN THEY ARE CUT, SHOT OR HURT. Rambo, Robo Cop, and Dirty Harry may not, but the man who lives next door or across the street does. CONTRARY TO WHAT YOU MAY HAVE BEEN TOLD, THAT TOUGH HIDE IS REALLY SKIN AND HIS HEART IS NOT MADE OF STONE.

As little boys, males are told things like, "Don't be a sissy and don't be a cry baby." "Don't let anybody push you around." "If there is a fight, make sure you get the last lick in." "Don't play with girls or their toys, and don't play with dolls." This last commandment is interesting, however, in as much as (with their fathers' blessings) boys have been playing with dolls for years, like G.I. Joe, different cowboys, and even "Mr. T." dolls. And women, who did not play with guns as little girls, are learning to use weapons as adults.

NOT ONLY ARE BLACK MEN NOT EXPECTED TO HURT OR CRY OPENLY, THEY ARE AGAIN NOT EXPECTED TO FREELY DISPLAY AFFECTION OR ANY OTHER FORM OF GENTLENESS. If they don't do it on television, and generally they don't, it's not for real. Many of these lessons they learned from their fathers, too, more by example than through father-son conversations.

Even if you lose your job, do not let anyone see that you are hurt and vulnerable. Just pretend that everything is alright and that you have everything under control. Damn the fact that you are about to be evicted, just hang tough and be cool. And remember that women love the strong, silent type, so whatever you do, if you want to stay in the game, act like one of the players.

Many black men believe that even though black women say they want a man who is sensitive and caring, when they find a man with a heart they can't wait to see how long it will take to break it. And why? Simply because he has one. Men with hearts are not exciting. They are no challenge. While they claim to loathe men who are unfeeling, they will slice up a good man's heart with the precision of a surgeon, then hang it publicly in the sun, on a meat rack to rot.

Unfortunately, however, what does not come out one way will come out another way, perhaps in the form of child

103

abuse, substance abuse, or mental or physical abuse as men retaliate.

LITTLE BLACK BOYS WHO WERE PRESSURED TO CONFORM EVEN THOUGH THEY HAD SO MUCH LESS, BECAME THE ULTIMATE MACHO-MEN, SHOWING NO PAIN, NO MATTER HOW MUCH THEY SUFFERED. At least so it seemed. Lynch me, no problem. Castrate me, no problem. Rape my wife and my daughter, no problem.

How could there possibly not be a very serious problem for anyone that badly abused? Moreover, how could anyone be so stupid as to even think for one moment that there would be no ramifications? BLACK MEN WHO HAVE HAD TO ENDURE SO MUCH STILL HAVE NOT YET LEARNED TO LET GO, AND TO BE HONEST ABOUT THEIR OWN FEELINGS.

FROM THE OUTSIDE HE MAY APPEAR TO BE UNAFRAID, SELF-SUFFICIENT, DECISIVE, ASSERTIVE, IN CHARGE, IN CONTROL, AND MAYBE EVEN BRAVE, BUT DEEP DOWN INSIDE HE MAY BE THE CLASSIC EXAMPLE OF THE LITTLE BOY WHO HAS GROWN UP PRETENDING AND EVEN BELIEVING THAT "HE IS INVINCIBLE." But what he really is, is a very dangerous powder keg just waiting to be ignited. Are black men who have never really been allowed to let loose truly volatile? What do you think?

One curious thing that many of them did admit to me was how much they had depended on women. Even though they were supposed to be strong and self-reliant, whenever they did talk it was usually to a woman who was a close friend. Finding another man to talk to was rare, especially because of the competition among men and because of black men's unwillingness to admit they have problems that they cannot solve alone. Again, it does happen, but not often. Men, and especially black men, do not like to admit that they have feelings and that they can be sensitive, and while men do not generally listen anyway, a woman who is a good friend will. Because women are historically gentle and more open themselves, a black man may feel that she, "a good friend rather than a lover," is sincere and truly cares, without all the games and thoughts about his inadequacy. Because her expectations of him are different from those of another man, or even his lover, he feels less threatened and less vulnerable. And why not? After all, one of his first "best friends" was a caring mother who felt the same way.

Kevin, my ex-wife's cousin, said that his wife truly was his best friend. He told me that he could talk to her about anything and that he could even cry in front of her if that's what he was feeling. After all they had been through together and will go through together, she deserves to know him better than anyone does. Kevin said their relationship is based on love, respect and trust, and who could be better as a real partner than his own wife.

Other black men who do not have a good male or female friend or a loving wife like Kevin's, often resort to other measures for release. SOMETIMES MEN WHO CANNOT CRY USE DRUGS OR DRINK INSTEAD, OR FIND OTHER WAYS OF DEALING WITH THEMSELVES, SUCH AS ACTING LIKE FOOLS TO CONCEAL THEIR HURT. By being a clown he is proving to the world that he has it all together, because he is having more fun than anybody else is. Remember, though, that a clown hides behind a mask.

Do black men cry?. Everyday. SHOW HIM THAT YOU CAN BE HIS FRIEND BY HELPING TO HEAL HIS PAIN.

CO-DEPENDENCY AND OBSESSION

Have you ever loved a woman too much, and been so miserable at the same time that your own life was actually falling apart, and there seemed to be nothing you could do about it? IF YOU CANNOT GET HER OFF YOUR MIND AND IT IS CONTROLLING YOUR EMOTIONS, IF YOU ARE NERVOUS, YOU LACK MOTIVATION, AND ALL YOU WANT TO DO SOMETIMES IS SLEEP, YOU MAY WELL BE INVOLVED IN A CO-DEPENDENT RELATIONSHIP.

If fact, your life may have come to a screeching halt because you have become so caught up in her problems that your only purpose now is taking care of her. She may treat you like dirt, and even cheat on you, but still you cannot leave her. IF YOU KNOW THAT SHE IS OUT OF CONTROL, AND NOW YOU TOO ARE ONLY HOLDING ON BY A SLIM THREAD, THEN IT SHOULD BE OBVIOUS THAT YOU TOO HAVE A VERY REAL PROBLEM.

106

For example, if she has a drug or gambling problem and you know that she does not intend to stop, but you spend every waking hour wondering what she will do next or agonizing over ways to help her, then you are allowing her problems to create problems for you.

An older gentlemen I know, Cedric, was dating a much younger woman who was addicted to drugs. He said that they had lived together for a while and that she had him feeling like he was losing his mind. Cedric said that no matter how hard he tried, he just couldn't make her understand that what she was doing was wrong, and that he spent most of his time worrying about her.

Twice he had found her in bed, using drugs with other men, and on both occasions she had physically attacked him. On this particular day he was especially disturbed because she had been arrested for arson, and her bail had been set at $500. He said that he just didn't know what to do, because he would have to borrow the money, and then pay it back. He also said that even though he knew that she did not intend to change, he still couldn't leave her, in spite of the fact that she had even threatened to burn him out. Cedric said that she was always lying to him, and even though he resented it, he still had to take care of her. As I observed his uneasiness and listened to tragic story after story, I realized that this "good guy," had become Sampson, in a co-dependent relationship with Delilah.

If you are always thinking about her, where she is, what she's doing, who she's doing it with, and it is constantly nagging at you, then there is a very good chance that you just might be in an obsessive relationship, too. Important work goes undone and you develop health problems, but you still cannot let go.

You are always calling her on the telephone. If she doesn't answer you drive to her house. If she is not home you either go everywhere you think she might be or you park outside of her home and wait. You bring her gifts and tell her how much you love her, but she seems to care less as the challenge of uncertainty sucks you deeper into its grip. LURKING SOMEWHERE NEARBY IS THE SHADOW OF LOW SELF-ESTEEM. Does she need you or do you need her? A popular black singer, Bobby Womack, once released a hit tune called "Nobody Wants You When You're Down and Out," and it is especially during those down and out times that we latch on to something or someone else. When things are not going well, that is when we need them most. IRONICALLY, THE SAME THING THAT MAKES YOU FEEL GOOD, ALSO MAKES YOU FEEL BAD, BECAUSE OBSESSION IS ABSOLUTELY DEPRESSING. This Goodpussy can kill you!

IN BOTH INSTANCES OF CO-DEPENDENCY AND OBSESSION YOU'VE GOT TO LEARN TO BE SELFISH. Let other people live their own lives and solve their own problems. They have made it this far without you, they will make it the rest of the way. YOU SHOULD CONCENTRATE ON TRYING TO GAIN CONTROL OF YOUR OWN LIFE.

Good men who often feel that they should be kind, loving and supportive are often the victims, because they are caretakers who simply want to protect and make their loved ones happy. They are easily seduced into giving up themselves in order to control their mates. WHEN OTHER PEOPLE'S PROBLEMS AND LIVES DO NOT WORK OUT AS WE THINK THEY SHOULD, THAT DOES NOT MEAN WE MUST STEP IN AND TAKE OVER.

Many men who have been taught "ladies first" do just that. They put ladies first and forget about themselves. These are the 90's, however, and if some women are out of control as alleged, it's up to each man to remember himself. Just think about those Rottweilers, Dobermans and Pit Bulls we met earlier in this book. As a grown woman, she is an adult just like you are, and the life raft you keep frantically throwing out to her, you may soon need for yourself.

Besides, this same little pussy cat just might let you drown if she were safe on shore and you were going down for the third time... Gurgle... Gurgle... Gurgle.

PARTIAL REINFORCEMENT IS A S.O.B.

She loves me... She loves me not... She loves me... She loves me not... She loves me... She loves me not. Hell, let's be real. If she left you she probably doesn't love you. She just didn't want you anymore. Did you leave her? No. But now she wants to talk, right? After three months. She says she still loves you. Well, maybe, but does she really love you or does she love whatever it was you were doing for her? She loves her children. Did she leave them? She loves her new Toyota. Did she leave it? Today's black woman leaves first, and considers the consequences later, if it becomes necessary.

When she calls after two weeks of nothing, the first thing she says is, "Don't hang up," followed shortly thereafter by, "I just wanted to hear your voice." She hangs up, leaving you hanging, and you do not hear from her for another three weeks.

Men, good black men, learn early in life to be loyal, to cover each other's backs. Little girls grow up in wonderland playing with their pretty little baby dolls. They comb their hair and dress them up, and when they are finished with their dolls they put them away. Little boys are taught to hang in there when the going gets tough. Little girls are painted pretty little pictures and given pretty little dresses. Everything is pretty. Perhaps one of the reasons why men and women are having so many problems is that they seem to have different ideas about reality and what love and devotion are.

Today I find that many black men are willing to work two or three jobs if necessary to take care of their loved ones. Women, however, still connected to their childhood visions, need those same frills. So while the man appears to be paying more attention to business instead of her, she impersonally puts him away, too.

The more demanding she is, the angrier he gets. The more complacent she becomes, the more frustrated he gets. Finally, there is too much distance between them, and she leaves, often with the blessings of other women who believe that she is rightfully entitled to more. This is true, however, of some black women, not all of them. There are obviously others who do know that there is life beyond being selfishly spoiled.

Jake, 41, had been dating Carla for two and one-half years when he finally decided to call it quits. They would make-up and break-up and make-up and break-up over and over again, for no less than 15 times. But he would take her back each time even though he knew it would never work. Carla had been abusing him both mentally and physically, often battering him and cursing him out in public. Even if he went to the store she would send one of the children with him to make sure he came right back and he found himself constantly checking his watch as he raced home from work. Jake, a bodybuilder, said that he refused to hit her back because he knew that he would hurt her. But each time he left her she would call him and tell him that she had been praying; that she missed him and how much the children loved him. She would seduce (pu--y whip) him again and he would be right back where he started.

Like Carla, your lover already knows how to master you, too. You have taught her how. She knows what it takes, how to act and what to say to make you do whatever she wants you to do. The only way you can escape is by not listening in the first place - by not giving her a chance to set you up. You cannot make a person do something they do not want to do, and she already knows that you care.

But before you let her come back, ask yourself, is she really coming back because she loves me and wants to be wherever I am, or is it simply easier to be here with me than it is to be out there with them?

111

NOTHING PERSONAL

How could she have done this to me? How could she have just walked out on me like that? And what about the kids? What kind of person is she anyway? WHAT SHE IS, IS A GROWN WOMAN WHO IS DOING WHAT SHE WANTS TO DO, AND IT'S "NOTHING PERSONAL."

She is not going out of her way to get you. She has just made up her mind that what she wants, or thinks she needs, is more important than you are. And again, it's "nothing personal."

You put yourself through many, many sleepless nights and all kinds of changes trying to figure out what went wrong, or what you might have done differently. Maybe you didn't have to argue so much. Or maybe you could have spent more time at home. You really didn't know that things were that bad, or that you were so terrible.

But maybe you weren't! It takes two, remember. You're taking all that old baggage and loading in on your own back when she has a back, too.

On the other hand, you may be putting all the blame on her. None of it was your fault, and she is the bitch who left you. None of this would have happened if it had not been for her screwing things up.

Well, whichever way it happened, it still may have been a matter of being "NOTHING PERSONAL." When she left did she do something to you, or something for herself? Did she pour scalding water or battery acid on you, or are you the one who is making it personal because you were humiliated and dishonored in the eyes of your family and friends? If she did you in on purpose, then it was definitely personal, but if she did not, her actions may have been no more personal to her than changing clothes, moving on to a new job, or putting out the garbage.

Jules, 28, came home after work to find all his clothes and shoes slashed, in a smoldering pile of ashes in the middle of the family's two-car garage. The neighborhood too was filled with the fragrances of 50 bottles of his prized colognes which lay broken on the front lawn.

Along with a stack of overdue bills on the dining room table, he found a foreclosure notice and a letter from his wife Juanita. Essentially what it said was that she had exhausted every way she knew how to make him understand that their marriage was over. Having a locksmith change all the locks had not worked. Hiding his car so that he would have to catch a ride to and from work had not worked either -- in spite of the fact that her car was parked out front and she refused to drive him.

Finally, she just made up her mind to leave, and she stopped paying bills for several months to get the money she needed. Juanita explained in the letter that she did not have anything personal against him. She just didn't love him anymore. She also wrote that her lawyer would be contacting him soon.

Our egos and our self-esteem tell us that we are important, and a significant reason for another person's actions. In truth, the other person really might just "care less." So while you frantically search for answers, the truth may be staring you squarely in the face... "NOTHING PERSONAL!"

LONELINESS IS A FORM OF
MENTAL ILLNESS

According to a recent study by Yuanreng Hu and Noreen Goldman of Princeton University, unmarried men had significantly higher death rates than married men. The average death rate for unmarried women was one and a half times that of married women. Married women with children were generally healthier and missed fewer days from work. Unmarried women with no children were sick more often while unmarried women with children were somewhere in the middle.

Divorced people, especially men, had the highest death rates among all the unmarried groups. The death rate for divorced and widowed people in their 20's and 30's was up to 10 times higher than that for married people of the same age. The study compared death rates as far back as 1940, confirming a long-held theory that married people live longer than unmarried people.

ONE EXPLANATION OFFERED FOR THIS PHENOMENON IS THAT PEOPLE WHO HAVE PARTNERS COPE BETTER WITH TODAY'S STRESSES AND HAVE SOMEONE WITH WHOM TO SHARE THEIR LIVES. Often when single people complain about being alone, saying how empty their life is, no one really listens.

Loneliness is a lingering feeling that leads to despair and even self-hatred sometimes. You often find yourself asking questions like "Why me?" And you feel that the pain will never end. You feel hopeless, helpless and worthless. BECAUSE LONELINESS HAS NEVER SERIOUSLY BEEN SEEN AS A "REAL ILLNESS," THOSE WHO ARE LONELY NEVER SEEK PROFESSIONAL TREATMENT. Lonely people are not healthy people, and like any other sick person they have no appetite, they cannot sleep, they lose interest in everything, and they are often depressed and suicidal.

Suppose that every day of your life, for the rest of your life, you knew that when you walked into your home there would be no one there to greet you. No hug, no kiss, no warm and friendly smile, nothing but an empty house. Of course, some people like it that way. But there are others who slowly die a little bit more each day. They are just as empty inside as their houses, and only someone who has been there truly knows what it is like.

Man is both instinctively and intrinsically a social being. He needs the interaction or companionship of others like himself. When a lady friend of mine had a home security system installed, she playfully remarked "All I need now is a dildo." Even our cave dwelling ancestors knew that coming home to an empty cave after a hard day of hunting was no fun. Surveys of modern man still prove that our desire for companionship is even more important to us than sex.

I submit to you at this time that loneliness is truly a form of mental illness, and that it is equally as destructive as stress, another "silent killer." Whereas stress is aggressive, I believe loneliness is more subliminal or passive, because there is no numerical or medical way to scrutinize it. As the statistics do support, however, people do die a slow and painful death by being alone. THEIRS IS NOT A DEATH BY STROKE OR HEART ATTACK BUT "DEATH BY HEARTBREAK." A broken heart is just that -- a heart that is broken. Whether it was caused by pressure or neglect, what is the difference?

If our society is plagued by loneliness and the black man is at the bottom of that society, then what is happening to him? He has been dehumanized and demoralized and gotten his a-- kicked from one continent to the next for nearly four centuries. If the single white male, who is at the top of the chain, suffers miserably, then surely the black male suffers horrifically. And while his nightmare is the worst of all, he receives the least sympathy. WE HAVE BEEN TAUGHT THAT HE IS AN ANIMAL, AND AS WE KNOW ONLY TOO WELL, ANIMALS DO NOT HAVE FEELINGS -- OR FEEL ANYTHING. Just like a chicken, a catfish or a worm, you cannot hurt him. Whales, porpoises, eagles and even some turtles have gotten more support than the endangered black male. He is abused, exploited and victimized like no other animal ever has been.

Black males are even killing each other at a staggering rate, because they too have read society's billboards saying that "you are worthless." Killing a big roach or a little roach is alright. Killing a big rat or a mouse or even a snake is still alright. Killing a black man or a black boy is alright, too, while killing a white man or a white boy is a grave and a tragic loss. Again, the black man is alone, all by himself.

Unlike older black women, white women, or even white men, old black men have few peers. Their good friends have long since disappeared. There is no one to play golf with, to walk in the park with or to travel with, and even the father that some of the others may have had had never been there for him.

Recently, in a restaurant, I observed an elderly black gentlemen dining with several well-dressed elderly black

116

women. I watched as he bounced up and down bounding to and fro eager to accommodate their every whim. It appeared to me that even though he was with the group, he was still not a part of it. He seemed to be validating himself by serving them, and I wondered as I watched him, "Is that all that's left when you get to be an old black man?"

I know of one situation in a mental health group home where Mr. Sims, an elderly gentlemen, actually pretends to be mentally disturbed so that he might have a place to live with companionship and attention.

LONELINESS DOES KILL AND WHEN IT DOES IT IS A SLOW AND AGONIZING DEATH. THE BLACK MAN HAS BEEN ALONE AND DYING FOR FAR TOO LONG. Far too long. It's time to change all that.

DETACHING

IF THE LOVE OF YOUR LIFE REALLY IS OUT OF CONTROL, IT MAY WELL BE CHEAPER NOT TO KEEP HER. In fact, she may actually succeed in turning your very life into a state of bankruptcy. IF SHE IS NOT THE "RIGHT ONE," MAYBE YOU SHOULD LET HER GO, BEFORE YOU END UP LOSING YOUR CAR, YOUR HOME AND EVEN YOUR MIND. Men who have always been told never to give up may have to learn to do just that, to "give up" on something that will never work anyway. Just as women have learned to put us away, "like their dolls and other play things," we must learn to put them away as well. YOU MAY FIND YOURSELF HAVING TO THINK AND RETHINK ALL THOSE OLD DO'S AND DON'TS ABOUT BEING A MAN. Even in today's movies, the good guy who would never shoot first has learned to just pull the damned trigger. You, too, may have to learn to detach -- not to turn the other cheek and get slapped again, but to walk away.

A young police officer I know, Louis, is having his life fall apart before his very eyes. The cause is not stress or crime. It is his wife. Every day in the line of duty he puts his life on the line, a life that he feels is no longer worth living, because she has moved out of their apartment to pursue a relationship with another man. This older man has his own business and treats the depressed young officer as harshly as his wife does. He has pleaded with the older man to release the woman he loves from the grip he has on her, but the older man laughs impersonally, saying, "You lose."

What Louis needs to realize, however, is that neither his wife nor her new lover is worth all the grief they are causing him. The truth is that if he takes her back, he really will be losing. He even sleeps at his brother's house occasionally because he cannot bear going home alone. Louis has to decide for himself whether it is better to be hurt now or to be hurt more later. "When a man loves a woman she can do no wrong." Those are fine lyrics, but in real life it doesn't always work that way. She may well do wrong, over and over and over again, so it is important to know when to let go and when enough is enough.

As a police officer and a man, Louis is humiliated, and the life that he feels is no longer worth living, he really may lose. Yes, it hurts, but it's going to hurt anyway whichever choice he makes. WHAT MOST OF US NEED BEFORE WE ENTER A NEW RELATIONSHIP IS A GOOD THERAPY SESSION OR AN INSURANCE POLICY.

One of the best ways, however, to deal with a bad situation like this is to detach. "BREAK AWAY!" SEPARATE YOURSELF MENTALLY, EMOTIONALLY, PSYCHOLOGICALLY AND EVEN PHYSICALLY AND SPIRITUALLY FROM THAT WHICH IS CAUSING YOU SO MUCH PAIN. It's going to hurt anyway, remember. No, it won't be easy, because you really may be in love with her, but do yourself a favor, give it your best shot. There will be over one million divorces in the United States this year alone, and while you may not want to be in that number, you may absolutely have no choice in the matter. Thirty percent of the woman who are killed in this country are murdered by husbands or boyfriends.

DETACH, LET IT GO. Start getting rid of the pain so that you can begin to heal. No, it won't happen overnight, but in time it will happen. If your rafts are tied together and she is about to run hers over the falls, cut the rope. It may save your life.

DO WHAT YOU CAN - NOT WHAT YOU CANNOT. KNOW WHEN TO SAY ENOUGH IS ENOUGH. I believe that people hang on because they are afraid of letting go, of falling off. Mama was always there when you were sick and when everybody else was too busy. But, remember, she is not mama. And even if mama is not doing right, it may be time to cut the cord.

ONE OTHER IMPORTANT CONSIDERATION: YOUR LOVER MAY ALREADY HAVE DETACHED FROM YOU. If she is already gone, what are you waiting for? Is anything better than nothing? Lisa, 29, a recently separated friend of mine, said she is already going on with her life and does not understand why her husband, Nick, isn't doing the same with his. Many black women want men, but they don't think they need them. They remember only too well being called bitches and whores and being treated like old clothes. And some black women who remember will cut your d--k off before a white man will.

There is one last redeeming thing you should remember as you painfully sever your life line from the woman you once believed was your Goodpussy. IT IS SAD TO BELONG TO SOMEONE ELSE WHEN THE RIGHT ONE COMES ALONG. Get rid of all that old baggage, especially the hatred that will haunt you like a rusty anchor.

ANOTHER BIT OF ADVICE THAT I HAVE FOR YOU IS THAT YOU REALLY DO TRY TO KNOW AS MUCH AS YOU CAN ABOUT YOUR MATE BEFORE THINGS GET TOO SERIOUS. For example, things like, yes, believe it or not, her astrological sign and her family background. For instance, did she grow up in a matriarchy? And how does she feel about God?

As I stated earlier, I have dated thousands of women and I have made some interesting observations at times. On the topic of astrology, for example, I do not follow day-to-day predictions, but I have seen that people born under the same sign can be alike. My second wife, whom I dated for seven years, and a girlfriend, with whom I shared a serious relationship for seven years, were both born on the same date and were identical in mannerism, temperament, and even loyalty, all the way down to their love for small animals. Similarly, the woman I was in love with but incompatible with was the sign both the regular arabic zodiac and the Chinese zodiac calendar said I was least compatible with.

IF SHE WAS RAISED IN A MATRIARCHY, IF SHE IS NOT REASONABLY FLEXIBLE AND WELL-ADJUSTED, THERE IS A VERY REAL POSSIBILITY THAT YOUR RELATIONSHIP IS IN FOR SERIOUS PROBLEMS, BECAUSE SHE MAY HAVE VERY LITTLE KNOWLEDGE OF HOW MEN AND WOMEN INTERACT WITH EACH OTHER IN REAL LIFE.

IS SHE A FEMINIST AND HOW STRONGLY DOES SHE BELIEVE IN WOMEN'S RIGHTS? And dear merciful God, is she spoiled? If she is, you may never be able to live up to her expectations or give her what she wants.

DID SHE COME FROM A DYSFUNCTIONAL FAMILY? HAS SHE EVER USED DRUGS OR HAS SHE EVER BEEN SEXUALLY ABUSED? These are important questions and you need some answers, because blind faith does not always work.

AND FINALLY, HOW DOES SHE FEEL ABOUT GOD? If she is secular rather than spiritual, she may prove to be more worldly than personal. She may understand the difference between good and bad, but the difference between right and wrong may be cloudy. If she does not know who God is how can she possibly know who she is or who you are either? Or is God all she ever talks about?

BLACK MEN WHO DO NOT KNOW WHERE THEIR WOMEN ARE COMING FROM AND BLACK WOMEN WHO DO NOT KNOW WHERE THEIR MEN ARE COMING FROM MAY DISCOVER THAT A LITTLE BACKGROUND INFORMATION CAN BE A PRICELESS INVESTMENT.

There is still one other thing to consider. If that old axiom is true about the acorn not falling far from the tree, take a long hard look at your mate's mother. If girls do grow up to be (like) their mothers, seeing her mother you may be looking at your lover 20 years from now.

There are two other words that I would like to discuss briefly with you. They are RELEVANCE and RELATIVITY. Relativity is "what could have been," "should have been," "would have been," while relevance is simply "what is." She may love you. She may not love you. But she did leave you, for whatever reason. DEAL WITH THE FACTS FIRST. SAVE YOURSELF.

LEAVING YOUR MATE BECAUSE
SHE WON'T DO "THE WILD THING"

SOME MEN, AFTER LEARNING A FEW NEW TRICKS OUT IN THE STREETS, ARE TURNING ON THEIR MATES, OR RATHER, TURNING AWAY FROM THEM SIMPLY BECAUSE THEY ARE NOT SPOILING THEM WITH THE SAME FREAKY FAVORS. Imagine that after 15 years of marriage your husband decides to change the way you make love to each other, and he wants you to do things that both of you have always looked upon as wrong.

Because you will not, or quite literally cannot accommodate him, he decides to leave you. This is precisely what has happened to several women I know. Because women are generally more traditional in their roles as housewives and girlfriends, there is usually less emphasis

122

placed on "outside tricks," and with their inner circles their relationships may be comfortable already.

THE MALE, HOWEVER, WITH NO REAL INNER CIRCLE IS ALONE AND OPEN TO NEW ENCOUNTERS AND DIFFERENT EXPERIENCES. When he meets a new women with new interests and energy, as well as a body that is different from his mate's, he often becomes intrigued and compelled. Each day is another exciting first day of the rest of his life, and he hopes that it will never end.

NOW THAT HE HAS DISCOVERED THESE NEW TREATS, HE IS NOT GOING TO GIVE THEM UP EASILY. When his wife refuses to do the same things his new lover does, she is history, just like yesterday's bad news. Stacey and Jack had been married for 22 years when he met Gloria. Gloria loved both oral and anal sex, and whenever Jack would come over she would seductively ask him which hole he wanted, and then proceeded to give it to him, whichever hole it was. As a matter of fact, Jack said that she would actually go to sleep whenever they were together with his penis in her mouth. He said that his groin was her pillow. Well, of course, Jack loved it and when Stacey refused to favor him similarly, he deserted her. Six months later Jack was sick and unemployed, and Gloria left him. He called Stacey asking if he could come back home, but realizing that she could no longer satisfy him, she said no.

AND SPEAKING OF NEW TRICKS, WHAT DO YOU THINK WOULD BE A BLACK MAN'S ATTITUDE IF HE CAME HOME AND HIS WIFE HAD A FEW NEW TRICKS OF HER OWN, OR EVEN ONE NEW TRICK? His d--k would probably be as soft as a rubber band as he worried about where she had been, who had been teaching her, did she enjoy her lessons, what other tricks was she holding back, exactly what was her relationship with her new teacher, precisely how much more did he know, how did she feel about his instructional tools, and, finally, now that she had a new teacher did she find him dull, boring and unsatisfying?

OFTEN BLACK MEN CAN DISH IT OUT BUT WHEN THEIR TURN COMES AROUND IT'S ANOTHER STORY. Putting the shoe on the other foot sounds like a fine idea that the two of you can talk about sometimes, but when that shoe is in his behind and hurting, he's likely to say, "let's stop wearing shoes."

The next time you want her to do something that she says she cannot do, try swapping shoes. Just ask yourself if you would be willing to be sodomized and let her watch if that was what she wanted you to do for her.

REMEMBER, LIFE IS A TWO-WAY STREET AND TRAFFIC IS MOVING IN BOTH DIRECTIONS. "Goodpussy is carefully watching your step and making sure you're not fatally run over by something you can't possibly handle."

INTERRACIAL DATING

Well, this is going to be a very, very, very tricky chapter, but for the sake of simplicity, let's just consider dating between blacks and whites in the United States for a moment. Before I move on however, I want to tell you about a little joke friends shared with me. Let's call it "Nature's Joke." OVER THE YEARS I HAVE HEARD SEVERAL EMINENT DOCTORS I KNOW LAUGHING AT THE FACT THAT THEY BELIEVE DEAR OLD MOTHER NATURE IS DOING A NUMBER ON ALL OF US.

According to them, white women are generally built wider (the area between their legs) while black women are built closer. White men tend to generally have smaller penises while black men are usually more well endowed. So, IT WOULD SEEM, AT LEAST ACCORDING TO THEM AND MOTHER NATURE, THAT BLACK MEN SHOULD BE MATING WITH WHITE WOMEN WHILE WHITE MEN SHOULD BE MATING WITH BLACK WOMEN.

I am not entirely unfamiliar with this idea myself. Just as black men and white men are built differently in some areas, black women and white women are, too. For example, we all know that black women usually have bigger behinds, that is they stick out farther and have more rounded rears. But while black women usually look better from the side and rear, white women generally look better from the front, because their hips are more serpentine and pronounced.

Other differences that I have observed are the way some white women's nipples are made, almost like beautifully shaped cones sculptured to the breast with a raisin-like nipple attached at the end. On the other hand, I have seen black women with wonderfully well-rounded voluptuous breasts and exciting nipples as large as the caps on a two liter bottle. But, getting back to the subject, if indeed I have not forgotten my physics, opposites do attract.

Let me ask you another one of my brilliant horse questions. If a rancher had a corral full of horses ready to mate, would all of the white horses only mate with other white horses and all of the black horses only mate with other black horses? Would brown horses only mate with brown horses, Appaloosas only mate with other Appaloosas and would Pintos only mate with other Pintos? And would the thoroughbred only mate with other thoroughbreds and the quarter horses only mate with other quarter horses? I may be wrong, but I don't think so, and why not? That's another easy one. They would not mate according to color or classification, because to do it that way would be unnatural. THE PROBLEM WITH THESE DUMB ANIMALS IS THAT THEY ARE TOO STUPID TO MAKE UP GOOD RULES AS MAN HAS, NO MATTER WHAT MOTHER NATURE MAY SAY. Classification, as we know it, is a man-made concept, and whether it comes naturally or not, we must all obey the rules that somebody else has made up.

Modern man (homo sapien) is only 50 to 100 thousand years old while the earth is 5 to 10 billion years old and the broad universe is 5 to 13 billion years old. In all that time and in all that space, man alone asserts himself as the authority in this vast cosmos. In his egotistical self-centeredness he uses race and color, rather than species and gender as determinants in procreation.

But let's talk about what people want, not what they say they want, but what they really do want in their hearts. Let's consider black women and what they really want and white women and what they really want. Let's also take a look at black men and white men too, to find out what they truely desire.

First, let's consider the white woman. I think that she appreciates the good manners, the good looks of her Caucasian counterpart, and the status and the security she enjoys with a white man. But I also think that she longs for the natural virility, the intrinsic animal chemistry and the dark, serious magnetism that the black man seems to exude. That twangy little, "Darling, can I get you anything else?" gets to be just a little bit too sweet sometimes, and she wants to be

126

handled more firmly and in a less "he's kissing my a-- again" manner.

And what of the black woman? Well, I think that she just plain gets tired of being handled sometimes, period. She loves her black man's manliness but she wants some sweetness too, and a little consideration and kindness.

The black man loves his strong black woman, but sometimes he wants some soft pink frailty that lets him know he is still a force to be reckoned with.

The white male loves the dominant role he commands over his white woman and the others as well, but sometimes he wants the fire and fight that the black woman can give him when he goes too far.

And yet the white male has always been vigilant and relentless in trying to maintain possession and authority over his Goodpussy, that is, his power and his white woman. He has tried and done everything to keep the black male and the white female apart. Two hundred years ago his ancestors must have indeed been dumbfounded to find a prized white female (they were rare in those early days), being attracted to what they considered a dirty, uneducated, wild black animal, a heathen who was neither civilized nor socialized as she was. (For the sake of example, I am speaking primarily of the black slave.) He was not well dressed, he was not well educated or articulate, he did not own vast stretches of prime real estate, he owned no live stock - not even a single chicken, and he did not come from a fine old family with tradition and a wonderful name, at least not one that he knew of. He was neither an eminent public figure nor a successful business man. In fact, he was not even a home owner. He was not highly respected, and he had no foreseeable future. The only clothes that he had were the rags on his back, and somebody had given them to him. The only visible means of support that he had was his job as a slave, with no benefits and no paycheck.

Outside of the cities, black men and white women did not generally grow up in the same neighborhoods in 1790, or meet at school functions or get introduced to each other by a mutual friend at some fabulous party. Indeed, she may have seen him at work, but they did not meet on the job at the water cooler, at least not "well to do" white women. She was up in the big house while he lived in slave quarters that were always falling down. Surely the black man and the white woman could not possibly have been any more different -- opposite. Oil and water will never mix, and so it would seem with velvet and burlap or fine silk and tattered rags.

It is understandable that white males, who saw few females during those days, would exercise their options with Indian squaws and with black females whom they thought of as property. But what was the lure for pristine white females and for others who knew that the answer then for them was the same as it is for their descendants today, more or less?

I know of several white women who generally find black men unsavory and undesirable, but who confessed that they would be willing to have sex with the right black man, if they could find one, just so they could find out for themselves if those old rumors and myths that they had heard were true. The same thing happened to their great, great, grandmothers and to their great, great, great, grandmothers as well. They knew what they wanted and they were determined to get it. It is also important to remember that the slave did not have very much mobility, so he did not do very much traveling, especially at night, in white man's country. So if the white man sneaked away from home by the back door, which door did the white woman use?

Once again, it is important to know history, and to be able to transfer that information to other similar situations so that you may better understand them sometimes. For example, blacks began to appear in movies after Al Jolson's famous rendition of Mammy in The Jazz Singer at the beginning of the "Talkie" era in movies (1929). What better character to portray a dim-witted black man singing, dancing, and making a fool of himself, than a real black man.

Similarly, most of us are inherently creatures of desire who secretly court visions of wild, passionate, riveting sex, and what sex partner could possibly be wilder than a "wild thing," whose body was powerful and whose genitals were huge and uncontrollable, or wild?

The black male was the missing link. He may have been an animal alright, but he walked erect and he could be given commands. He was just close enough, and although sex with him was taboo, it was within reach. Thomas Jefferson once wrote of the black man that "They are more ardent after their females; but seem with them to be more an eager desire than a tender delicate mixture of sentiment and sensation." To paraphrase a line by Denzel Washington in Spike Lee's movie, "Mo Better Blues," "It had to be a d--k thing."

In addition, however, we must not forget one other very important factor that sealed the black man's fate. He was an expert, a professional whose natural instincts as well as his indoctrination made him a superb sexual machine. He had all the power and skill of the blacksmith, and could do the job with one stroke of his big, hard, powerful, built-in hammer. IT WAS SIMPLE, IF YOU WANTED TO LIVE OUT YOUR FANTASIES OF WILD SEX, GET A GOOD START BY DOING IT WITH SOMETHING WILD.

As a matter of fact, during the earliest days black men and white women barely spoke the same language, but there was only one language that he needed to speak, and he knew that one only too well. After all, they had not taken long leisurely strolls together where they could talk and listen and get to know each other better and become good friends, but they had found each other anyway.

Miscegenation was very common among the lower classes but every class did it. Southern planters openly kept Negro women and when they had guests they would often give them a girl for the night. Josiah Quincy, a young man from Boston, stated that "The enjoyment of a Negro mulatto woman is spoken of as quite a common thing; no reluctance, delicacy or shame is made about the matter." W.E.B. Duboise wrote "Where all the best of the Negroes were domestic servants in the best white families, there were bonds of intimacy, affection, and sometimes blood relationships among the races."

In every city in the South blacks and whites lived side by side, constantly interacting. At night black men and white men mingled freely in back rooms and in grog shops with black women and white women often joining them. But there was always an imbalance of the sexes in both races, an imbalance which was always more white men than white women and more black women than black men, because the men had been sold or were living in rural areas. So white men and black women frequently lived together, having mulatto children whose blood was often considered "polluted."

White men ran after black women while placing their own women on a pedestal. It was alright for them to have sex with black women, but they absolutely condemned any black man who dared to be with a white woman, even though white women often sought out black men, frequently marrying them or having children by them. During the Colonial period white women were even whipped at the post because there were so many of them persuing black men, with mulatto children running around everywhere. Some white women were even willing to be slaves to be with black men who were enslaved. Back then too, a white woman might have married a free black man if he had enough money. Again, white women had also been forced to marry black slaves to produce more slave children. A Negro man could lose his life if found with a white woman, or be castrated. One of the main reasons was the white man's insecurity and perceptions of black men with larger penises being better lovers. Another reason was that white men felt if they lost sexual control everything else might follow. Ultimately, sex with white women became a political rationale for subjugating black Americans.

TODAY BLACK MEN AND WHITE WOMEN ARE STILL TOGETHER, AND OVERALL SOCIETY IS STILL NOT VERY HAPPY ABOUT IT. White men are still turned off, as are black women who say that they cannot find enough good black men. But black men are sometimes having an easier time with white women, because many black women and men are defensive and restrictive with each other. Society has told the black woman that the black man is worthless and that he only wants to use her, while it has told him that she is a whore who will lie on her back and make babies for any man who comes along. HE IS AN OVERSEXED MALE WHORE WHILE SHE IS AN OVERSEXED FEMALE WHORE AND NEITHER ONE TRUSTS THE OTHER. Society has told both of them that they were trash and trouble and they believed it.

But who could possibly be any trashier or any more oversexed than white males who created pornographic magazines and x-rated movies, and who are incestuous, group sexers, exhibitionists, peeping Toms and beastialities? And the list goes on and on and on and on. But again, we were accused of something and the label stuck.

Today, however, black men and white women do sometimes live in the same neighborhood, or work on the same jobs and meet at the water cooler or at the snack bar. They speak the same language and often do have a mutual friend who may introduce them or put in a good word. SIMPLY STATED, BLACK MEN AND WHITE WOMEN ARE TALKING, GETTING TO KNOW EACH OTHER BETTER, AND BECOMING FRIENDS. Other black men and white women who are not interested in getting to know each other better in any way but sexual are getting to do that too because of a simple thing like opportunity. If you are interested in finding someone or something, you merely go where they are or where it is, and nobody else has to know unless you want them to.

MANY BLACK MEN WHO ARE MAKING IT AND ESPECIALLY THOSE WHO ARE MAKING IT BIG ARE FORMING BONDS WITH WHITE WOMEN. Some are validating themselves personally,

131

some are chasing the proverbial forbidden fruit, some are trying to distance themselves from their past, some of them have found a new doormat to walk on or a new urinal to p--s on, while others have really found a true friend. Whoever she is, unless she is the poorest white trash, if she is with a black man she is going through some social unpleasantness. And her very presence at his side is living testimony that he is important to her, for whatever reason.

Even though Miss Ann may seem to have an edge over the black women because she is new and different and interesting and exciting, and generally better off, the black woman has still not gone down for the final count yet.

PEOPLE, INCLUDING BLACK MEN, ARE STILL MORE COMFORTABLE WITH FAMILIAR THINGS THAT THEY KNOW ABOUT, AND THE BLACK WOMAN CAN BE AS COMFORTABLE AS WARM HONEY SLIDING DOWN HIS THROAT. With a little creativity, a little kindness, a little understanding and just a bit more cooperation, anything is possible, and indeed Goodpussy may be Goodpussy again.

YOUNG MEN - OLDER WOMEN
OLDER MEN - YOUNG WOMEN

One of the advantages, if there are any, of living in the 90's is that some people really are getting their lives together for themselves. Without hurting anyone else they are openly defying antiquated social norms and doing what makes them happy. YOUNG BLACK MEN ARE NOW CHOOSING TO SPEND THEIR TIME WITH OLDER WOMEN WHILE OLDER BLACK MEN ARE DATING MUCH YOUNGER WOMEN.

Older men are seeing younger women for many different reasons. An older man who is single may be financially secure, and thus be able to finally pursue some of those dreams that have been hidden away in his closet for all those years. That includes a pretty young girl who is still fresh and filled with vitality. A young woman is also a good companion with whom he can explore new experiences. He can do some of the things with her that he may feel he has missed as a younger man -- without feeling stupid or foolish. This works well for the younger woman, too, because she generally finds a man who is more supportive and less likely to be playing games, with enough resources to be there if and when she needs him. One older black gentlemen said that every woman he knew who was his age smelled like Ben Gay and was constantly complaining about aches and pains. Today's older black man is also younger feeling now, because he is eating healthier foods and taking better care of himself -- that is unless he is one of those unfortunate males who now finds himself isolated and plagued by loneliness.

Younger men sometimes enjoy the company of an older woman for many of the same reasons. Usually she is more stable and supportive than a younger woman, and he finds it easier to trust her also. While she enjoys doing things for him, a woman his age wants to know how much he is going to do for her. The older woman has by now raised all of her children, and gets the action she may have missed during her child-rearing years with someone who is very much alive and fun loving as well.

Along with the good, however, also comes some bad. Friends and relatives of the older person often feel that he or she is being exploited for whatever savings or security he or she may have. The younger person is usually criticized and laughed at for being with someone who is their senior and "over the hill." MANY PEOPLE FALSELY BELIEVE THAT OLDER BLACK MEN ARE NO LONGER VIRILE AND THAT THEY HAVE LOST THEIR SEX DRIVE, BUT MANY OLDER MEN SAY THAT SEX, LIKE A FINE WINE, GETS EVEN BETTER WITH AGE. Some agree that it may take a little bit longer to get ready and that their erection may not last as long or be as hard, but their younger lover definitely helps to keep sex more interesting and exciting. And while many of the older black men I talked to said that they were not as strong sexually, they definitely felt that they

134

were better lovers because of the knowledge and the experience they had gained over the years.

As older men, they are not expected to be studs either, so they are free to be more relaxed and less pressured by unreasonable expectations and competition. Older black men may not f--k or make love as much, but what they really appreciate is the closeness and having someone special there, and a younger woman definitely makes them feel special. Another thing is that as a man gets older he becomes less obsessive about setting traps to see how many female prizes he can catch, which I'm told is really one helluva' relief.

Meteau, a retired 67-year-old chef, was married, but he said that he loved younger women because his wife's sexual desires had declined much more than his had. He told me that she was usually not interested and that some of his friends were having the same problems, as their women appeared to be more interested in their relationships with old girl friends. FOR SOME OLDER BLACK MEN, THE BOTTOM LINE WAS THAT YOUNGER WOMEN WERE JUST MORE FUN TO BE WITH, AND THEY MADE THEM FEEL YOUNGER.

AGAIN, WHAT YOUNGER BLACK MEN FOUND IN OLDER WOMEN MANY TIMES WAS A CARING LADY WHO HAD GOTTEN PAST THAT SELFISH "GIRL-STAGE." She was wise and worldly in her own way, but she still maintained a certain innocence and naivete, because when she was coming up things really were different. An older woman may be both a lover and a friend as well as a counselor and a confidant who shares the interests and dreams of her younger lover. He eagerly welcomes her desires to explore her life with him, and like the older man she is sometimes financially secure herself and will be there for him if he ever needs her. Like the younger woman, the younger black male has less fear of being involved with someone who is playing games when he dates an older woman, and the warm nurturing closeness he needs she freely gives. He also worries less about flirting and competition because she already knows who she is. She understands him and will never be guilty of saying something callous like, "If you want to be mothered, you should marry your mama." She is not afraid to give love, and he loves it. And she is as willing to experience the exhilaration and passion of her younger partner's sexuality as he is eager to give her what he has. Relationships such as these are often mutually rewarding because, in a sense, both partners are teachers with something special to share with the other person who is usually open enough to receive it.

If the old axiom, "Life is what you make it" is true, then these Spring - Autumn and Summer - Winter partners are doing just that, making life what they want it to be, their way. They are designing their own Goodpussy.

HOMOSEXUAL RELATIONSHIPS
AND SODOMY

I'm afraid I'll have to play this one by ear too, but because homosexuality is the very real lifestyle of some black males, especially in popular, easy-going metropolitan areas like San Francisco and New Orleans, I'll do my best by taking a stab at it. Most of the homosexual black males I talked to were very eager to tell their side of the story.

IN A CONTEMPORARY SOCIETY THAT SEES THE BLACK MALE AS BEING A ROUGH AND TOUGH ULTRA-MACHO SEX OBJECT, THE BLACK MAN WHO PROJECTS FEMININITY AND HOMOSEXUALITY CATCHES IT FROM ALL SIDES. In addition to just not being liked simply because he is another worthless black male, he is a freak too. So if black men in general have no value, what could a black homosexual male possibly be worth? Heterosexual black males naturally refuse to see black gay men as one of them, because historically the only thing that they have seemingly been able to hold on to was their black masculinity, and the black homosexual male is soiling and spoiling that. I don't really think that they care whether he is a homosexual or not, as long as he is a homosexual somewhere else. Black women, who complain that they cannot find a real man are disappointed in him too, and see him as a pitiful waste. While there are not enough men to go around, and those remaining continue to diminish, it is truly disgraceful to find a man who wants to be a woman, and who is competing with them for the same man. And feelings often run a passionate gamut from "Somebody oughtta' kick his a--," to "How can I kill him?"

Not everyone is against the homosexual black man, however, because some black heterosexual males do accept him -- as long as he does not make any moves on them. IT'S FINE WITH THEM IF HE WANTS TO BE ONE OF THE GIRLS BECAUSE THAT'S JUST ONE LESS BLACK MAN TO COMPETE WITH. Some black women like him too, because he is not just one more macho-thinking, macho-acting black male with a stud mentality. He is fun to be around (those who are out of the closet), because he sincerely does want to be one of the girls, and what better girl friend can there possibly be to really let you know what men are all about. SWAPPING NUMBERS IN THE LADIES' ROOM IS FINE, BUT SWAPPING NUMBERS IN THE MEN'S ROOM IS PRICELESS.

Some authorities insist that homosexuality is a matter of sexual orientation, while others believe it is just a matter of basic sexual preference. IS HE A HOMOSEXUAL BECAUSE HE WAS BORN THAT WAY, OR IS HE A HOMOSEXUAL BECAUSE THAT IS WHAT HE WANTS TO BE? Many experts argue that just as you cannot go to sleep tonight and wake up tomorrow and decide to be gay, it did not happen that way for homosexuals either. There is also a prevailing belief that environment has absolutely nothing to do with one's homosexuality or heterosexuality. Others, of course, vigorously disagree. SOME EXPERTS CLAIM THAT HOMOSEXUALITY MAY INDEED BE GENETIC AND THAT IT CAN BE ATTRIBUTED TO CERTAIN HORMONAL FACTORS. It is known that homosexuality is not unique to man and that it does exist in other mammals as well, with a corresponding range of frequency, so that homosexuality in its natural physical state may not be unnatural at all. Those who believe in biblical teachings and social morality would still disagree with this hypothesis, I'm sure, but it is still a commonly-held view.

WHATEVER THE CAUSE, HOMOSEXUALITY USUALLY MANIFESTS ITSELF IN THE FORM OF A PASSIONATE, OVERT LOVE OF MANLINESS AND AN OFTEN CORRESPONDING EXPRESSION OF FEMININITY. The key players are the mouth, the anus, and the predominating male penis. In many ways sex is much like a giant grab bag where you do not know exactly what you are going to get until you've gotten it. It is like that wonderful Christmas present that you do not have to wait for all year. This delightful Christmas gift may very well come every day, or several times a day, and homosexuality, like heterosexuality, may be based upon a physical attraction or an emotional need or desire.

WHEN YOU THINK ABOUT HOMOSEXUALITY, ONE OF THE THINGS YOU NEED TO CONSIDER IS ENVIRONMENT, NOT THE KIND OF ENVIRONMENT THAT MAY HAVE PRECIPITATED IT, LIKE BEING RAISED AROUND TOO MANY WOMEN, BUT RATHER THE SOCIAL ENVIRONMENT IN WHICH IT EXISTS, IN AMERICA IN OUR CASE. To the outside world homosexuals are vulgar little sex perverts. In prisons, however, homosexuality is something that strong, aggressive, sometimes dangerous and virile men openly participate in. What is considered unnatural and abnormal outside comes naturally and normally inside. These men achieve erection. They achieve orgasm. Life goes on. Their society and ours is different, that's all. Homosexual men who have broken one of the old rules (don't be a sissy), have learned to live by some new ones, rules that now sometimes make them Goodpussy.

Homosexuality, I believe, is something that people are just not honest about. IN OUR AMERICAN CULTURE, IN THE HOME OF THE BRAVE AND THE LAND OF THE FREE, WE PRIDE OURSELVES ON STEPPING ON MINORITIES WITH OUR BIG BOOT. We kick butt, and what better butt to kick than the one attached to some little queer who is not like us. Attitudes about homosexual sexuality and homosexual behavior may just be the results of conditioning and social pressures rather than a natural consequence. Each of us is an individual capable of making our own decisions about our own lives, which I believe is fair enough as long as we do not knowingly harm someone else. Society, with its big boot and its big glove, sometimes steps right up and grabs the bull firmly by the horns -- or testicles. All the way back to the "good book," it was written that way, although it did not always happen that way. In fact, homosexuality was once an accepted religious way of life in certain European cultures, becoming immoral only after mores began to change. White history's super heros, Greeks and Roman gladiators, fought side by side, bathed side by side, and even slept side by side, sexually. We see them, however, as powerful men of muscle and courage, because that is the image Hollywood created for its white heros.

The example that I am about to cite may seem to be just a bit overly simplistic, but a rose by any other name is still a rose. Like oral sex, if your eyes are closed and there is no beard, can you tell whether a man or a woman is sucking your penis? If you are blindfolded and bite into an apple, can you be sure what color it is -- red, golden or green? Similarly, if you are blindfolded and make love to a woman, can you tell what color, race, and age she is? And still wearing that same blindfold, if you penetrate your lover rectally, is your penis so sophisticated that it knows whether it is inside a man or a woman, even though he or she might have tiny little hairs on his or her behind? I think not. You probably could not because the function is the same as are the surrounding muscles, so that whatever your attitude is, whether pro or con, it is due in large measure to your own personal orientation. The matter itself is really more of a social issue than anything else, that is really quite ludicrous. In Great Britain, you drive from the right side of the car on the right side of the road, and in the good old U.S.A., you drive from the left side of the car and keep to the right side of the road. So what's the big deal? THE BIG DEAL AGAIN IS OUR SOCIETY AND ITS BELIEF THAT HOMOSEXUALITY IS UNNATURAL, UNCLEAN AND AGAINST THE LAWS OF NATURE AND GOD. I also need to remind you here of society's ethnocentric belief that inappropriate sexual behavior will absolutely lead to lawlessness and its ultimate demise. THIS IS TRUE OF SOCIETY'S VIEWS OF THE SEXUAL PRACTICES OF THE HOMOSEXUAL AND OF THE SEXUAL PRACTICES OF THE BLACK MAN AS WELL. By their very nature, which is naturally considered to be corrupt, the inference made is that anything they touch will go bad or be ruined, or, "absolute corruption corrupts absolutely."

And in America, even the way we are socialized is different. Young white boys sometimes find nothing wrong

140

with mutually masturbating each other, even to orgasm, or sucking each other, or of having anal intercourse with each other. That is not considered homosexual behavior, but innocent fun and experimentation. Touch a little black boy's prize, however, or even look at it too hard, and you've got a real fight on your hands, because there is no doubt that something is wrong with you, and before long everybody else would know it too. Sex wasn't for fun, not even with yourself.

JUST TO SHOW YOU HOW THINGS ARE CHANGING, HOWEVER, CONSERVATIVE ESTIMATES ARE THAT AT LEAST 50% OF ALL CATHOLIC PRIESTS, THE GUARDIANS OF CHASTITY, ARE HAVING SOME FORM OF SEXUAL ACTIVITY, EITHER HETEROSEXUAL OR HOMOSEXUAL. The news is out. The truth has not changed, it is just out of the closet. Maybe admitted homosexuals were being more honest all the while and society is just beginning to catch up.

Emotionally, psychologically, mentally and physically, men and women are brothers and sisters of the same species. Who is to say that their wants and needs are not, similarly, the same.

In discussing his thoughts about having a man's penis in his rectum, Jason, a 46 year-old contractor, had many of the same answers other black homosexual men had given. He said that it was probably the same warm full feeling a woman experiences when a man's penis is inside her. Other black men as well who participate in homosexual activities said that oral stimulation and touching usually proceeded anal intercourse. In addition to describing the usual oral activities and feelings that accompany fellatio, they said that they felt like letting a man insert his penis into their rectum was a feeling of closeness and of trust. This, too, seemed to be basically the same feeling some heterosexual black men had as they described eating their women.

Bruce, a slightly built dental assistant, said that he is not a homosexual, but that his wife penetrates his rectum with her finger and masturbates him at the same time. He said that

141

she often rims him, licks his a--hole to excite him just before they get into regular vaginal sex, and that by that time he is ready to explode with passion. Other black men who were homosexuals said that they just loved the feeling of having fingers, penis size objects like smoked sausage, dildos and penises inside them. In the male role most of them said that they enjoy the tight feeling of the anus as it clung to the shaft of the penis, and the feeling of dominance.

Lawrence, who admits to being bisexual, confessed that he started doing men to pick up a few dollars when he was laid off from his job. He said that he likes to grease his penis down real good with either Vaseline or K-Y Jelly, with his lovers on their backs and their legs resting on his shoulders. He says that this position really allows him to plunge deep and that he can watch his partner's expression while he is coming, and also that he likes the tight slippery feeling when it pops out, which does not happen with vaginal intercourse.

Like other forms of sexuality, there were some men who wanted to try certain things like sucking another man's penis, or feeling another man's penis in their rectum, but for most of the usual reasons it had not happened yet, though they were still open to it and hopeful.

Whatever the case, homosexuality among black males is a reality. In the selection of a mate many of these men have decided that they too need to be complete and fulfilled, and they are willing to buck whatever tide they must to get to their own Goodpussy.

LESBIAN RELATIONSHIPS

Even as youthful teenagers, my buddies and I sat around after playing ball, talking about lesbians and their girl friends. Way back then, and inexperienced, we were smart enough to figure out at least one thing. If a real woman (any female) was able to get close enough to your woman, your a-- was grass. We didn't know exactly what a lesbian was or what she did, but we did know that she had a connection that we did not have.

I LATER LEARNED THAT A LESBIAN IS SIMPLY A WOMAN WHO LOVES ANOTHER WOMAN. I also learned that society felt basically the same way about homosexual women as it did about homosexual men. Some people argued that lesbian behavior was a matter of sexual orientation while others still believed that it was just another example of sexual preference. Some people, in fact, feel that lesbians are women who have become what they are because they did not have successful relationships with men. This, indeed, need not have been the case. Again, lesbians just love other women. They do not hate men, necessarily.

BECAUSE SHE IS A WOMAN, HOWEVER, SHE INSTINCTIVELY UNDERSTANDS ANOTHER WOMAN BETTER THAN MOST MEN CAN. The lesbian understands the other woman's moods, her feelings, and even her erogenous zones, while the male would have to learn and practice, or guess. After all, it took thousands of years of watching birds before man learned to fly. For the bird flying came naturally.

OUR MISTAKE AS MALES WAS IN THINKING THAT A PENIS WAS A GUIDED MISSILE TO FEMALE GRATIFICATION. In our EGOTESTICLE haste we forgot about the rest of her, but her lesbian lover did not. When we went left, she moved to the right. When we were defensive, she was compassionate. Those times that we should have been listening, we were out drinking or finding our own pleasure.

AS IS THE CASE IN ISSUES SUCH AS ABORTION, WOMEN NOW BELIEVE THAT THE LIFE THEY ARE LIVING IS THEIRS, AND THEY ARE CHOOSING TO MAKE THEIR OWN CHOICES. "Do I do without because there are not enough men to go around, or do I make adjustments for a more fulfilling life?" Again, in prison what was abnormal outside becomes normal inside. Lesbians, as well as bisexual women, realize that they have been held morally captive by many of those who were secretly exercising their own choices behind closed doors.

AS A COLLECTIVE UNIT, MEN ARE TYPICALLY INSECURE, NO MATTER WHAT KIND OF MACHO FRONT THEY PROJECT, AND THEIR INSECURITY CAN BE TRACED BACK TO THE BASIC OLD "FEAR OF THE UNKNOWN." And certainly what can be any more unknown than trying to understand why a woman would want another woman, and what would she do with her that was so great? After all, she didn't even have a penis, at least not a real one with a man on the other end of it. White men were afraid of black men being with their women. Black men were suspicious of white men with their money and power, and I suspect that all along both had been cautious of the close, secret sorority or sisterhood that all women seem to share. MANY BLACK MEN HAVE EVEN BECOME HOMOPHOBIC, THAT IS, THEY HAVE DEVELOPED AN IRRATIONAL HATRED AND FEAR OF GAY MEN AND LESBIANS, BOTH EXTERNALIZED AND INTERNALIZED. Many lesbians, in fact, believe that it is more difficult being lesbian than a homosexual male. There may be some truth to this because many men do not like someone unlike them trying to be one of them, and because many of these women who are trying to be just like him are competing for the same prize, a good woman. In that case, she presents more of a problem for the black man than a homosexual man, because he is having enough problems with his woman already. The last thing he needs is some woman "bad mouthin'" him and putting her hands between his woman's legs.

Another question still looms on the horizon however. Lesbians are a concrete reality and their numbers seem to be rising. So are they really that good? MEN, AND BLACK MEN TOO, WHO ARE ALREADY CONCERNED ABOUT HOW GOOD OTHER MEN ARE, ABSOLUTELY AND EMPHATICALLY DO NOT NEED TO WORRY ABOUT HOW GOOD SOME WOMAN IS. In another man, he knows what kind of competition to expect, but how does he compete with a woman?

Bambi, a firmly built black lesbian friend of mine, explained that heterosexual men and women often change roles, especially in love-making, with one partner being dominant and the other one being subordinate. She said that she simply switched to a permanent dominant role leaving out one simple ingredient, the man. She said that she has always been captivated by the soft, sweetness of other women, by the feel of their breasts and by the wonderful taste of their pu--ys, and that as long as she stayed in the closet and kept a low profile nobody really bothered her.

Julie, a subordinate lesbian, said that she felt more secure with another woman than with a man who was out to

145

stick his d--k in anything that had a hole in it. She said, "Why should I have to run behind someone that I might die for, with AIDS being out there the way it is and men being what they are?"

And if all that is not enough, a lesbian may still feel closer to her sister, another woman, than she does to men who have been trying to f--k her all her life. If she is going to be f--ked, she might as well let a friend do it. AND EVEN IF THE OTHER WOMAN USES A DILDO, "IT IS ONLY AN IT," AND NOT A PART OF HERSELF THAT SHE IS IN LOVE WITH AND TRYING TO GRATIFY.

She has a common bond, a trust with the other woman, a feeling of security, that she may not have with a man. In fact, more women, including straight heterosexual women, are choosing to seek out female gynecologists and obstetricians because of mutual trust and the belief that another woman understands them better and can appreciate what they are going through better than a man can. For example, as women "it is us." With a man, "it is him."

Even bisexuality is common in the 90's, and many experts agree that there is the potential for homosexuality in most human beings, especially in our sexually permissive and more relaxed society which emphasizes and encourages individual freedoms. Several black lesbians, however, told me that as they traveled about the country, they soon found out that they were not free at all, and that they had been discriminated against in bath houses and in gay night clubs. It was for this reason that many of them still chose to identify with being black first and lesbian second.

More and more however, as people seek out their own individual rights and options in their lifestyles, being gay or lesbian is becoming less deviant and more of just a matter of being sexual, and one more American minority. Times are hard and getting harder for all minorities, and each is simply trying to find and secure its own place in our system, and generally it is the person or group with time on their hands who are stirring up all the dust.

MASTURBATION AS GOODPUSSY

MASTURBATION IS QUICK, IT'S CHEAP AND IT'S PROBABLY THE SAFEST SEX YOU CAN HAVE, AND ALTHOUGH MANY BLACK MEN DO IT DURING THEIR LIFETIME, YOU WILL ALMOST NEVER HEAR THEM BRAGGING ABOUT "BEATING THEIR MEAT." For many reasons, mostly societal, they are embarrassed about admitting that they have sex with themselves, no matter how much they may enjoy it or how often they may do it. BECAUSE THEY ARE ASHAMED, THEY TRY TO HIDE IT. If I do it by myself everyone will think I am perverted, that something is wrong with me, but if my lover does it for me then I'm "the man" who is in control. Masturbation, in fact, is even mentioned in the bible in the book of Genesis where Judah ordered his son Onan to marry and sleep with his slain brother's wife Tamar, but instead Onan spilled his seed on the ground.

THE WORD MASTURBATE ACTUALLY COMES FROM THE LATIN, MASTURBARI, MEANING TO POLLUTE ONE'S SELF, AND AGAIN THIS IS THE PROBLEM THAT MANY BLACK MEN FACE, FEELING DIRTY ABOUT PLAYING WITH THEMSELVES. Unlike declared heterosexual white males who experience a wide range of sexual experiences with each other as children or as teenagers, such as mutual masturbation, oral sex and even anal sex, black boys were taught that any such behavior was absolutely homosexual. Experts agree that ½ of all boys and ¼ of all girls masturbate by age 15 and that number rises to 85% for males and 60% for females by age 20. I believe too that white people use terms to protect them from reality as well, neutral terms like fellatio and anal penetration instead of blow job and being f--ked in the a--. These words are unclear labels that allow them to do whatever they want to while avoiding feelings of guilt. "Oh, by the way Hal, I sodomized my little brother yesterday." "Hey, that's really great, Brad..." Do they even know what the hell they are talking about?

White boys jerked each other off for fun, sucked each other off for fun and even f--ked each other because that was fun too, while black boys knew that other black boys would kick their a--es and that their parents would whip their behinds when they got home. Black boys knew that their families, who tended to be proud and moralistic, would not just sit around and talk about "something nasty" calmly over the scrambled eggs, and that there was definitely no eighty-dollar-an-hour analyst sitting by the telephone waiting for their call. LOVING, CONCERNED BLACK PARENTS PERFORMED THEIR OWN THERAPY ON THEIR CHILDREN'S BEHINDS, BECAUSE MEANINGLESS TERMS LIKE HEALTHY EXPERIMENTATION WERE NOT A PART OF THEIR VOCABULARY.

What was considered fun for white boys was a taboo symbolically punishable by death for black boys. You didn't get caught looking at anybody else's penis or touching anybody else's penis, and you knew better than to let anybody else touch yours either. His d--k was his d--k, your d--k was your d--k and that was the end of it. THESE WORD GAMES THAT WHITE PEOPLE PLAY TO KEEP EVERYBODY ELSE OFF BALANCE ACTUALLY BACKFIRE AND KEEP THEM OFF BALANCE TOO. This is probably one of the reasons they have so many problems with incest and child abuse, and have to qualify things like "inappropriate touching." Because they consider themselves so liberal and forward-thinking, it is difficult to tell sometimes where right ends and where wrong begins. For example, if it is alright for the entire family, mom, dad, little 10-year-old Billy and voluptuous 14-year-old Betty to go nude bathing together, is it alright for dad to embrace Betty or for Billy to fondle or experiment by touching mom? Curiosities and libidos will arise. "Billy, I see that's a fine erection you have there. May I touch it, and kiss it for you, and you can put it inside mommy to see how wonderful it feels." Bullshit!

WHILE WHITE BOYS OFTEN PLAYED WITH EACH OTHER UNTIL THEY GOT UP ENOUGH NERVE TO GO AFTER GIRLS, BLACK BOYS STARTED OFF TRYING TO BE TOUGH LITTLE MEN LOOKING FOR FEMALES. They didn't have soccer and hockey and tennis and traveling, but there were lots of little girls who didn't have those things either, all over the place. That was who they wanted to experiment with. As a young man in college, I had worked on the children's ward of a mental health hospital where I had frequently discovered young white boys fondling each other's penises and young black boys telling them they were crazy. I believe that this kind of experimentation leads to confusion about what is sexually correct behavior as well as what is morally and socially proper.

MOST OF THE ADULT BLACK MALES I TALKED TO WHO ADMITTED THAT THEY MASTURBATE SAID THAT THEY DO IT BECAUSE THEY KNOW BETTER THAN ANYONE ELSE WHAT MAKES THEM FEEL GOOD AND BECAUSE THEY HATED THE IDEA OF DEPENDING ON SOMEONE ELSE ALL THE TIME FOR SEXUAL GRATIFICATION. Some of them said they felt just a little bit guilty if they had not made love to their wives or their girlfriends instead of "jerking off," while others said that masturbating was a fair trade when females either held back or were not available. SOME BLACK MEN FELT THAT THEY HAD THE RIGHT TO PLEASE THEMSELVES IF THEIR PARTNERS COULD NOT OR WOULD NOT SATISFY THEM, AND THAT MASTURBATION ACTUALLY KEPT THEM FROM PRESSURING THEIR WOMEN FOR SEX SOMETIMES.

Huey, a student and part-time taxi driver, said he liked to "beat his meat" because his schedule was so sporadic and because he could get himself off whenever and wherever he felt like it without all the trouble of trying to find a date for sex. He said his usual routine when he got home was to grab the vaseline and a towel, drop his pants, pick out a fantasy and go at it. He said he had been "milking himself" since he was about 13 and that masturbation also helped him to sleep. Most black men felt that according to society, men who have their act together with women are not supposed to masturbate. Many of them felt that was the main reason black men didn't admit to doing it. Some of them confessed that they only began to feel more at ease and relaxed about giving

150

themselves "hand jobs" when they realized their lovers or wives were playing with themselves too.

MANY BLACK MEN, HOWEVER, WHO WOULD NEVER CONSIDER MUTUAL STIMULATION (PETTING), OR MUTUAL MASTURBATION WITH ANOTHER MAN, LOVE BEING MASTURBATED OR JERKED OFF BY A WOMAN. Men who enjoy jerking themselves off and not being responsible for pleasing someone else also enjoy being jerked off without being pressured to perform.

"Women do not take the initiative often enough, so it's wonderful when you find one who does, who just wants to please you sometimes without expecting anything in return," said one man. Again, most black men enjoy any consideration their lover gives to them and their penises, in fact, to their entire bodies, a truth that is often lost to women who also do the same old wham, bam, thank you man.

"Let's get this over with as quick as we can..." Yes, women do that too. "Do not treat it like an it. Handle it with care like you love it as much as I do, because it is a very special part of me that you can touch with your hand, your mouth, your body and even your heart." That's the way Dennis felt.

MASTURBATION CAN INDEED BE WONDERFUL WHEN PERFORMED BY A WOMAN ON A MAN WHEN HER HEART IS IN IT AND HER HANDS KNOW WHAT TO DO. It is an exciting turn-on for a man to watch as his lover manipulates and controls his penis, especially if she knows how. Masturbation is immensely personal, because unlike genital, oral or even anal sex, the woman actually gets to feel the power of his contractions and see what is coming out of her man. It is much like the woman who is standing nearby watching as the man urinates versus another woman holding his penis, actually guiding and feeling the flow and the warmth of his organ as he expels. It's like getting your back scratched in just the right spot by somebody else. Sure, you may be in tune with your own body, but it is real Goodpussy knowing that someone else is on such good "touching terms" with it too.

OFTEN DURING MASTURBATION, BLACK MEN DO THINGS TO THEMSELVES THAT THEY MAY BE UNCOMFORTABLE ASKING SOMEONE ELSE TO DO, LIKE MASSAGING THEIR NUTS OR TOUCHING THEMSELVES IN OTHER PLACES. The usual technique in giving yourself a "hand job" is to grip the shaft with the right hand (fist) using subtle pumping up-and-down motions until the come can be felt in the shaft. From that point use either long or short strokes near the head and the first inch or two of the shaft, as many black men feel that this area -- including the underside and the area just below the hole where the shaft and the head meet -- are the most sensitive. A lubricant such as vaseline or hand cream is sometimes used and even saliva if there is nothing else available because dry masturbation often results in soreness. Most black men do fantasize and some have even admitted to tasting their own semen.

Masturbation has and always will be Goodpussy for many black men, and whether they admit it publicly or not their secrets will remain hidden between them and their right hands.

IS PENIS SIZE IMPORTANT?

Well, I think it is, but then I'm only a man, what do I know? After all, every little white housewife that I have ever seen on television or read about claims that the size of a man's penis is not important. These women say that "It's not what you have but what you do with what you have." BULL SHIT!... TO EVERY MAN I KNOW THE SIZE OF HIS PENIS IS A BIG DEAL, AND NOT JUST FROM THE STANDPOINT OF WHAT YOU DO WITH WHAT YOU HAVE.

It is crucial to a man that he have something to do something with in the first place. AS MEN, SOCIETY HAS EXPECTATIONS OF US, AND AT THE SAME TIME WE HAVE EXPECTATIONS OF OURSELVES. One of the things we do not expect is a boy's penis with a man's body. Expectations for black men are even greater, because of myths that have been handed down from generation to generation about the size of his organ, and about his proficiency with his enormous tool. Again, some white women I know, who generally loathe black men, said they would be willing to have sex with "one of them" just to see if the old tales were true.

Even as children, this naive curiosity about sex permeates our society. Little girls and little boys say things like, "Show me yours and I'll show you mine" while playing doctor. Or some woman is always bragging to her girl friends about how well her lover is hung. But size isn't important, right?. Wrong. In fact, it's even important to her, whether she knows it or not. Not all women, but some women actually validate themselves by being able to take "all his penis." Because she could take all he had she knows that she is a woman, and the bigger his is the more woman she is.

For other women it works just the opposite. These women believe that a woman should be timid and frail and the mere fact that they cannot comfortably handle his "plunging organ" tells them that they are indeed real women. PENISES -- THEIR SIZES AND COLORS AND DIFFERENCES -- ARE A NATURAL CURIOSITY TO MOST WOMEN, AND TO SOME MEN. And magazines like Playmate are making tens of millions of dollars by literally showing what men have.

Penis size isn't important. Who do they think they are kidding? When she gets him excited she would really like to see it, and really like to feel it, where it counts. And these women who claim the size of their mate's organ is not important want to maintain a facade of normalcy for their friends as well. They would hardly share the fact that their man's penis is only two inches long on full erection because they do not want to be pitied or laughed at. Some women really may not care, however, because they really love the man and everything else is incidental. Some others may feel that the smaller his penis is, the more equal she is to him. Have you ever, in your entire life, heard any woman say, "Oh Helen, Jim's penis is only three inches long but I love it to death..." Somehow, I don't think so. She is not about to let anyone know that those prized family jewels are only watery paste or simple costume jewelry.

The size of a man's penis is at least as important to him as the size of a woman's breasts are to her. It is not necessary to be the biggest, but every man wants to be reasonably represented. Tommy, another friend of mine, is a physical therapist. He told me of one occasion where he had to give a 6'4", 250-pound man a sponge bath, and that this huge man's penis was no bigger than a woman's little finger. Imagine the sexual, psychological and emotional problems that he must have. As his new lover passionately waits for him to whip it out, he must be terrified. All he can do is pop it out.

At the same time, there is the other side of that coin. My 89 year old uncle, my Uncle Johnny, told me about a young man he once knew out in the country. He said that this fellow would sit in a tree and "beat his meat." He said that the boy's penis was as thick as his wrists (which were large from house painting), and as long as his arm up to the elbow, like a mule. He said that his friend was ruined, and that he had to go from town to town looking for unsuspecting girls and women who didn't know him, because once he had struck and word got around, he couldn't go back. So, the grass is not always greener on the other side. It's just different grass.

And for those of you who think this is only a black man's fortune or misfortune, think again, because you are seriously mistaken. Another friend of mine, Claire, who was recently separated, told me that she was alone one night, and lonely, so she went to this bar near her apartment complex where she met a very nice white gentleman whose name was Phillip. She told me that they had a few drinks and laughed and talked and that she invited him to have a nightcap at her place. When they got to her apartment and he undressed, she said her eyes almost popped out of her head as she exclaimed, "And just what do you think you are going to do with that?" He had a 12-inch penis.

155

I remember yet another story about another friend of mine. His name is Don too, and he jokingly told me about one of his frequent midnight escapades. Well Don, who was pretty popular with the ladies, always traveled with his gym bag. Whether it was 7 o'clock in the morning or 11 o'clock at night, if you saw Don, his gym bag was nearby. I had often wondered about it, but just blew it off as a tooth brush, deodorant, you know, the usual things, but what I found out was that everywhere he went he carried a 10-inch dildo with him. Imagine that, a grown man walking around carrying a gym bag with a d--k in it. He said that he used it to break the monotony and to keep from wearing himself out. And he said that most of his girlfriends actually loved being a little freaky.

On this particular evening, as he put it, he knew that he was really laying some serious meat, so he confidentially asked his lover, "What about me, baby, I mean compared to your old man?" She thought carefully for a moment then answered, "Well, my hand can fit around your wrist, so he's bigger than that."

Don said that he actually started to panic. He told me he became so curious that he even wanted to know how long the other man's penis was. He said that when she asked him if he had a yard stick, he just PETERED OUT. He said that his own penis had gone limp and that her last words to him as he was leaving were "NEXT TIME YOU COME, DON'T FORGET THE D--K... AND BRING SOME FRIENDS WITH YOU."

The point here is that even when you are well-equipped and you know that you know what you are doing, you can still be intimidated by a simple thing like size.

OVERALL, MOST BLACK MEN SEEMED TO BE SATISFIED WITH THE SIZES OF THEIR PENISES, AND SOME OF THEM EVEN THOUGHT THAT THEIR PRIZES WERE HANDSOME OR BEAUTIFUL. Some preferred circumcision while others did not. For uncircumcised men, hygiene was sometimes a problem, but they thought the added sensitivity they believed they felt when the foreskin was pulled back more than made up for any inconvenience. Some of the black men I talked to liked the way the head was shaped while others were more pleased with the length and thickness, buying into that old idea that the bigger it is, the better it works and the more powerful you are.

BIGGER, LIKE BEAUTY, HOWEVER, IS IN THE EYE OF THE BEHOLDER, BECAUSE WHILE THE MAN MAY BE HAVING A LOVE AFFAIR WITH HIS HUGE ORGAN, AND SOME WOMEN MAY ENJOY FONDLING AND LOOKING AT IT, AND MAYBE EVEN LAUGHING AT IT, THEY STILL PREFER AN ADEQUATE LOVER WHO SATISFIES THEM.

How big is big, anyway? And while women may playfully tease about a big penis, they do not want the pain or medical problems that go with having their insides destroyed. Some men, including some black men, said that they had become self-conscious and had actually developed hang-ups because of the size of their penises, compared to other men, especially if they felt that a wife or a girlfriend had been lost to a bigger, more experienced, more powerful penis.

Other black men, friends whose names I dare not call, even admitted sneaking a look to compare sizes in showers and in rest rooms, saying that they just wanted to check out the competition, to see how they stacked up.

There is one other thing that I would like to say about the size of a man's penis, and especially about the size of black men's penises, and it is a social statement. In all the world, the only thing that the black man in America is revered for is his sexual prowess. He is not renowed as a builder, scientist, an educator or a thinker. To the world community he is someone who makes babies, who does not work, who is ignorant and undesirable. He and his African brothers are the only men on the face of the earth who are revered for what is between their legs, but unlike the African, the black man in America often places little value on developing his mind. Black men's penises have become bigger than life. Collectively it is the biggest and most powerful penis on earth. It is a ten trillion ton whopper that can knock missiles from the sky, sink entire fleets of battle ships, and one drop of semen from its powerful head can annihilate entire civilizations. It is the ultimate weapon. But what good is it? Can it buy food or provide shelter? I think not. Bigger is not always better. The Japanese have shown us that, with their economical and efficient compact and sub-compact cars and their vast micro-technology. And like the white male, they too despise the black man as they are buying up and colonizing America. Unlike his predecessor, however, the Japanese have no use for the black man. White males, not all white males, but those who have made careers of castrating black men, now have a partner who is equally up to the task, and many black men do not even know that their penis is laying on the table and that the butcher's knife is about to come down on it, too. MOST BLACK MEN ARE SO BUSY EITHER TAKING THEIR PENISES FOR GRANTED OR SHOWING THEM OFF THAT THEY DO NOT EVEN KNOW WHAT IS HAPPENING TO THEM. AND IT IS INDEED TIME TO WAKE UP, BEFORE IT IS TOO LATE, AND OUR BLOOD IS DRIPPING ON THE FLOOR.

In all fairness to black women, in this chapter I did not say that they were the ones doing most of the complaining. Generally, they too are satisfied with the sizes of their men's penises, even though they may be dissatisfied with their collective ineffectiveness.

One thing that all black men should remember is that you are not your penis, and that it is not you. You are the one who should be doing the thinking. IF YOU HAVE A PENIS, AND IT WORKS THE WAY IT SHOULD, BE HAPPY WITH WHAT YOU'VE GOT, AND THANK GOD.

DO BLACK MEN EAT PU--Y?

Does a bull have nuts? NEXT TO THE USUAL
CURIOSITIES ABOUT THE SIZE OF THE FAMILY JEWELS, THIS
QUESTION IS PROBABLY THE MOST PROVOCATIVE ONE ON THE
LIST. Many black men become very defensive and irate if you
ask, however, exclaiming, "No, man, I don't eat no f--kin' pu--
y! If the good Lord had meant for me to be eatin' pu--y he
would have put a knife and a fork over my top lip instead of
a mustache."

I call many of these black men CLOSET GOURMETS. By
contrast, many white men are saying "Show me a man who
doesn't eat it and I can show you an unsatisfied wife or a
girlfriend I can take away." Black men are embarrassed while
white men openly brag, with not so much as a hint of shame.
SEX IS AN INTEGRAL PART OF WHO AND WHAT WE ARE AND HOW
WE EXPRESS OUR SEXUALITY IS EQUALLY AS IMPORTANT.

There are several reasons why most black men still deny that they perform oral sex on women. The most obvious reason is that some black men really do not do it, and they probably never will. ONE OF THE REASONS WHY THOSE WHO DO CONTINUE TO SAY THAT THEY DO NOT, HOWEVER, IS THAT THEY SEE ORAL SEX AS "A WHITE MAN'S THING." In fact, they know black people in general believe anything that is not normal is something that sick white people do. They have learned that even as teenagers many white boys participate in oral sex rather than intercourse so that their girlfriends will still be considered virgins. Historically black men have felt that white men have had to resort to using their tongues and mouths because they were not equipped to cut the mustard using straight sex, so they had to resort to other tricks. So, many black men do not admit that they participate in oral sex because they do not want the same aspersions cast against them. White men who are not manly eat pu--y, therefore, because I am manly, I do not.

ANOTHER REASON FOR DENIAL IS THAT MANY BLACK PEOPLE TEND TO BE MORALISTIC, AND ANY SEX ACT THAT IS NOT MISSIONARY IS WRONG. Doing it any way but the right way is nasty. And there is nothing any filthier or low down than putting your mouth on somebody else's genitals. Many of these men admitted to being repulsed by the smell of the woman's vagina and thoughts of the horrible taste it must have. ALSO, THEY FELT THAT DOING SOMETHING THAT NASTY AND DIRTY MEANT THEY WERE NASTY AND DIRTY AS WELL.

YET ANOTHER REASON WHY BLACK MEN DO NOT ADMIT TO CUNNILINGUS IS THAT THEY FEAR RIDICULE AND HUMILIATION. "If anybody finds out they will laugh at me." They think other black men will see them as weaklings who will stoop to doing anything to get close to a woman. While some women may see it that way too, others will see him as a man who knows how to please a woman, as a man who is willing and anxious to do what he has to to give her what she wants. This type of black lover knows that there are things he can do with his mouth and tongue that he cannot do with his penis and hands. He truly wants to satisfy her, realizing that just as a woman loving his penis turns him on, loving her vagina turns her on.

JUST AS THERE ARE THOSE MEN WHO DENY IT, OTHER BLACK MEN BOLDLY ADMIT THEY DO IT. These men use the direct approach. EXPERIENCE ITSELF HAS TAUGHT THEM THAT WOMEN ENJOY ORAL SEX TOO, AND THEY ARE BETTING THAT THEY CAN CUT RIGHT THROUGH ALL THAT RED TAPE AND GET RIGHT DOWN TO "LICKING THE JAR." Many times this is true, because a woman who feels cheap if she just sleeps with a man, can somehow justify her actions if she believes that she is getting something too. No, she may not just let a man f--k her, use her to get his rocks off, but if she thinks that she is going to get her rocks off too, then that's another story. EXPERIENCE HAS TAUGHT HER TOO, THAT THE MAN WHO IS WILLING TO FORGET ABOUT HIS PRIDE AND EAT HER PROBABLY DOES WANT TO PLEASE HER, WHILE THE OTHER MAN, YOU KNOW THE ONE WHO WON'T, MAY JUST BE INTERESTED IN PLEASING HIMSELF. The man who is willing to get down on his knees is also viewed as a more worldly, sophisticated and interesting lover. If he does that, what else does he do, and how good is he at it? This nasty old man is really the fox in the hen house. He understands that when this woman opens her legs like that, letting him see her most private parts close up, she is revealing both confidence and trust in him. He knows that with just a little more skill and patience he will get what he wants too, Goodpussy.

But what does he really want, this dirty old man, or dirty young man, as the case may be? Is he just out to add another notch to his belt or is there more? I think that there is. I believe that this black man truly enjoys the taste, the texture and the smell of a woman's genitals. I believe that just as some animals scent each other (and remember that man is an animal too), there is a similar connection between men and women. (In saliva a substance called cebum has been isolated which is a driving force in the desire for deep kissing.) I FEEL

THAT A WOMAN HERSELF PRODUCES A NATURAL APHRODISIAC THAT MAY BE COMPELLING TO A MAN. I suggest also that feeding herself to her lover is as gratifying emotionally, sexually, psychologically and spiritually as breast feeding her own young. She gets to give all of herself to him. INDEED A WOMAN WHO HAS NOT EXPERIENCED THE JOYS OF GIVING BIRTH AND FEEDING SOMEONE FROM HER VERY OWN BODY GETS TO DO JUST THAT -- FEED HIM... And just that is what bothers a few black men the most. You cannot eat it without tasting it and smelling it, and doing it right means getting the taste of her and the smell of her all over your face.

Some black men are eager to try oral sex, but for any of the aforesaid reasons, they hesitate. A couple of other reasons is that they may not feel they know what to do, or they may not think they know anybody to do it with. Others want to but their mates do not.

Those black men who did admit it, however, gave a wide variety of reasons for orally stimulating their lovers. Topping the list, of course, was the fact that they enjoyed the taste and even the smell, while others said that they enjoyed spreading their lover's legs and manipulating her vagina, labia and clitoris with their mouths and tongues, listening to her moaning and gasping and looking at her face and convulsive spasms as she comes. Their bottom line was sensual pleasure for their lovers, watching and feeling them being weakened and seduced by their power, and the feeling of ultimate intimacy and closeness they derived from the act. These black men felt, overall, that they were showing their love for their woman, while others merely felt that penile stimulation alone might not provide the total gratification their lovers deserved. Still other black men enjoyed a different kind of control, his control as he uses his mouth to manipulate her, or her control as she uses her body to feed him. Terry, a disc jockey, said that just eating pu--y itself excited him, and that he had come many times that way. Another good friend of mine, Robert, one of those nasty old men, says that while he is licking,

162

kissing and sucking breasts, belly buttons, lips, noses, fingers, toes and eyelids, he might as well do pu--ys and a--holes too. He said that he also liked watching women masturbate while he ate them and the way they buried his head between their legs when they got excited.

Do black men eat pu--y? After reading this chapter I think you can draw your own conclusions. If white men can learn rhythm by dancing, I'm sure black men can learn a few new tricks too. Noah, a close friend of mine, says, "There are two kinds of men: those who do and those who lie. Which one are you?"

DO BLACK WOMEN GIVE H--D?

Some do, some don't, but then we already knew that, didn't we. But why or why not? And why do some black women swallow every drop of semen, while others will only suck?

Well, first, I think some black women just down-right love the licking, sucking and biting, and the feel of the man's throbbing penis pulsating in their mouths, teasing the head, the shaft, the balls and even the nipples and anus with their tongues. For others the thrill comes from doing the unspeakable without fear of getting pregnant.

SOME BLACK WOMEN SEEM TO INSTINCTIVELY UNDERSTAND THAT FOR MANY BLACK MEN THE ULTIMATE FANTASY IS GETTING "SUCKED OFF." Its only equal, for some other black men, is to be loved and sucked by more than one woman at the same time. THE MOST EXCITING AND PLEASURABLE SEXUAL EXPERIENCE THESE BLACK MEN CAN IMAGINE IS HAVING A WOMAN'S WARM LOVING MOUTH ON THEIR PENISES. These women realize that their mouths can be just as erotic and gratifying as a warm loving pu--y. A woman whose heart is in it can do things with her mouth and tongue that she could not begin to do with her vagina. I'm sure for others sucking is just a simple psychological matter of pacification, much like sucking one's thumb or any other oral fixation.

For other black women I believe that the turn-on is control and making the man's penis transform from flacid to fully erect. She gets to see and touch the results of her labor, and actually reap the benefits if she so desires. She is the vixen who transfixes her lover as they marvel at her rigid accomplishment. And there is nothing any more commanding at that moment than her performance. She is the absolute base of power, hers and his. HE WOULD HAVE NO LIGHTS WITHOUT HER SIZZLING ELECTRICITY.

164

Other black women, I believe, see sucking a man's penis as complete sex. IF SHE IS GOING TO DO PART (B) SHE MIGHT AS WELL DO PART (A). If she is going to turn him on, she might as well turn him all the way on. Why pick up the keys if you don't intend to drive the car? Like some black men who genuinely enjoy performing oral sex on women, there are black women who derive excitement from sucking a man.

Some black women suck their men's penises even though they may not want to. They may in fact even hate it, but do so to keep their men. "If I don't suck his d--k, he might get someone else to do it or even worse, he might leave me."

Finally, some black women give the men in their lives h--d for reciprocity. "If I don't do him he won't do me." Some of these black women and black men enjoy performing oral sex simultaneously, or the old faithful "69."

And what about ejaculation and swallowing (drinking) a man's semen? Of course we know that some women genuinely enjoy sucking, but they will not swallow. Some, in fact, cannot swallow. They literally get sick, or choke or throw up, and sometimes all three happen. I personally know of a woman who had a passion for men in uniform, and one day after servicing too many police officers, she choked to death.

And while some women love the taste of semen, which is supposed to be influenced by the man's diet, some black men were turned off because their lovers complained that theirs tasted nasty. Some of them complained that these women didn't know what they were doing anyway, and that they either moved their mouths off at the last minute leaving them to shoot off in space, or they take it in their mouths and run to the toilet to spit it out, in spite of the fact that they want men to eat their juices.

A few black men said that they had never tried it. Others said they thought it was a filthy habit, and that any woman who did it was a nasty bitch.

Again, in my long list of associations, I know of another little story. An acquaintance of mine, Dale, and his very lovely lady, June, were making love, but when she went down on him to show him how much she adored him, he threw her out of a second story window causing her serious injury. Because he was such a cosmopolitan type, my friends and I were surprised that his attitude about oral sex was so volatile.

SOME BLACK MEN DO, IN FACT, FEEL THAT WHEN A WOMAN MAKES LOVE TO HIS BODY SHE IS INDEED WORSHIPPING AND PAYING TRIBUTE TO HIS MANLINESS. Others feel that she is paying tribute to herself, by taking this black man's manhood, which is the best that he has, and bringing him to his knees.

Again, not being a woman, I cannot feel what she feels or know precisely what she is feeling either. I only offer what I believe to be true. I do know, however, that whether it is done for him, for her, or for the two of them, women do perform fellatio on men, and for them it is true Goodpussy.

PRE AIDS VS POST AIDS

Attitudes have changed, yes they have. Before AIDS (Acquired Immune Deficiency Syndrome) everything was fair and the one-night stand was still more of the stuff some black men's dreams were made of. SOMETIMES THE PENIS REALLY WAS THE BRAIN AND SOME BLACK MEN HAD MANY CAUSAL PARTNERS. And not only did they have many casual partners, these men were also less concerned about what kind of sex they had. The only thing that was important was "having sex," hence the old saying that "A stiff d--k has no conscience." But remember that society had played its part in making him that way too.

As a result of AIDS, black men in general have become more responsible, at least for themselves. Overall, many of them may not really care who they screw over, but they are concerned about not being screwed over themselves. In the past, if a man got infected (burned), it was no big deal, and certainly nothing that a visit to the doctor's office and a quick shot of penicillin could not cure. BECAUSE AIDS CANNOT BE FIXED, SELFISH SEX REALLY HAS BECOME TRULY SELFISH. Men are screwing around less, not because they appreciate women more, but because they do not want either the pain or the devastation of a deadly disease visited upon themselves.

BLACK MEN TODAY ARE HAVING CLOSER AND FEWER SEXUAL PARTNERS. Before AIDS, a man might have four or five casual encounters in the course of a year. That number has now dropped to more like two or three. He may have a primary relationship with a wife or a girl friend, a second or side relationship with someone he knows well whom he has been seeing for some time, and a casual relationship that just happens either on the job, while he is out with the guys, or while he is just driving down the street.

Another big change is in the area of prophylactics. BEFORE AIDS MOST BLACK MEN ENJOYED THE THRILL OF EJACULATING INSIDE THEIR LOVER, MAKING HIS MARK OR

LEAVING PART OF HIMSELF WHERE HE HAD BEEN. Receiving his semen also let him know that his lover had enjoyed him too and that he was being accepted. USING A RUBBER WAS ALMOST LIKE NOT BEING THERE AT ALL BECAUSE THERE WAS NO TRUE CONTACT. Today, if you do not use a rubber, it just might be better not to be there at all.

In the 90's, both men and women are "packin" prophylactics. While opening up her purse and taking out several different brands, Lynn, 23, told me, "He may not have his but I've got mine." THESE DAYS ANYONE WHO HAS GOOD SENSE AND IS SEXUALLY ACTIVE WITH MORE THAN ONE PERSON CARRIES A "RAINCOAT."

Because we once thought that AIDS only killed homosexual men, the disease did not really bother the rest of us too much. But when the truth was known -- that it affected heterosexuals as well -- panic began to strike closer to home. Many people believed that homosexuals had caused the AIDS crisis, and that these men were only getting what they deserved.

At the top of the fault list, however, was of course the black male, who naturally gets blamed for everything. The African was accused of having started the whole thing by having sex with the green monkey (just as he was accused of having sex with the orangutan centuries ago). This theory too, about the green monkey, has been scientifically disputed while the real villains, America's sexually permissive attitude and racism, sleep undisturbed.

The World Health Organization and not the green monkey is responsible for the Aids virus, charges Dr. Theodore A. Strecker, an expert on the subject. According to Dr. Strecker, the virus was introduced in Africa through an immunization policy using hepatitis B and smallpox vaccines which were thought to have been developed at Ft. Detrick, Maryland. It was at Ft. Detrick that biological and chemical warfare research was being conducted. Experts believe that one-third of the African population, or 75,000,000 (seventy-five million) people could be infected with the virus.

THE (HIV) OR AIDS VIRUS IS TRANSMITTED ONLY THROUGH INFECTED BODY FLUIDS SUCH AS BLOOD, SEMEN AND VAGINAL SECRETIONS. THE VIRUS ATTACKS THE BODY'S NATURAL IMMUNE SYSTEM LOWERING ITS RESISTANCE SO THAT IT CAN NO LONGER PROTECT ITSELF AGAINST INFECTIOUS GERMS. Anyone infected with AIDS cannot be cured, and the virus is passed on by receiving transfusions from contaminated blood, sexual intercourse and intravenous drug use. A pregnant mother who is infected may also pass on the deadly disease to her unborn child either during birth or in her womb through her blood. The fear now is that people's pasts will start catching up with them as experts predict that almost 200,000 people will have died of AIDS in the United States by 1991.

TWO OF THE HIGHEST AT-RISK GROUPS ARE YOUNG PEOPLE AND THE HOMOSEXUAL COMMUNITY. A study by Robert Coles and Geoffery Stokes, called "Sex and the American Teenager," determined that many teenagers participate in masturbation, oral sex, same-sex experimentation and anal sex as well, and that even 12-year-olds were having sexual intercourse. Approximately 2.5 million teenagers are affected by sexually transmitted diseases in the United States each year with about 1 million unplanned pregnancies. So they, the teenagers, are both sexually active and sexually naive at the same time. Most homosexuals generally practice anal sex, and the sensitive lining of the rectum is easily susceptible to contamination or infection. Many of these persons also change partners frequently, but those who maintain faithful monogamous relationships are as safe from AIDS as heterosexual couples who are monogamous. AIDS cannot be contracted by kissing, not by drinking or eating after someone who is infected, not from a swimming pool, a toilet seat or from a water fountain. It can only be contracted by those means I described.

Again, there is no cure for AIDS, but the drugs AZT (azidothmidine) and DDI (dideoxyinosine) do prevent the virus from multiplying and prolong and improve the quality of the infected person's life.

Two associates of mine, Lewis and Larry, had recently died of AIDS, and as I thought about them I recalled something that I had heard another AIDS victim say. He said that it was a terrible thing to look around and see that all of your friends had died. This truly is a tragic situation, but we must remember that even though AIDS is getting all the headlines today, there are many, many other sexually transmitted diseases out there just waiting for us to make the wrong move. And Goodpussy is about not making the wrong move.

GENTLEMEN, COVER YOUR NUTS

Just about everybody out there wants them, but not for the reasons you might think. IF YOU ARE A BLACK MAN AND A REAL MAN, YOU MAY BE VIEWED AS A THREAT TO WHITE MEN AND TO YOUR BLACK SISTERS AS WELL. History has taught us about the white male, but why our own black women? The answer is obvious. Black men may upset the apple cart.

WHITE MEN ARE STILL AT THE TOP OF THE SOCIAL, POLITICAL AND ECONOMIC CHAIN, BUT LIBERATED BLACK WOMEN WHO ARE ANXIOUS TO GET AHEAD REALIZE THAT STRONG BLACK MALES MAY BE THE ONLY OBSTACLE COMING BETWEEN THEM AND THEIR GOALS. Knowing you down may be all she has to do to get to her own Goodpussy. Black males too, who are weak, share her sentiments as well, because they do not want any problems from you either. Black faces are fine, but not black faces that may rock the boat.

171

SOME WOMEN, INCLUDING BLACK WOMEN WHO ARE IN POSITIONS OF AUTHORITY, SOMETIMES FEEL INSECURE AND INTIMIDATED WHEN THERE ARE INDEPENDENT-THINKING BLACK MEN UNDER THEIR SUPERVISION. In fact, some black women in management and co-workers as well, actually hate black men.

SHE KNOWS WHO YOU ARE, BUT SHE IS AWARE THAT YOU KNOW WHO SHE IS TOO, AND THE BEST GOODPUSSY THAT SHE COULD POSSIBLY IMAGINE WOULD BE YOUR BALLS BRONZED AND MOUNTED ON THE MANTLE OVER HER FIREPLACE BESIDE HER SMILING PORTRAIT. You have peeped her card. You know that she is trying to be something she is not, and she doesn't like it. She may be talking white and acting white because she knows that is what white people like. She may even secretly want to be white, and even though the white people around her do not know it, you do. And you know that practicing someone else's culture may just be a different kind of slavery. Even her name which was Linda is now "Lin." You are the deadly switch that undermines her security and stability. In short, you make her down right uncomfortable if not paranoid. You truly are her worst nightmare. YOUR BALLS, THE ONES SHE DOES NOT HAVE, AT LEAST NOT YET, ARE NOW IN HER WAY. She liked them before. She thought they were cute. She even liked playing with them, but now she won't even play with you.

SOMETIMES BLACK WOMEN ACTUALLY DESPISE BLACK MEN WHO TRY TO SUCCEED, HELPING TO LABEL THEM AS TROUBLEMAKERS. Again, some of us want to be something that we are not, and she wants to be you. Often, too, there is nothing feminine about women in power. Like the man who washes dishes and cleans up all the time, she seems to have lost something, too.

BLACK WOMEN, HOWEVER, HAVE HISTORICALLY HAD A LONG STANDING TRADITION WITH WHITE MEN EVER SINCE THE DAYS OF SLAVERY. They often bore his children and some black women had white men who were there protectors. In New Orleans, during what is called the "Golden Era" beautiful young Creole girls would be taken to the elegant Quadroon

Balls by their mothers to meet Frenchmen or Spaniards to enter into an arrangement called placage. These women would have families for their white men, educate their children and live in elegantly appointed homes as second wives. The results of this mixture or miscegenation are still quite obvious in Louisiana, with its briques, mulattos, griffes, octoroons and quadroons.

Again, strong white males are leaders, while strong black men are bad news. This was the case in 1891 as it is in 1991, and just as white males who have treated blacks unfairly fear reprisal, so do self-serving black women. The best way to handle your kind is to eliminate you.

Society is saying, be a man and make something of yourself, while all the time its foot is planted firmly on your neck. Less than 150 years ago black men were still wearing chains and being treated like animals. We have, indeed, come far without going very far. All things considered, white people have always been free, so why are they all not equal to the Duponts, the Gettys or the Rockerfellers? Surely if all whites are not equal, blacks could not possibly have caught up in such a short time, even though they have made phenomenal gains.

Those phenomenal gains are the problem. Our successes testify to our ability to adapt and go forward. Strong black males are a clear and present threat to the status quo. STRONG BLACK MEN REALIZE THAT THEY DO NOT HAVE A GOD-GIVEN RIGHT TO BE INFERIOR, BUT TO BE EQUAL. This attitude poses a problem for white men who have been comfortably leading without opposition -- and for some black women who want to be leaders. It's like the relay race where all the other runners are saying, "Oh Lord, whatever you do, please don't give that black man the baton."

Here again is still more evidence about the importance of historical perspective. Knowing about our fathers and mothers helps us to understand who we are. White people understand that if we do not know who we are, we do not know what to expect of ourselves, because family ties help to determine our obligations and responsibilities.

That is why it is so important that the minority races be kept apart, so that we do not come together to find out what we have in common. LIKE THE SLAVES WHO WERE NOT ALLOWED TO BE GROUPED TOGETHER IF THEY SHARED A COMMON LANGUAGE, AMERICAN HISTORY IS REPEATING ITSELF WITH THE RACES. Keep minorities separated. Divide and conquer is still the policy of the day, even with our women.

THE BLACK MAN CAN BE THE KEY, AND THAT WHICH HAS DONE HIM SO MUCH HARM -- HIS COLOR CAN ALSO DO HIM THE MOST GOOD. That which has separated him from everyone else could polarize him to others like himself, because just as it was easy for them to spot us, it is just as easy for us to spot each other.

And those black women who find themselves in opposition to black males should know a few things about other women as well. For example, at least 15% of the world's cultures are matrilinear. What that means is that in those societies it is the mother's family line that is important, and descent is from a common known female ancestor. The Navaho Indians for instance are matrilinear. Women control the economy and make most of the money, and everyone in the group is responsible for everyone else. The point is that anyone can respect anyone else, if they know who they are and how they are expected to behave. BLACK MEN AND BLACK WOMEN NEED NOT BE AGAINST EACH OTHER.

The black man in America is indeed unique in all the world, and if he truly knew how unique he is, he would be a serious force to be reckoned with. KNOW WHO YOU ARE!

POWER AND SEX, SEX AND POWER

Power is a strange and compelling entity. It is control, it is authority, and for much of our lives most of us court it, never to bask in its wondrous radiance. Power gives the illusion of esteem, however, because believing that you are powerful is a purely subjective matter. For example, you may be influential on your job, but a nobody in your community. Or you may be the dominating force in your home, and just one more poor soul stuck in a rush-hour traffic jam. POWER IS AN ABSTRACT CONCEPT, AN ILLUSION HELD BY SECULAR MEN AND WOMEN WHO HAVE GRANDIOSE DELUSIONS ABOUT THEIR OWN LOFTY SELF-WORTH OR THAT OF SOMEONE ELSE.

OFTEN MEN WHO BELIEVE THEMSELVES POWERFUL ALSO BELIEVE THAT IT IS THEIR RIGHT TO HAVE WHATEVER IT IS THAT THEY WANT, INCLUDING YOUR WIFE OR YOUR GIRL FRIEND. These men believe that the world belongs to them. And because it is already theirs, it is naturally theirs to use. Society generally feeds and nurtures this kind of fallacy. YOU ARE STRONG, YOU ARE SUCCESSFUL, YES, YOU CAN TAKE WHAT YOU WANT. It is your right. You deserve to have your way. Society, and women, lie on their backs spreading their legs so that he, the almighty conqueror, can indulge the sweet taste of victory again as he sows his wild oats, simply because he has them to sow.

SOCIETY HAS TAUGHT US AND WE ARE TEACHING OUR SONS THAT THEY ARE POWERFUL, THAT THEY ARE HEROES AND THAT THEIR REWARD IS SEX. Being a nice guy, that is, being too nice will get you nowhere. Women, too, encourage their own abuse when they walk right past a nice guy to get to a bad guy. EVERYTHING HE SEES TELLS HIM THAT THE STRONG MAN GETS THE WOMAN, AND ANY YOUNG MAN GROWING UP IN AMERICA WITHOUT REALLY LISTENING WITH AN OPEN MIND MAY NEVER REALLY LEARN TO APPRECIATE ANY WOMAN.

America is allegedly the land of the free and the home of the brave, where men are taught to do their own thing.

AND IN AMERICA, THE GREATEST COUNTRY ON EARTH, SOME BLACK MEN NOW SEE THEMSELVES AS THE STUFF DREAMS ARE MADE OF. Women sometimes accuse men of thinking that they are God's gift to women and that may well be true. Way, way back when, when he was born, he was God's gift to his mother, remember. IF HE WAS THAT IMPORTANT TO THE MOST WONDERFUL WOMAN HE HAS EVER KNOWN, THEN SURELY HE MUST BE IMPORTANT TO OTHER WOMEN AS WELL.

Add to that all the messages he has been given all his life and we get a reasonably clear picture of who he is. He has become the best thing that has ever happened to himself, since the day he was born. And he knows that is true because society has told him so every day of his life. MAN HIMSELF HAS BECOME HIS OWN GOODPUSSY.

Many influential men, politicians, businessmen and even clergymen have fallen from grace because they have succumbed to this foolishness. Just as Sampson had his Delilah, Jim Baker had his Jessica Hahn, Gary Hart his Donna Rice, and on and on and on. Because of their high profile, these influential men, too, believed that the world was theirs to use, including the women, and sometimes even the men in it. They have greedily eaten the bullshit they have been pushing, and have fallen frail prey to their own vanity. And again, what was the reward for their accomplishment? It was always sex. The world, their world, the one they owned, was supposed to always love and honor them because they were her favorite sons.

RAPE, ONE OF THE MOST HORRENDOUS CRIMES, IS OFTEN PAINTED AS A CRIME OF VIOLENCE. CERTAINLY VIOLENCE MAY BE AN ELEMENT IN ESTABLISHING CONTROL, BUT IT IS NOT ALWAYS THE SINGULAR MOTIVATION FOR THE ACT ITSELF. I, MYSELF, MAINTAIN THAT RAPE MAY ALSO BE A CRIME OF PASSION, OF POWER AND OF REWARD.

As an example of passion in rape, let us consider the rapist who has a loving wife and family at home. He may commit the crime because his home life is too perfect, too

176

boring, and he needs the excitement and the exhilaration of passion felt when a woman resists him. His wife is willing, but she just lies there like a three-week-old steak. He may, in fact, love his wife very much, but not consider the intimacy they share real sex, the sex he is entitled to as a man and as a good husband.

DATE RAPE, ESPECIALLY ON COLLEGE CAMPUSES, IS APPROACHING EPIDEMIC PROPORTIONS. YOUNG WOMEN ARE ALMOST OPENLY BEING OVERPOWERED BY MEN THEY KNOW. They are not being preyed upon by sinister figures who pounce upon them in dark alley ways, but are often abused in familiar surroundings they presume to be safe. THEIR ATTACKERS (MEN THEY KNOW) ARE NOT JUMPING OUT OF BUSHES, THEY ARE SIMPLY, SIMPLY, TAKING SOME SEX. Many of these men do not feel that they are doing anything wrong, and who knows, maybe they really do not see it that way. ACCORDING TO THE GOODPUSSY THEORY OF DEVELOPMENT DISCUSSED BACK IN CHAPTER III, THESE YOUNG MEN HAVE BEEN TAUGHT, ENCOURAGED AND EVEN REINFORCED TO BELIEVE THAT SEX IS THEIR REWARD FOR ACCOMPLISHMENT. They have been good boys who have completed one phase of their education. They have done their parents proud, now they are collecting their customary reward -- sex. WOMEN WHO HAVE ALWAYS BEEN HIS PRIZE, CONTINUE TO BE JUST THAT, TO BE USED AS HE SEES FIT. Just as the hunter bags his prey, our young hero gets to bed, or bang the girl, only needing now to have her "stuffed and mounted" for his collection.

HE HAS BEEN BRAINWASHED ALL HIS LIFE SO THAT NOW HE NO LONGER SEES FORCIBLE SEX AS A CRIME, BUT RATHER AS HIS RIGHT. To the victor belongs the spoils, and he is only collecting what is rightfully his, even if that prize happens to be someone else's body.

After being reported to campus authorities for raping her, Jeff had burst into Jill's dormitory shouting, "How could you do this to me? I thought you were my friend!" He had raped her, but now felt betrayed because she had reported the attack.

BLACK MEN MUST LEARN WHEN TO TELL THEIR EGOS TO F--K OFF. When a woman says "no" she probably knows what she means and you'll just have to take her word for it. And yes, all your life you've been told that when she says "no" she means "yes," but if she is viciously trying to knock or yank your nuts off, let it go.

A MAN IS SUPPOSED TO BE AGGRESSIVE, YOU'VE BEEN TOLD THAT, TOO, BUT KNOW WHEN TO USE A LITTLE COMMON SENSE. Sure, you may have the sweetest peter in America, but be smart and save it for somebody who really wants it.

SO YOU TOOK HER OUT TO DINNER OR YOU BOUGHT HER A COUPLE OF DRINKS, HER PU--Y STILL BELONGS TO HER, UNLESS SHE DECIDES TO SHARE IT WITH YOU. When you paid the tab it didn't automatically include her a-- for dessert.

Like everything else, rape, too, has a history. DURING THE EARLY DAYS OF SLAVERY, WHITE MASTERS, OF COURSE, HAD SEX WITH THEIR FEMALE SLAVES. IT WAS NOT VIEWED AS RAPE BUT RATHER AS THEIR RIGHT, BECAUSE SHE WAS CHATTEL PROPERTY. White men also argued that when they had sex with a female slave (raped her) it was not so much their fault as it was that of the lascivious, passionate black temptress who had made them do it, even though she was forced to go around half-naked. Reported incidents of forcible rape are on the increase, especially among white females by white males, and I believe that there exists another historical implication here as well. WHEN WHITE MEN COULD HAVE THEIR WAY WITH BLACK WOMEN, THEY DID NOT NEED TO RAPE WHITE WOMEN, BUT SINCE THEY CAN NO LONGER FREELY GO INTO BLACK NEIGHBORHOODS AND TAKE BLACK WOMEN (NOT WITHOUT RISKING THEIR LIVES) THEY ARE DOING WHAT THEY HAVE BEEN DOING ALL ALONG TO BLACK WOMEN TO THEIR OWN WHITE WOMEN. Did white men just start raping women? We know better, don't we. They just started raping their own mothers and sisters. My own grandmother told me that as a young girl working out in the fields she would always hide when the white men would come by on their horses, and that many of her young playmates had been sexually assaulted by white men. Historically, many things that white men had accused black men of they themselves were guilty of. COINCIDENTALLY, OTHER FORMS OF ABUSE BY WHITE MALES AGAINST THEIR OWN WOMEN AND CHILDREN ARE ALSO ON THE INCREASE AT THIS TIME. Is there an historical connection there as well?

Often, men who commit forcible acts of rape do so for many reasons. BECAUSE MANY BLACK MEN ARE POWERLESS IN THEIR EVERYDAY LIVES AND LACK SELF-ESTEEM, CONTROLLING OR DOMINATING A WOMAN GIVES THEM THE TEMPORARY ILLUSION OF POWER. Maybe the victim was a woman who was a "DT" (d--k tease), or a "bitch" that they wanted to put in her place, or a "nice girl" who was simply out of their league, or maybe she was a woman who just happened to be in the wrong place at the wrong time. THE VICTIM'S VERY ACTIONS VALIDATED HIS MASCULINITY, SO HE THOUGHT.

AND WHILE SOME BLACK MEN BELIEVE THAT RAPING SOMEONE MAKES THEM FEEL MANLY, OTHERS BELIEVE THAT RAPISTS ARE MEN WHO ARE TRULY INSECURE AND INADEQUATE. I believe this is certainly true.

George, a successful black businessman, said he had raped a woman one night after he and his girlfriend Charise had broken up. He said he knew that he might get caught, but that he was so angry about the way Charise had treated him that he was just driven to punch someone, to make her cry and hurt the same way he was hurting. He had waited in a deserted parking lot that same night and pounced upon a young Spanish woman as she got into her car. She kicked and scratched and scuffled, but he still raped her, like she wasn't another person at all, for that one moment of dominance and control.

IT IS ALSO INTERESTING THAT HISTORICALLY THE WHITE WOMAN HAS ALWAYS BEEN PICTURED AS THE ULTIMATE OBJECT OF SEXUAL DESIRE FOR THE BLACK MAN RATHER THAN AN

179

OBJECT OF RETALIATION AGAINST THE WHITE MAN FOR ALL THE ATROCITIES HE HAS COMMITTED. "You raped our women now we are going to rape yours." White men fearing "payback," have set it up to make it look that way to protect their women and their illusion of power at all costs. To guard against this "payback," during the early days they would castrate a black man and even Indians who would rape or attempt to rape a white women, or burn the black man alive, cut off his ears, boil him or lynch him. BECAUSE OF THE BLACK MAN'S VIRILITY AND ANATOMICAL SUPERIORITY, HE WAS CONSIDERED A REAL THREAT WHILE THE INDIAN WAS NOT LOOKED UPON AS BEING ESPECIALLY PASSIONATE WITH AN EVEN SMALLER PENIS THAN THE WHITE MAN. This fear and jealousy of the black man who was seen as a big d--ked animal also made white men envious, a sentiment which often prevails today.

Women, too, use "Power and Sex" and "Sex and Power." OFTEN WOMEN MAY WITHHOLD SEX AS A FORM OF PUNISHMENT (I'VE GOT A HEADACHE, OR I'M ON MY PERIOD), OR USE IT, AND LET'S PAY CLOSE ATTENTION TO THIS, AS A REWARD. They also use sex sometimes to establish their own power base because they, too, have learned early on that sex is one of their powers.

THE DOOR THAT SWINGS OPEN REALLY DOES SWING BOTH WAYS SOMETIMES, BECAUSE LIKE SOME BLACK MEN, SOME BLACK WOMEN, TOO, HAVE BEEN SEDUCED BY POWER AND ITS ILLUSIONS. They have tasted control and, like any other addict, they are controlled and cannot get enough of it. THESE ARE SOME OF THE WOMEN WHO ARE OUT OF CONTROL. Much like young black males who are being controlled by a stronger force, these women are in a similar arrangement.

BLACK WOMEN TRULY ARE POWERFUL, HOWEVER, IN TERMS OF BUILDING OR DESTROYING BLACK MALES. On the positive side, one black woman can motivate three generations of black men. On the negative side, she can destroy three generations of men. If she uses the same language on her husband or her man that society does to tell him that he is worthless, that's one down. If she tells her son that "he's going to be just like his good-for-nothing daddy," that's two down. If her grandson is exposed to this, that's three down, and if there is a son-in-law around somewhere he makes four.

BLACK WOMEN WERE RAPED BY WHITE MEN AND THEIR BABIES SOLD, BUT THE BLACK MAN IS THE ONE THEY ACCUSE OF BEING NO GOOD. Their mothers told them to marry a doctor or a lawyer, someone who had made something of himself. Don't marry a nobody (anybody else). THIS PROBLEM DID NOT START YESTERDAY, BUT IT WILL CONTINUE AS DAUGHTERS STRIVE FOR ACCEPTANCE FROM THEIR MOTHERS WHO ARE PASSING ON OLD BAGGAGE THAT SABOTAGES HEALTHY BLACK FAMILY LIFE.

Black men are running in a race with white men and expected to keep up with one arm and one leg twisted behind their backs, as black women make gains with only an arm tied. How can the black man possibly win? But black women, who are looking for their own power, couldn't care less.

There is an old axiom that goes, "You are today the results of the thoughts you had yesterday and will be tomorrow the results of the thoughts you have today." IF BLACK MEN AND BLACK WOMEN IN THIS COUNTRY DO NOT REVISE THE WAY THEY VIEW EACH OTHER, THE NEXT GENERATION AND THOSE WHO FOLLOW ARE INDEED IN FOR TRAGIC LIVING. Men and women, all men and all women, must again learn to love, honor and respect each other.

BLACK-ON-BLACK CRIME

YOUNG BLACK MALES ARE KILLING EACH OTHER AT AN ALARMING RATE BECAUSE BLACK-ON-BLACK GENOCIDE IS A SAFE CRIME. They commit these acts because they know they can and get away with them. They may not get off Scott free, but they will come close enough. THEY BELIEVE THE BENEFITS THAT THEY MAY GAIN MORE THAN COMPENSATE FOR ANY INCONVENIENCE THEY MAY HAVE TO SUFFER AS A RESULT OF THEIR ACTIONS. A black person who steals from another black person may get sentenced to a year in jail. And if he kills that person or sells them drugs, he may do equally little time, if any at all. IN EITHER CASE, THE OBVIOUS MESSAGE BEING SENT IS THAT A BLACK LIFE IS NOT WORTH VERY MUCH AT ALL.

WHEN COMMITTING CRIMES, THE BLACK PERPETRATOR WILL GO RIGHT PAST A WHITE PERSON TO GET TO ANOTHER BLACK PERSON. And the reason for this is equally as clear.

THE WOULD-BE CRIMINAL UNDERSTANDS ALL TOO WELL THAT THE SAME RULES DO NOT APPLY WHEN YOU INFRINGE UPON A WHITE PERSON. Doing a white person wrong means that you will be prosecuted to the full extent of the law. Even when the family lacks the funds to adequately prosecute the black perpetrator, things will still go badly for him for wronging that particular individual, because the system itself (including the judge who sits on the bench) will step in to see to it that he gets punished and that society's unyielding message to people of color is not lost. Justice in America may be wearing a blindfold, but she is anything but "colorblind." IF A BLACK PERSON IS RELEASED FROM A MENTAL INSTITUTION HE STILL KNOWS BETTER THAN TO ASSAULT A WHITE PERSON. NO MATTER HOW CRAZY HE MAY BE, HE STILL IS NOT THAT STUPID.

Most responsible blacks feel that black-on-black crime is making young black males an endangered species, and that these young men are out of control. I suggest to you that they may well be out of control (of themselves), but that they are predictably under the control of someone else. Young black men are attacking other black people and leaving white people alone. Is this simply by chance or is it by design?

WHEN YOU HEAR BLACK PEOPLE TALKING ABOUT THE CAUSE OF BLACK-ON-BLACK CRIME THEY INTELLIGENTLY BUT UNINFORMEDLY SPOUT OFF REASONS LIKE DRUGS, FRUSTRATION AND UNEMPLOYMENT, NOT REALIZING THAT THEY ARE TALKING ABOUT INGREDIENTS, AND NOT THE REAL CAUSE. These ingredients are like the slices of a pie, and when placed back together neatly in the pie pan they clearly spell out genocide, or self-destruction.

To really begin to get to the heart of the problem, I'll ask this question: WHAT IS THE ALTERNATIVE TO BLACK-ON-BLACK CRIME? Jobs, education and drug prevention, right? No, wrong. Like the other slices of that pie, these are constructive steps and theoretically they will help to bring about a change, but they are not the alternative to black-on-black crime.

It is my belief that there are only two alternatives. One of them is "No Crime At All," which is highly improbable, if not downright impossible. The other alternative, the real one, is "Black-on-White Crime," which is equally as improbable. I hardly see our white brothers and sisters welcoming black criminals into their homes with open arms so that they can be robbed blind. THE ONLY WAY THAT WHITE NEIGHBORHOODS CAN BE SAFE IS IF BLACK NEIGHBORHOODS ARE UNSAFE. THE ONLY WAY THAT WHITE CHILDREN CAN BE SAFE IS IF BLACK CHILDREN ARE UNSAFE. It is as simple as that and it may be "nothing personal." IT IS JUST US VERSUS THEM AS THEY BLAMELESSLY WATCH US VAINLY SEARCH FOR ANSWERS THAT WILL NEVER COME. We are going down the wrong road, and they know it.

IN FACT, I BELIEVE THAT IF A CRIME IS BEING COMMITTED IT SHOULD MORE APPROPRIATELY BE CALLED "WHITE-ON-BLACK CRIME." But why the label "Black-on-Black Crime?" Well, white people are experts at using words. They wrote the book, literally, and any books that they did not write, they destroyed. They understand better than anyone else that words create images and that images create thoughts and ideas. And white people are experts at creating images, too. THAT IS ONE OF THE REASONS WHY THEY SWITCH TO NEW WORDS AS SOON AS WE BEGIN TO LEARN THE OLD ONES, TO KEEP US IN THE DARK (TO MAKE SURE WE STAY IN OUR BLACK PLACE). For example, "preferential treatment" for white male English speaking Protestants becomes "quotas" when applied to blacks and other disadvantaged minorities who are simply trying to catch up.

A simple example of this might be either verbal or written instructions to inject the primary component A into the recessive receptor B, rather than merely saying plug the cord into the socket. IT IS THE SAME THING THEY ARE DOING WITH THAT STICKY LABEL CALLED "BLACK-ON-BLACK CRIME."

When the whites slaughtered millions of buffaloes on the American plains, did they call that "White-on-Buffalo

Crime?" When they massacred the Indians, was it called "White-on-Indian Crime?" When six million Jews were eliminated, was that "White-on-Jew Crime?" And finally, when blacks in Africa and blacks in America were senselessly executed, and when blacks in America were brutally attacked and lynched by the Ku Klux Klan, did they even call that "White-on-Black Crime?" So, why now is there so much emphasis being placed on "Black-on-Black Crime?" Well, they told us that we were "low lifes," and we listened. They told us that everything around us belonged to them, and we listened. WHY NOT TELL US THAT WE ARE OUR OWN PROBLEM, BECAUSE WE ARE LISTENING AGAIN ANYWAY, AREN'T WE?

Even our leaders, you know, the people who get invited to attend conferences because they are supposed to be important, are not wise enough to see through the SMOKE SCREEN. Sitting high on their pedestals, they are so consumed with themselves that most of them do not realize that there is no such thing as "Black-on-Black Crime." IT IS JUST ANOTHER WORD GAME DESIGNED TO DISTRACT US INTO BELIEVING THAT WE ARE SOME NEW SUB-HUMAN STRAND OF MUTANT CANNIBAL TEARING OURSELVES APART AND THAT BLACK-ON-BLACK CRIME IS A PROBLEM WE ARE CREATING FOR OURSELVES.

ONCE MORE, WHERE OH WHERE ARE OUR LEADERS WHO ARE SUPPOSED TO BE OUR EYES AND OUR EARS AND WHO WE DEPEND UPON TO PROTECT US? AND AGAIN, THE ANSWER IS EMBARRASSINGLY SIMPLE. THEY ARE SITTING AT THE CONFERENCE TABLES WITH THEIR HAIR COMBED AND THEIR TEETH BRUSHED (LIKE GOOD LITTLE NEGROES) AND DRESSED IN THEIR BEST BLUE OR GRAY CONSERVATIVE BUSINESS SUIT WITH THE RIGHT MATCHING TIE. Having been invited because they are such intelligent and civilized people who speak English so wonderfully, they are not the slightest bit aware that even though they so beautifully and eloquently articulate the language, they are missing the entire conversation. It's just simple business. THEY HAVE BEEN INVITED TO A MEETING AND ASKED TO PARTICIPATE, NOT REALIZING THAT THE REAL MEETING

WAS HELD ALREADY, BEFORE THEY ARRIVED. They are only there for the show.

For example, when the President of the United States has a summit conference, or before a treaty or any legislative decision is reached, do you really believe that he has not met painstakingly with his advisors and with his cabinet members? Of course he has. Again, that is just doing business, something most blacks unfortunately have very little knowledge of or experience with. LIKE BLACK YOUNGSTERS WHO SELL DRUGS AND MURDER EACH OTHER, WE HAVE BECOME COMFORTABLE WITH LETTING OTHER PEOPLE DO OUR THINKING FOR US, AND BELIEVING THAT WHATEVER HAPPENS IS JUST THE WAY IT IS.

Henry Clay once said "Negroes are rational being like ourselves, capable of feeling and reflection and of judging what belongs to them as a portion of the human race." But in the 1800's it was Gustave de Beaumont who wrote "As long as philanthrophy on behalf of the Negroes resulted in nothing but useless declamation, the Americans tolerated it without difficulty; it mattered little to them that the equality of the Negroes should be proclaimed in theory, so long as in fact they remained inferior to the whites." SO 150 YEARS AGO IT WAS FINE TO TALK ABOUT SOLVING BLACK PROBLEMS, AS LONG AS IT WAS ONLY TALK...DOES THAT SOUND FAMILIAR?

"BLACK-ON-BLACK CRIME IS PROBABLY THE BEST CON GAME AND THE BEST EXAMPLE OF REVERSE PSYCHOLOGY EVER KNOWN TO MAN, AND WE HAVE FALLEN FOR IT HOOK, LINE, SINKER AND EVEN TUGBOAT OR STEAMSHIP." Again, white people are simply doing things differently.

What we are really seeing, however, is that white people who have reasons for almost everything they do, are still thinking. Remember, "If you want different results, do things differently." WHY WASTE TIME AND BULLETS ON BLACK PEOPLE WHEN YOU CAN HOOK THEM ON DRUGS, THROW THEM IN PRISONS, TAKE AWAY THEIR JOBS AND THEIR HOMES, DESTROY THEIR FAMILIES AND SEND THEM OFF TO WAR. Black-on-Black

186

Crime is just the latest plan for eliminating the black man. White America has no intention of ever stopping it.

Even the slaves were smart enough to know that they were not going to willingly be puppets for their masters. Of course they were told that it was wrong to steal your master's corn or to raise your hand to a white person, and they generally listened because they had no choice. And again, if the master said something was right it probably was not. But one thing the slave knew was wrong was to harm or steal from another slave.

During the days of slavery blacks didn't strike a white man and run. They ran first so they would not strike him. Many slaves had considered murdering white people, but they did not do so because even back then the message was clear. As children they had already been taught not to strike little masters and mistresses. So today, descendants themselves abuse, not white people -- but each other.

If the ever-menacing black penis truly was the ultimate weapon that would destroy genteel society, then they have finally found a way to quietly and inconspicuously disarm and silence it. (Castration, the old way, was definitely too obvious, too messy and sometimes too costly.) With this subtle new strategy, white America gets the same advantages without having to dirty its own hands. OBVIOUSLY, WITHOUT BLACK MALES THERE CAN BE NO BLACK BABIES, AND WITHOUT BLACK MALES, ESPECIALLY STRONG AGGRESSIVE ONES, THERE WILL BE NO ONE LEFT TO DEFEND BLACK PEOPLE AGAINST WHITE ATROCITIES OR TO POSE A THREAT TO WHITE SECURITY. There will never be another "Santo Domingo," or a "John Brown's Raid," or another "Watts Riot." Blacks without leaders (generals) will be even more helpless without followers (troops). And all the while, blindly confident black men still dumbfoundedly say to each other "What it is," "Whas' goin' on," or "Yo, hey man whas' happening?" But most of our so called "black leaders" do not know either.

And what about black people's dreams for their children? What are they? College, an exciting career and security with a beautiful family. I think not. Forget it. What parents have always wanted for their children was independence and the ability to take care of themselves. That was "Family Goodpussy."

TODAY, HOWEVER, BLACK CHILDREN GENERALLY ARE NOT EXPECTED TO LIVE BETTER THAN THEIR PARENTS HAVE, AND THE DREAM FOR BLACK BOYS IN PARTICULAR IS THAT THEY AT LEAST LIVE LONG ENOUGH TO REACH ADULTHOOD, SO THAT THEY MAY FULFILL NATURE'S PROCREATIVE PLAN FOR THEM, JUST LIKE THE GIANT SEA TURTLE, THE WHALE, THE BALD EAGLE, OR ANY OF THE OTHER CREATURES ON THE ENDANGERED SPECIES LIST. But it would seem that white America's goal is once more in direct conflict (remember the horses and their color) with nature's design. After all, nature delicately balances, sustains itself and believes in reproducing one's own kind for continued existence, but that is not the fate intended for black Americans.

OBVIOUSLY, WHAT IS A PROBLEM FOR BLACK AMERICA IS A SIMPLE SOLUTION FOR WHITE AMERICA. "Black-on-Black Crime," or rather black people violating and destroying each other, is the best Goodpussy that some whites could possibly hope for. For that reason, it is incumbent upon those of us who do understand words and concepts and their implications to share our knowledge with others and to hope that they will listen.

So called "Black-on-Black Crime" is only a label that makes us look the other way. It was never the real issue. Black Americans need to find their own solutions for the real problem, not for the symptoms.

Black-on-black crime is destroying both black relationships and black families. Once again black women are being left alone to raise and discipline their children in "fatherless" homes. Many of these children are boys and without black male influence they will freely exercise their own aggression. Ultimately they too will turn to a life of crime and violence. THOSE BLACK BOYS WHO SURVIVE MAY ALSO BECOME PLAYERS IN A CYCLE OF RELATIONSHIPS THAT ARE DOOMED TO FAILURE.

CITIES, AN ABNORMAL HABITAT

How would you and your family feel about moving to the jungle? Before you answer, however, let me make just one more point for you. **IF YOU LIVE IN A BIG CITY, YOUR SURROUNDINGS ARE PROBABLY AS UNNATURAL FOR YOU AS THEY WOULD BE FOR A RAT LIVING IN A MAZE.** In fact, both you and the rat are really one in the same, both products of your environment. Curiously enough, the city has often been referred to as the asphalt jungle, a title it well deserves. **IN HOSTILE URBAN AREAS, BLACK PEOPLE ARE TRYING TO BEHAVE NORMALLY IN AN ABNORMAL SITUATION.**

After rising early to leave the box you live in, you go outside to get into the box you ride to work in, or you use a public transportation box crowded with other anxious riders like yourself. At any rate, as you negotiate hectic rush-hour traffic in your cubicle, you are continuously barraged by aggressive commuters who are just as agitated as you are. There are both real and imaginary lines and boundaries everywhere you go that signal do's an don'ts, property lines, speed zones, traffic signals and even your space at work. JUST HOW EASY DO YOU THINK IT IS FOR YOU OR ANYONE ELSE TO MAINTAIN A REALLY NATURAL RELATIONSHIP WITH ANOTHER HUMAN BEING IN A SETTING THAT IS SO INTRINSICALLY ADVERSARIAL? The only normal or natural thing about a city is its parks, unless there is an ocean or lake nearby. And what about the serenity and peace of mind you experience while you are in the park just watching the other animals being themselves? That's right. It makes you feel good.

What many people see as success is being able to retire and live the good life out in the country, or having a summer or a weekend home. OFTEN THEY FEEL THAT THEY ARE GETTING AWAY FROM URBAN PROBLEMS, NOT REALIZING THAT URBANIZATION ITSELF IS THE REAL PROBLEM. Due to urbanization, strangers have been thrown together and people do not even know who their neighbors are anymore. People become preoccupied with self-gratification and their own self-interests, consequently losing respect for anyone else. BLACK PEOPLE LIVING IN CITIES OFTEN FEEL THREATENED AND BEHAVE DEFENSIVELY. EXPERIENCE HAS TAUGHT THEM NOT TO BE TOO TRUSTING AND THIS TRUSTLESSNESS IS TRANSFERRED TO PERSONAL RELATIONSHIPS AS WELL. People living in fast paced metropolitan areas incessantly wear facades or faces all over their bodies, having learned early in life about the urgency of sending out the right signals, whether it is true or not. Realizing how important body language is, they believe, "If I look like a wimp somebody will surely get me." EVEN IN RELATIONSHIPS WHERE BLACK MEN AND BLACK WOMEN ARE SUPPOSED TO BE CLOSE, WE HAVE LEARNED TO "KEEP OUR DISTANCE" TO SAVE OURSELVES.

Are you more likely to tenderly hold your lover's hand while strolling leisurely through the park or near a lagoon, or while walking down a busy, crowded city street? (If you are holding her hand on the street it is probably to keep from losing her or having someone else grab her.) CITY LIVING PROMOTES AGGRESSION, DEFENSIVENESS AND DOING THINGS IN A HURRY, WHILE NATURE LENDS ITSELF TO TAKING IT EASY AND LETTING THINGS HAPPEN MORE PEACEFULLY IN THEIR OWN TIME AND AT THEIR OWN PACE.

CITIES OR LARGE METROPOLITAN AREAS, WHICH ARE GENERALLY UNKIND TO EVERYONE, HAVE BEEN ESPECIALLY HARSH TO BLACK AMERICANS. Because they owned no real property, poor rural blacks packed up their few belongings and moved to the city, where they still owned nothing. Jobs were menial whenever they were able to find work so that their standard of living was still sub-human. The homes that they lived in were owned by wealthy absentee landlords who cared little whether the property was maintained or not, so as things fell apart they were not repaired, services were cut and things kept going downhill. WHY SHOULD BLACK PEOPLE, WHO DID NOT HAVE ANYTHING ANYWAY, FIX SOMETHING THAT DID NOT BELONG TO THEM, SOMETHING THAT WAS ALREADY RUN DOWN AND THAT THEY WERE ALREADY PAYING TOO MUCH FOR. Others clearly broke things because nothing belonged to them. Like black boys who were not always bad and who had no one to lead them, black people are rebelling because they have no help either. Society is still playing it's old game of rewarding women for having babies, but today it is called welfare. BLACK PEOPLE ARE STILL BEING HERDED INTO DILAPIDATED AREAS WITH INVISIBLE FENCES AROUND THEM, BUT INSTEAD OF BEING CALLED SLAVE QUARTERS, THEY WEAR THE LABEL OF PROJECT OR GHETTO. Like "Indian reservations," these run down, demoralized areas could more aptly be called "Black reservations."

Having Negroes around has always been a problem, and nowhere was this more evident, even in the 1800's, than in urban areas where poor blacks lived. In 1842, James Freeman Clark, a Unitarian reformer wrote:

A worse evil to the slave than the cruelty he sometimes endures is the moral degradation that results from his condition. Falsehood, theft, licentiousness, are a natural consequence of his situation...He goes to excesses in eating, and drinking and animal pleasures; for he has no access to any higher pleasures, and a man cannot be an animal without sinking below an animal - a brutal man is worse than a brute. An animal cannot be more savage or more greedy than the law of his nature allows. But there seems to be no limit to the degradation of a man. Slavery is the parent of vices...

Surely black people in cities were leading a nightmarish kind of life, and they responded accordingly, almost 200 years ago. Black people who were treated criminally behaved criminally and perhaps developed criminal minds as well. Many black men who could not find work simply turned to stealing. It was the same thing that they had done on the plantations. But were they the ones who were the criminals?

In the 1830's, Professor Thomas R. Dew of William and Mary College stated: "Declare the Negroes of the South free tomorrow, and vain will be your decree until you have prepared them for it...the law would make them free men, and custom or prejudice, we care not which you call it, would degrade them to the condition of slave." TODAY BLACKS LIVING IN INNER CITY GHETTOES ARE STILL BARELY BETTER OFF THAN THE SLAVE WAS. Freedom may be their passion but slavery is still their condition.

BLACKS WHO ARE NOT FORCED TO LIVE UNDER SUCH CONDITIONS ARE LOOKING AT LESS FORTUNATE BLACKS JUST AS WHITES DO AND ASKING THEMSELVES, "HOW CAN THOSE PEOPLE LIVE LIKE THAT?" What they should remember though is, "But for the grace of God there go I." DEMOCRACY IN AMERICA IS

AN ILLUSION FOR BLACK PEOPLE, INCLUDING SO CALLED MIDDLE CLASS BLACK PEOPLE. And many white people, who think that because of the color of their skin they are on the A-team, do not realize that for all practical purposes, they are pushing the broom too.

Without the black man in America as the lower class, all white people would not be equal. Some white men would be the peasant class. Without racism they could not be democratic with each other. In the 1800's Thomas R. R. Cobb said of the whites that "It matters not that he is no slave holder; he is not the inferior race; he is a freeborn citizen...The poorest meets the richest as an equal; sits at the table with him; salutes him as a neighbor; and stands on the same social platform." And the lower classes should always stay in their place. Being born white was the only claim all white people had for being superior.

AMERICA IS STILL JUST ONE BIG PLANTATION OWNED AND OPERATED BY A FEW GREEDY PEOPLE AT THE TOP. The rest of us are busy running fast to keep up while they take vacations. Make no mistake about it, we are their slaves. White collar workers are the house servants. The blue collar worker is the artisan or mechanic, while the common laborer is the field hand. IT IS THE SAME SYSTEM, IT IS JUST BEING FED TO US DIFFERENTLY.

BLACK PEOPLE IN AMERICA ARE NOT AMERICANS, THEY ARE BLACK PEOPLE. They are destroying their surroundings because it does not belong to them, and they are painfully aware that after nearly 200 years it never will. AMERICA BELONGS TO SOMEONE ELSE AND THAT MESSAGE IS MOST APPARENT IN ITS CITIES.

Willie, 27, a habitual offender, laughed as he talked about today's urban problems. He said, "More police officers on the streets is not the real solution for problems of crime in big cities. But better management and better trained officers (people who know what they are doing) can make a difference." A football team with 50 lousy players will lose

194

just as many games as a team with 100 lousy players. Why is it that State Police officers tend to be effective, courteous, professionals while city policemen are amateurish goons? "QUALITY AND TRAINING CAN MAKE A DIFFERENCE," WILLIE CONFESSED, "NOT MORE JERKS ON THE STREETS WITH GUNS AND FRESH, NEW UNIFORMS."

A hostile environment breeds hostile inhabitants. Instead of letting cities fall apart our leaders should find ways to prop them up. Like the bum who feels better after he has had a shave and a bath, if our cities are cleaned up, they, too, will feel better. Most black leaders, however, white-wash the ghettoes too, because they do not live there.

Many people in large urban areas never visit their parks or enjoy any of the other natural resources that may be available. They are too occupied with the more immediate problems of survival and day-to-day living. What they fail to realize, however, is that if they cannot go to the country, parks are the next best thing to at least temporarily give them a different focus. GETTING BACK TO NATURE AND THEIR OWN TRUE NATURE MAY BE THEIR ONLY ESCAPE. IT IS THAT SPECIAL, SPIRITUAL COMMUNION OR GOODPUSSY WE ALL NEED.

DRUGS AS GOODPUSSY

AFTER TWO CENTURIES OF TRYING TO DESTROY THE BLACK MAN IN AMERICA, A "LETHAL WEAPON" HAS FINALLY BEEN FOUND. White men who wanted different results simply started doing things differently. Strong black males and their proud ancestors were always too courageous, too durable and too resilient to be destroyed no matter how inhumanly or how brutally they were treated. Lynchings, burnings, whippings, imprisonment and even mutilations -- nothing could break their spirit. And white America was wearing itself out trying, breaking its own back and becoming just as resentful as the blacks who were being victimized. Bearing the harsh marks of punishment as well as signs of physical deprivation and mistreatment, these determined black men and black women just kept on getting stronger and stronger as they inched their way forward.

BLACKS WHO WERE ONCE VALUABLE PROPERTY DURING SLAVERY BECAME AN EVER PRESENT NUISANCE AFTER EMANCIPATION, AND AN EVER PRESENT REMINDER TO WHITE AMERICANS OF ALL THAT THEY LOATHED, EVEN TODAY. What they loath also is the constant visual reminder by impoverished blacks that they (the whites) have done this to them as well as their (the blacks) begging and constant pleas for help which will only place an added burden upon them (the whites). The idea that black people need to be disposed of is not a new one, however, because even back then when there were too many "worthless blacks" running around, white people knew that something had to be done before they were outnumbered. GREEDY WHITES HAD CREATED THEIR OWN FRANKENSTEIN MONSTER, NOW THEY JUST WANTED IT TO GO AWAY, BUT IT WAS TOO BIG.

The black man, who had been stolen from his own land and worked like a mule, was now a social burden and a financial liability, plus he was an ugly eyesore who was contaminating and stinking up their environment. UTOPIA, OR

196

RATHER GOODPUSSY, WOULD BE FOR THE ENDANGERED BLACK
MALE TO BE THE EXTINCT BLACK MALE.

After many years of trying unsuccessfully to rid
themselves of this hideous black plague, a logical rather than
emotional solution is being applied. Remember, if you want
different results, do things differently. SOCIETY, WHICH HAS
ALWAYS ATTEMPTED TO EMASCULATE OR DISMEMBER THE BLACK
MAN BY PHYSICAL MEANS, HAS TURNED TO A MORE
SOPHISTICATED CHEMICAL METHOD TO MAKE HIM
DYSFUNCTIONAL. It has been alleged that the AIDS virus was
manufactured (chemically) to dilute the numbers of
undesirables like blacks and homosexuals, and, as we all know,
the common denominator or catalyst is always sex, drugs or
both. While that may not seem especially significant, closer
inspection as well as a recent study indicates that people who
do not feel good about themselves or about their environment
(blacks in particular) are more likely to become addicted to
drugs. One reason, of course, is that they do not have the
same options that others have, and secondly, drugs do help
them to forget how bad things are, at least for a little while.
IT IS IMPORTANT TO REMEMBER THAT PEOPLE WHO ARE WELL DO
NOT TAKE DRUGS, LET ALONE GORGE THEMSELVES WITH DRUGS.
SICK PEOPLE TAKE DRUGS AND BLACK PEOPLE WHO ARE NOT
WELL ARE BECOMING "DRUG GLUTTONS."

Giselle, a 14-year drug user, says she is an addict and
she knows it while many others might deny it. She says
anybody using anything that long is addicted to it whether they
want to admit it or not, just like an alcoholic who refuses to
believe he has a drinking problem. She says that over the
years she had bought it all, from baking soda to sheet rock,
and explains that that is just the way it is because the only
thing poor blacks have access to is church, food, sex and of
course drugs.

And whether that chemical theory about AIDS is true
or not, there may be yet an even more immediate form of
chemical warfare poised against black Americans and setting

itself up for that fatal strike which will be the final kill. BLACK MEN WHO HAVE ALWAYS BEEN REVERED FOR THEIR SEXUAL PROWESS ARE NOW IN BED WITH A NEW GIRLFRIEND. She is mysterious, she is compelling and erotic and they love her even more than sex itself. Even black men who have always loved their penises have finally found something they love more. In fact, when they are with her nothing else is important. If their adorable prized penises were to be laid gently on a cold chopping block to be whacked off they would not even flinch, because their resolve to be with her is so intense that they are both unmoved and unafraid. SHE IS THE DEVIL'S OWN BRIDE, THE SULTRY "WHITE GIRL" HE IS ALWAYS ACCUSED OF HAVING WANTED. HER NAME IS COCAINE. These black men are like naive little boys and she is the rock candy that they cannot resist.

And why not? He deserves to feel good after all that has happened to him, and he has already tried just about everything else -- drinking, marijuana, wild sex, the whole bit. The only snag, however, is that drugs never really make things any better at all. Sure, drugs will give you an a-- kicking high that will even make you forget about pu--y, but you've got to come down sometimes and as the young people say today, "It ain't nothin' nice." THE POWER THAT YOU THINK IS YOURS REALLY BELONGS TO THE DRUG. You are merely its servant.

MANY BLACK MEN WHO HAVE NO MEANINGFUL PLACE IN THE REAL WORLD FEEL THAT THEY CAN MAKE A NAME FOR THEMSELVES ON THE DRUG TRAIN, NOT REALIZING THAT THEY WILL NEVER BE MORE THAN SIMPLE, SMALL-TIME DELIVERY BOYS. Their ancestors were proud people who were forced to work as mules, too, but these 20th century black males dishonor even the jackasses (work animals), whose legacy they carry. They have money, cars, jewelry, women and drugs to make them feel good, but are probably ignorant and uneducated and will never amount to more than a pile of shit in a cow pasture. NEXT TO REAL GOODPUSSY, DRUGS ARE UNDENIABLY THE SECOND

BEST COUNTERFEIT THING, BUT THEY ARE NEITHER REAL NOR GENUINE.

BLACK MEN -- WHOSE ANCESTORS WERE STRONG, PROUD AND HONORABLE -- ARE LYING, STEALING AND EVEN KILLING FOR DRUGS AND "PIPE DREAMS." Some of these men actually hate the "down side" of what drugs do to them but become addicted to the high and can never seem to get enough, even though they may want to stop. SOME HETEROSEXUAL BLACK MALES HAVE LOST EVEN THE SMALLEST PARTICLES OF DIGNITY AND SELF-RESPECT. These "brown bag men" wear paper bags over their heads while giving blow jobs to other men for a ten dollar rock of crack cocaine. These are not necessarily weak little men, just once-virile, aggressive black males who have become "drug slaves."

In one situation that I know of, both the husband and the wife were addicted to cocaine. When a drug delivery was made to their home one time, an argument ensued when they could not agree on whose turn it was to give the blow job.

AS A RESULT OF DRUGS, VIOLENCE IS RAMPANT AND LIFE MEANS NOTHING TO SOME PEOPLE ANYMORE. Young black boys selling drugs from dark alley ways, street corners and bicycles know that their lives are in danger but feel that if it happens, it just happens. This sentiment echoes throughout the black community. Children who are too young to buy expensive cars and weapons are getting adults to make the purchases for them, making hundreds of dollars in one day. The police are outnumbered, the judicial system does not work and there are not enough drug treatment centers for those who want to "kick the habit." There are no jobs or other financial options and black people are not properly educated about drugs. This education includes not only what drugs can do to them and their families but also how the system has designed itself to help black Americans destroy themselves. FOR THE BLACK MAN WHO IS POWERLESS, DRUGS ARE ONE WAY TO CREATE THE ILLUSION OF POWER, AND PEOPLE WHO ARE LOSERS AND FAILURES AT LIFE AT LEAST LOOK SUCCESSFUL.

MANY OF THE BLACK MALES WHO USE DRUGS AS WELL AS THOSE WHO SELL DRUGS DO SO BECAUSE THEY BELIEVE THAT THERE IS NOWHERE ELSE TO TURN. They have failed in school just as they have failed socially, personally and professionally. In fact, they are menacingly aware of their own dismal inadequacy as they fail life.

THE DRUG CRISIS IS NOT INCIDENTAL, IT IS DELIBERATE. SCRATCH OFF TENS OF THOUSANDS OF BLACK MEN WITH THE AIDS VIRUS, TENS OF THOUSANDS OF BLACK MEN IN JAIL, TENS OF THOUSANDS OF BLACK MEN MURDERED BY OTHER BLACK MEN, TENS OF THOUSANDS OF BLACK MEN WITH NO EDUCATION, TENS OF THOUSANDS OF BLACK MEN IN THE MILITARY, TENS OF THOUSANDS OF BLACK MEN HOOKED ON DRUGS, AND TENS OF THOUSANDS OF BLACK MEN SEVERELY DEPRESSED AND DYSFUNCTIONAL BECAUSE OF UNEMPLOYMENT AND YOU GET A VERY BLEAK PICTURE OF BLACK MEN'S PROSPECTS FOR THE FUTURE. What that also means is that young black boys growing up will have no fathers, grandfathers or uncles around to teach them or to protect them. White people, in general, are at least holding their own while black people across the board are suffering and feeling pain. Drugs (alcohol) destroyed the Indians. Drugs (cocaine) is destroying the black man. It is the same plan using a slightly different weapon. Or, are we to believe that that is just a coincidence too? DRUGS ARE NOT THE KEY TO SUCCESS, THEY ARE THE DETONATOR TO DESTRUCTION.

Louis, an unemployed airline executive, physically abused his wife and his two teenaged daughters, ultimately forcing them into prostitution to satisfy his $3,000 a week cocaine habit. DRUGS FOR BLACK PEOPLE MAY BE GOODPUSSY FOR SOME WHITE PEOPLE, BUT THEY ARE A DEADLY POISON THAT MANY BLACKS ARE GORGING THEMSELVES ON OF THEIR OWN FREE WILL.

200

WHY BLACK MEN CANNOT MAKE IT

Like almost everything else that has happened or is happening to the black man, the truth is veiled and confusing because of so many distortions. **THE REAL REASON THE BLACK MAN CANNOT GET AHEAD IS THE SAME ONE THAT MADE HIM DIFFERENT CENTURIES AGO, HIS PENIS.**

Hundreds of years ago the Europeans wrote about the black man's anatomical difference, describing his immense organ, a reality which was swept under the carpet in an American society where bigger is supposedly better and more valuable. **PERCEPTIONS OF LARGER BLACK PENISES MADE ALLEGED SMALLER WHITE PENISES LESS DESIRABLE AND LESS VALUABLE WHILE MAKING THEIR OWNERS MORE INSECURE.** Simply ignoring the problem would not make it disappear. The only way to neutralize this discrepancy was to eradicate its carrier.

If those who were in control had valuable penises and sexual power as well, then there would be no intimidation. The problem, however, exists because those who are powerless are in possession of nature's most valuable gift, at least in this society. Black men have been blessed with the Goodpussy and cursed because of it.

It's like the story of "The Emperor's New Clothes" in reverse. As he proudly displayed his beautiful garments everyone could clearly see that he wasn't really wearing any at all, but only a child spoke the truth. ALTHOUGH THE BLACK MAN'S PENIS IS STILL NOT OPENLY SPOKEN OF IN OUR "BIGGER SOCIETY," EVERYONE KNOWS THAT IT IS STILL THERE, AND THAT REALLY IS A PROBLEM. Throughout history the black man is basically the only man who had anything notable enough to cut off. MYTHS ABOUT THE BLACK MAN'S PENIS IS ONE OF THE REASONS WHY TODAY'S BLACK MALE IS DISAPPEARING.

The black man's penis is naturally not the only issue. ANOTHER REASON WHY THE BLACK MAN CANNOT MAKE IT IS RACISM, OR PREJUDICE, AND PERCEPTUAL DISTORTIONS BASED UPON SOCIAL ATTITUDES, VALUES AND NEEDS. White America's perceptual distortions are based on a need to protect what is theirs and to maintain their own self-esteem and healthy perceptions of themselves. In other words, no matter what they do to someone else, white people still need to feel good about themselves, so they make the other person look like the "bad guy."

A PERCEPTUAL DISTORTION IS AN INACCURATE INTERPRETATION OR A DISTORTED IMPRESSION OF THINGS OR PEOPLE, AND THAT IS EXACTLY WHAT THE WHITES HAVE DONE IN THE CASE OF BLACK AMERICANS. The victim is the criminal. The criminal is the victim. Today, many whites still see blacks as mentally inferior and dirty, and do not want to touch or come in contact with them.

Black people are also judged upon prejudices like selective perception. FOR EXAMPLE, A BLACK MAN RUNNING DOWN THE STREET AT MIDNIGHT IS A HARDENED CRIMINAL WHILE

A WHITE MALE RUNNING DOWN THE STREET AT MIDNIGHT IS AN ENTHUSIASTIC JOGGER. A BLACK WOMAN WITH FIVE CHILDREN AND NO HUSBAND IS A WHORE AND A DRAIN ON SOCIETY WHILE A WHITE WOMAN WITH FIVE CHILDREN AND NO HUSBAND IS A STRONG MOTHER WITH AN ABUNDANCE OF LOVE FOR HER YOUNG. That is "selective perception." Since most social attitudes are a matter of opinion and interpretation, they are easily maintained and not open to any evidence that will bring about a different point of view.

People simply tend to believe what they want to believe. It has also been shown that it is easier to learn things that you are in agreement with than things you are not. For example, it would be easier for a white racist to believe that a black intruder had raped and murdered his wife and kidnapped his 4-year-old daughter, than it would be for him to accept evidence that it was one of his white neighbors who had committed such a crime.

AN EXCELLENT EXAMPLE OF SELECTIVE PERCEPTION IS THE WAY MANY WHITES THINK THAT MOST BLACK PEOPLE ARE LAZY AND DANGEROUS SIMPLY BECAUSE THEIR SKIN IS DARKER. The same is true of blacks who believe that all white people are racists who are out to do them in. Both of these are obvious fallacies that are fueled by prejudices and a tendency to maintain order and uniformity by seeing what everybody else sees. IF ALL BLACK PEOPLE IN GENERAL ARE PERCEIVED AS BAD, THEN WHITE PEOPLE SAVE THEMSELVES BOTH THE TROUBLE AND THE RESPONSIBILITY OF HAVING TO FIGURE OUT WHICH BLACKS ARE WORTHLESS AND WHICH ONES ARE ALRIGHT. That is why white people often say that "black people all look alike." It also insulates them from guilt. "Black people, or at least most of them, are no good, so whatever happens, happens." "It's not my fault." "They brought it upon themselves." The media adds to this problem as it continues to spread malicious "one-sided" propaganda about today's black man. It's as if all white people have a Master Plan Handbook and we do not.

A white person driving his new Oldsmobile through the ghetto sees failure and destruction and renounces black people as being hopeless and derelict. It is in his best interest to insulate himself from the truth, the truth being that his new car was financed at a lower interest rate than a black man would pay. His fine home was also thousands of dollars less than a black man would pay for the same house, if he qualified, because naturally he might also be paid less even if he were doing the same job. His insurance premiums as well could be cheaper even though he might receive better benefits. HOW COULD AN HONEST BLACK MAN POSSIBLY KEEP UP WITH THESE "GOOD OLE BOYS" AND THEIR "PRIVATE CONSPIRACY?"

AND IT IS A CONSPIRACY BECAUSE EVEN THE "GOOD WHITE PEOPLE," WHO KNOW THAT THEY GET BETTER DEALS WHILE BLACK PEOPLE GET SCREWED, REMAIN SILENT BECAUSE IT IS IN THEIR BEST INTEREST TO DO SO. And let's not forget that the black man started from scratch, so how can he possibly compete? This is something that a few black women should remember while they are busy "brown nosing" some white man. Sure, black men are frustrated and angry, they are supposed to be. INSTEAD OF STICKING THEIR NOSES UP IN THE AIR, THESE BLACK WOMEN SHOULD BE BRINGING THEIR BEHINDS BACK DOWN TO EARTH, BECAUSE THEY ARE BEING OVERCHARGED TOO. Despite the fact that they are black, they too are buying into that same selective perception about the black man, their man, being valueless, because it expedites and best serves their own self-interests. Like everyone else, a perceptual distortion works out just fine for them too.

White men and white women still have each other while the black woman and the black man are cursing each other and dividing the furniture, but that's alright. IT IS JUST SIMPLER FOR THESE BLACK WOMEN TO SAY THAT BLACK MEN ARE NO GOOD AND PREJUDICE THEMSELVES AGAINST THEIR OWN MEN THAN IT IS FOR THEM TO ASK A FEW QUESTIONS, LOOK AT THE

204

TRUTH, AND TAKE SOME RESPONSIBILITY FOR WHAT IS GOING ON
TOO. Black skin is black skin, whether it is male or female.

In all fairness, however, many black women feel
cheated and are understandably angry. They have worked
hard, loved their men and been called all kinds of bitches and
whores. They wonder why black men are kicking them in
their behinds and how much more are they expected to take.
(First the white man called them bitches and whores. Now,
degraded black men do the same thing.) Many black women
have indeed been loyal and supportive but believe that their
only hope lies within themselves.

EVEN SUCCESSFUL BLACK MEN ARE NOT IMMUNE TO
STEREOTYPICAL AFFRONTS. James Bates, a black hospital
administrator, and one of his black doctors were dressed in
warm-up suits after leaving a health club one afternoon when
they encountered several white women who immediately
began clutching their purses. PRESTIGE, MONEY, EDUCATION,
FAME, ALL OF THESE THINGS OUGHT MEAN LITTLE TO BLACK
PEOPLE WHO SHOULD REMEMBER THAT THE BOTTOM LINE IS
ALWAYS THE SAME, NO MATTER HOW WHITE YOU MAY THINK YOU
ARE, YOU ARE STILL A NIGGER. In 1828 the African Repository
reported "The African in this country belongs by birth to the
lowest station in society; and from that station he can never
rise, be his talent, his enterprise, his virtues what they may."
All black people are in the same boat and "The boat ain't
movin'." It's sinking.

Malcolm X once asked an eminent black personality
with 57 degrees, what do you call a black man with 57
degrees? Malcolm answered the question himself simply but
honestly, "Nigger."

WHEN WE THINK OF RACISM AND PREJUDICE TODAY WE
TEND TO ASSOCIATE IT WITH OUR OWN REFERENCES, GENERALLY
CENTERING AROUND THE LATE DR. MARTIN LUTHER KING, JR.
AND THE CIVIL RIGHTS MOVEMENT. But black men did not
start getting held back in 1965, they were being held back all
along. Because it did not directly impact upon us, we usually

think of slavery simply as slavery, not remembering that slavery was a part of the beginnings of racism for blacks in America.

ALSO, BECAUSE OF OUR LIMITED EXPOSURE TO OUR OWN HISTORY, WE FAIL TO REALIZE THAT MANY OF THE PREJUDICIAL BELIEFS AND PRACTICES THAT WE NOW SEE ACTUALLY HAPPENED TO OUR ANCESTORS TOO. Nearly 300 years ago, there were white people who believed that black people had been treated so harshly that they would never be able to live harmoniously with white people. EVEN THOMAS JEFFERSON, GEORGE WASHINGTON AND ABRAHAM LINCOLN FELT THAT BLACKS WERE INFERIOR TO WHITES BOTH MENTALLY AND PHYSICALLY. President George Washington himself had over 300 slaves and President Thomas Jefferson had slaves as well, in spite of the fact that he hated slavery. Jefferson also kept one of his slaves, Sally Hemings, as a mistress, and fathered two children by her.

In our schools, we were generally taught that there were two kinds of white people. There were the bad ones who believed in slavery and the good ones who wanted to abolish it, with little being said of some of the others for instance who were environmentalists. The reason is simple, because over 200 years ago some white people were saying things that people still do not admit today. ENVIRONMENTALISTS, AS THEY WERE CALLED, WERE WHITE PEOPLE WHO BELIEVED THAT THE BLACK MAN WAS NOT INNATELY INFERIOR, BUT THAT HE WAS MERELY A PRODUCT OF HIS ENVIRONMENT, AND THAT WHATEVER HE HAD BECOME HE WAS THAT WAY BECAUSE OF HIS MISTREATMENT. IT WAS ALSO A COMMON BELIEF THAT IF THE BLACK MAN WAS PERMITTED HIS FREEDOM HE COULD NO LONGER BE CONTROLLED AND THE HATRED HE AND THE WHITE MAN FELT FOR EACH OTHER WOULD ULTIMATELY LEAD TO A RACE WAR, WITH BLACK MEN AND WHITE MEN KILLING EACH OTHER. Again, the more things change the more they remain the same, because that is exactly what is happening to the black man today, nearly 400 years later.

BLACK MEN TODAY ARE STILL BEING CONTROLLED SO THAT THEY DO NOT POSE A THREAT TO WHITE SOCIETY. There were basically three groups of whites who had very different views about the black man. They were the colonizationists, the abolitionists and those who favored slavery. The colonizationists believed that the best thing for all concerned was to send the black man back where he came from. Too many free "niggers" walking around was creating a burden on society, so they favored moving free blacks out, then gradually emancipating the slaves and getting them out too. The colonizationists did not have any real compassion for the slave, but simply saw slavery as a moral and economic evil that would someday destroy their social order. UNLIKE THE INFERIORITY ARGUMENT MADE BY THE SLAVE HOLDERS THAT SLAVERY WAS THE BEST THING FOR BLACK MEN, THE COLONIZATIONISTS BELIEVED THAT BLACK MEN WERE RATIONAL LIKE THEMSELVES AND THAT ONE DAY THEY WOULD DO THE SAME THING THEY WOULD DO UNDER THE SAME CIRCUMSTANCES, REVOLT.

Many of the colonizationists, in fact, believed that the Africans were geniuses in the arts and the sciences, pointing out accomplishments made by the Ethiopians and the Egyptians, which challenged myths about black inferiority.

Whatever their heritage and whatever their potential, free blacks were accused of being idle and disorderly, and blamed for causing the slaves (who naturally wanted to be free) to be disobedient and unruly. And then, as now, white power was the only thing that kept the black man in check. HENRY CLAY, ONE OF THE LEADERS OF COLONIZATION, BELIEVED THAT THE FATE OF FREE BLACKS WAS DUE TO THE "INVINCIBLE PREJUDICES" OF THE WHITES THAT DENIED THEM EQUAL PARTICIPATION IN SOCIETY BECAUSE OF THEIR DIFFERENT BACKGROUNDS AND THE FACT THAT THE WHITES HATED "SOOTY" BLACK SKIN. Some, in fact, equated the black man's color to dirt and claimed that he had a repulsive smell as well. OVER 200 YEARS AGO MANY WHITE COLONIZATIONISTS DID NOT

BELIEVE THAT THE BLACK MAN COULD MAKE IT IN AMERICA BECAUSE THE WHITES WERE TOO PREJUDICED TO ALLOW THAT TO HAPPEN. The problem of race was more difficult to solve than the problem of slavery because of color. AS THEY SAW IT, THERE WAS NO HOPE FOR THE BLACK MAN IN AMERICA.

In the 1850's, Alexis de Tocqueville, author of "Democracy in America" believed that even freeing the slaves would not solve this country's problems, because the slaves who were already hated, would have to be absorbed into a Negrophobic American society. But this could never be done because unlike others who had been freed with no visible signs of their heritage, the black man's color would never allow prejudice and his degraded past to die. Tocqueville wrote "His physiognomy is to our eyes hideous, "also" his understanding weak, his tastes low; and we are almost inclined to look upon him as a being intermediate between man and the brutes." During the same period Robert Goodloe Harper, another leading colonizationist said that the blacks "are condemned to a hopeless state of inferiority and degradation by their color, which is an indelible mark of their origin and former condition, and establishes an impassible barrier between them and the whites." Because the black man would never be accepted in a society where every other class hated him he would have to fight for himself.

Many believed that the Negro was an unassimilable alien who would never find a permanent place in their society. Only an all-white America could survive. Others who considered themselves more realistic believed that all white states might be possible. They succeeded in getting all-white towns and all-white neighborhoods all over America.

Unsupervised blacks would destroy order and produce chaos. In the 1850's, Whitelow Reid, editor of the Xenia, Ohio, News, wrote that "Where Negroes reside in any great numbers among the whites both parties are the worse for it and it is in the interest of both that a separation should be made as soon as practicable." The only solution was to exclude blacks from society while trying to find a way to eliminate them. EXTINCTION WAS THE REAL GOAL. THE SUPERIOR RACE WAS DESTINED TO EXTERMINATE THE INFERIOR RACES, BOTH THE BLACKS AND THE INDIANS.

Several statements made during that time are crucial in developing an understanding of why the black man is where he is today. Reverend J. W. Sturtevant, president of Illinois College in 1863 wrote of the disconnected lower stratum of the population that did not earn enough to support a family; that "the weak, the vicious, the degraded, the broken down classes would be weeded out." "He would either never marry, or he will, in the attempt to support a family, struggle against the laws of nature and his children, many of them at least, die in infancy." In 1857 Theodore Parker, a Unitarian minister, wrote, "In twenty generations the Negroes will still stand just where they are now; that is if they have not disappeared." And professor William B. Smith of Tulane University wrote that "The vision...of a race vanishing before its superior is not at all dispiriting, but inspiring rather...the doom that awaits the Negro has been prepared in like measure for all inferior races." Everything was planned.

Another very important thing to remember is the nature of the Anglo-Saxon compared to that of the African. Just as environment has played a key role in shaping the destiny of blacks in America, it has also been a determinant in shaping other men.

While describing the strong, fierce Anglo-Saxon, Theodore Parker spoke of "his restless disposition to invade and conquer other lands; his haughty contempt of humbler tribes which lead him to subvert, enslave, kill and exterminate; his fondness for material things, preferring these to beauty;" explaining the war-like and possessive nature of these men, these cold men from cold caves. Not unlike the Anglo-Saxons, the colonists, too, were greedy for wealth and power, no matter what the cost. Today, their descendants are the same way.

The Negro was viewed as just the opposite. He was gentle, patient and good-natured. In fact, because of his easy-going disposition he was often considered weak, inferior and even womanly. But, unlike the Anglo-Saxons, the black man had come from a garden where nature had been very generous. He was warm, hospitable and easy-going because he had everything he needed. He did not have to hoard and try to control everything. He did not have to own everything around him.

The Anglo-Saxon could not accept black sensibilities as anything but submission. The mere fact that the black man was there, and was the kind of man he was, meant that he was to be controlled and not respected as an equal. One official report stated that "The Anglo-American looks upon every acre of our present domain as intended for him and not for the Negro."

Like black men today who are discriminated against, black men who were considered free back then and living in poverty in the cities they had migrated to had very little and stayed in trouble. SIMPLY STATED, EVEN THOUGH THERE WAS NO SUCH THING AS A GHETTO, THERE WAS ALREADY A GHETTO MENTALITY DEVELOPING AS A DISPROPORTIONATE NUMBER OF BLACK MEN FOUND THEMSELVES BEING THROWN INTO JAIL. Sometimes when the slave was being transported from one place to the next he would temporarily be housed in a "slave jail." If he had had a choice it surely would have been to be somewhere else. So historically black men have a long standing tradition with jails, a pitifully unfair tradition.

According to William Jay during the 1800's, "The free blacks have been rendered by prejudice and persecution an ignorant and degraded class." And Reverend Robert B. Hall, an abolitionist said, "A prejudice is generated in our youth against the blacks, which grows with our growth and strengthens with our strength, until our eyes are opened to the folly by a more correct feeling." The poor living standard of free black men only confirmed what many whites believed all along, that whether it was his fault or not, the black man had become a degenerate who was not fit to be around decent white people, just as it is today. Of course, education and elevating the black man were considered then too, but naturally nothing happened.

IN ESSENCE, BLACK MEN WHO WERE NOT PREPARED FOR WHAT WAS CONSIDERED FREEDOM AND WHO WERE ABUSED AND BLAMED WHEN THEY DID NOT KNOW HOW TO ACT WHEN THEY DID NOT FIT IN, HAVE DESCENDANTS WHO ARE UNKNOWINGLY SUFFERING THE SAME ILLS.

TODAY'S BLACK MAN IS A PRODUCT OF HIS ENVIRONMENT TOO. He is still bound to his heritage, and giving him equality is still impractical and out of the question for white Americans. That, too, is why he cannot make it. The black man is a disobedient nuisance, and white America still fears him, believing that some day he may indeed snap.

WHITE AMERICA'S WORST NIGHTMARE CONTINUES TO HAUNT THEM AS BLACK AMERICANS SURVIVE. There are not enough boats, trucks, trains or airplanes to transport millions of black Americans somewhere else, and even if they had the capacity to do so, where would they send us? CONTROL UNTIL THEY CAN ERADICATE US IS THE ONLY ANSWER. It is just business as usual.

TODAY THE PREMISE THAT THE BLACK MAN IS NOT PREPARED FOR FREEDOM IS STILL HELD BY WHITE PEOPLE WHO BELIEVE THAT HAVING THE BLACK MAN IN A REPRESSIVE SOCIETY IS THE ONLY WAY. If they allow concessions they may give up too many, so it is just easier to leave things the way they are. NOTHING WILL MAKE WHITE AMERICA GIVE UP ITS SOCIAL, PSYCHOLOGICAL AND FINANCIAL ADVANTAGE, AND ITS FEELING OF WHITE SUPREMACY, UNSCRUPULOUSLY ARRIVED AT BY A PATTERN OF MISTREATING AND ABUSING OTHERS. They have the land because they stole it from the Indians, and they gained the rest of their wealth by forcing others to work for them while they thought up new schemes.

ACCORDING TO PLATO'S UTOPIAN PHILOSOPHY, "THERE CAN BE NO IDEAL SOCIETY WITHOUT RESTRICTING CERTAIN FREEDOMS FOR GOOD." If everybody gets ahead, who will do the dirty work? Black men cannot make it because they were never supposed to.

AFTER NEARLY 400 YEARS OF TRIAL AND ERROR, WHITE AMERICA FINALLY SUCCEEDED IN CREATING THE INFERIOR BLACK MALE THEY HAD BEEN LYING ABOUT FOR CENTURIES. What they did not plan for, however, was the moral and economic destruction of their own society, because of the cost of creating this mutant (welfare and crime), and white boys lost by black influence along the way. During the 1890's Governor Thomas G. Jones of Alabama said, "If we do not lift them up, they will drag us down." IF THE BLACK MAN HAD BEEN TREATED FAIRLY IN THE FIRST PLACE AND GIVEN HIS 40 ACRES AND HIS MULE AND ALLOWED TO PROGRESS, AMERICA PROBABLY WOULD UNALTERABLY TRULY BE THE GREATEST COUNTRY ON EARTH BY NOW, REAL GOODPUSSY.

BUT WE MUST TAKE SOME RESPONSIBILITY FOR OUR OWN ACTIONS, TOO, OR LACK OF IT. IGNORANT YOUNG BLACKS ARE MAKING FOOLS OF THEMSELVES AND EVERY OTHER BLACK PERSON AS THEY UNKNOWINGLY ADD FUEL TO THE FIRES OF PREJUDICE AND RACISM. Not realizing that prejudice and racism, against blacks in particular, is primarily based on being different, they are going to extremes to be even more different. Believing that looking like a fool is giving them status (which it may well do with other fools) they are destroying all of us.

UNKNOWINGLY, THESE 20TH-CENTURY PICKANINNIES AND HANDKERCHIEFHEADS ARE DEMOLISHING ANY SEMBLANCE OF DIGNITY AND SELF-RESPECT BLACK AMERICANS STILL HOLD IN THE WORLD COMMUNITY. Tragically, they feel that their profanity and their obscenity are in good taste (which it may well be for others like themselves). But we all need positive images of ourselves, and they certainly are not that. THEY,

TOO, ARE PART OF THE REASON WHY BLACK MEN CANNOT MAKE IT IN AMERICA TODAY.

"If we do not lift them up they will drag us down." And it is happening more and more every day. IGNORANT AND DEGRADED BLACKS ARE DRAGGING THE REST OF US DOWN. If all of us know, and recognize the fact that there is "poor white trash," why are we so defensive when someone suggests the idea of "poor black trash." Black people are not monolithic. WE ARE NOT ALL CARBON COPIES OF EACH OTHER AND THERE IS A LOWER CLASS GIVING THE REST OF US A BAD NAME AND DESTROYING ANY HOPE WE MIGHT HAVE. Naturally, it is to their advantage to make us feel guilty by saying things like, "You may think you are better than us, but you're still a nigger too." While we know that some white people will always consider us niggers, no matter what, we do not have to see ourselves that way. (Many whites believe that all blacks are niggers because they simply have never been close to decent black people who are equally good citizens, and because of one sided propaganda and "real niggers" they never will know the truth.) If you are not a junkie, a thief, or an ignorant, vicious low life, you may well be better than they are. But do not feel bad about it and stop being apologetic. If you are trying to make something of your life and they are not, do not allow trash to condemn you.

We must stop playing into their hands and into white America's hands as well. WHITE AMERICA DOES NOT ALLOW "POOR WHITE TRASH" TO DRAG THEM DOWN. BLACK AMERICA SHOULD NOT ALLOW "POOR BLACK TRASH" TO DRAG THEM DOWN EITHER. For example, niggers (poor black trash) are a reality. We have all seen them. Most of us have probably called somebody a nigger at some point in our lives. So why do we consistently make excuses for their behavior and deny their existence? Because when someone says nigger we take it personally too. But we already know, and the universe knows that "poor black trash" (niggers) exists. (Being poor and black, of course, does not automatically make a person trash.)

A study of so called "black-on-black" crime would support the fact that not all black people are committing crimes. It would show that overt criminal acts tend to be a class problem, and that "vicious and degraded" blacks are committing most of those acts. And every black person who is a criminal is not necessarily that way because the white man made him do it. Some of these "low lifes" would have become criminals anyway. Even if Polish or Chinese they would still be corrupt. They are not misunderstood blacks who simply became criminals, they are criminals who simply happen to be black. In fact, if "black-on-black" crime has to be expressed in a black context, why don't we call it "poor black trash on poor black trash" crime, and leave the rest of us, (the 75% who are innocent) out of it. And we should demand that the media report such crimes differently. Stop making all blacks look like potential criminals.

It is up to those of us who are not "poor black trash," (eating chicken and leaving the debris on somebody else's front porch) to save ourselves. Like many whites, "poor black trash" is dividing and defeating us. Those of us who are civilized and decent, and who are reasonable, should come together, become polarized so that we may become more productive and begin to see ourselves more positively. We need to clean our own house. IF WE STOP ALLOWING THEIR "TRASHY IMAGE" TO BE OUR IMAGE TOO, WE WILL BE WELL ON OUR WAY TO PICKING OURSELVES UP. Furthermore, our children need not grow up feeling like traitors, because they have not been intimidated into following the lead of "poor black trash," who want nothing. Although they are the most visible and the most vocal, we must not allow ignorant people at the bottom, with no knowledge and even less understanding to speak for us, no matter how long or how loud they protest. Their message is theirs. It is not ours, and they are a considerable reason why decent black men cannot make it.

Competition is another reason why the black man cannot make it, not sexual but economic competition.

214

Remember, for poor whites, working side by side with a nigger meant "working like a nigger." They unequivocally did not want the black man to be their master and that still holds true today. WHITE AMERICA STILL DOES NOT INTEND TO RELINQUISH ITS POSITION OF SUPERIORITY AND SUPREMACY TO ANY OTHER RACE. If the black man is given a chance he may do well. In fact, he may excel. The Welfare system, for example, is the opposite of competition. Giving blacks menial handouts means less headaches, in the long run, for whites who realize that fewer blacks will be looking for jobs, trying to improve themselves, or be able to move into their neighborhoods.

Throughout history black men and white men have been competing for the same jobs and that too is still true. When jobs are abundant and the economy is healthy, it is alright for a few blacks to get some of those "good jobs" the whites do not need. But when times get hard, they want (and need) those jobs back. Some major companies even have handbooks detailing for management proven ways to effectively get rid of undesirables...And guess who those undesirables are. Their solution is still the same today as it was then. NEVER GIVE A NIGGER AN EVEN BREAK. "The only good nigger is a dead nigger."

In 1892, three black men, Calvin McDowell, Henry Stewart and Thomas Moss - Memphis, Tennessee's first black postman, were lynched near there. Their crime was opening their own business, "The People's Grocery," and breaking up a monopoly previously held by a white store owner. White men tried to burn them out and they defended their property. When three of the perpetrators were shot, the black store owners were arrested as criminals and the black community threatened if the white men died. Ironically, the white men lived but McDowell, Stewart and Moss died anyway. McDowell, who had tried to wrestle a gun away from one of the assailants, was found with his eyes gouged out and the fingers of his right hand shot off.

Others like Horace Greeley had their own ideas about competition and the black man. His "root hog or die" theory was to give the Negro his freedom, then he was on his own. Greeley wrote "Give everyone a chance, and let his behavior control his fate. If Negroes will not work, they must starve or steal; and if they steal they must be shut up like other thieves." Men like Greeley believed that the fact that the black man had been disadvantaged as a former slave meant nothing. Some whites still feel that way today, as they continue to renounce issues like "Civil Rights" and "Affirmative Action," even though they have had their own affirmative action all along. They renounce (denounce) quotas today, because that quota is no longer 100% for whites. It appears difficult for many whites to comprehend that 80 + 20 = 100. They are more comfortable when 100 = 100.

In 1884 Senator John T. Morgan of Alabama had his own ideas about competition. He said that "The greater their personal successes may be, the more they will feel the pressures of caste, and their advancement in enterprises which may bring them personal honor and wealth will be checked by the jealousy of caste, so that race prejudice will forever remain as an incubus on all their individual or aggregated efforts." In other words, if blacks become too smart, too successful and too prosperous, competition between blacks and whites will increase, creating even more friction. As long as black men do not do well, there is no problem. If you are black, if you don't make it - you cannot make it, and even if you do make it - you still cannot make it. SO CLEARLY, COMPETITION AND BLACK MEN GETTING THEIR ACT TOGETHER WOULD BE A SERIOUS DILEMMA FOR WHITE AMERICA.

AND HOW ABOUT THE FUTURE? WHAT DOES THAT HOLD FOR THE BLACK MAN IN AMERICA AS THE JAPANESE, WHO MAY REINVENT SLAVERY, ARE BUYING UP EVERYTHING IN SIGHT? Like the whites, Justice Minister Seiroku Kajiyama compared black Americans to prostitutes and said that they were spoiling a Tokyo neighborhood. (It is interesting that while the

Japanese produce ½ of the cars sold in California, they do not care to sit beside a black person on public transportation.)

I BELIEVE THAT THE JAPANESE WHO REMEMBER LOVED ONES KILLED WHEN THE ATOM BOMB WAS DROPPED ON HIROSHIMA AND NAGASAKI HAVE A FUNDAMENTAL DISLIKE FOR AMERICANS. The Japanese people have strong family ties and a long kinship tradition. Unlike the United States, Japanese culture is, in fact, based on kinship and cooperation rather than individual self-reliance. Families, honor and loyalty are fundamental. Do we really believe that we are so wonderful, after destroying countless families, that the Japanese harbor no ill-will toward Americans? THE JAPANESE ARE SIMPLY DOING THINGS DIFFERENTLY. Bullets didn't work so they have decided to alter their World War II defeat with money, and America is taking all the wooden nickels she can get.

IN ESSENCE, THE JAPANESE ARE USING OUR MONEY TO BUY OUR OWN COUNTRY FROM US AND THERE WILL BE NO PLACE LEFT FOR THE BLACK MAN. And they are getting an even better deal than the United States got with the Louisiana Purchase. They are not buying worthless swamp land but some of the most valuable property in the world, one plot at a time, for what will be equal to pennies in the future. And how much of their country are they selling us? YES, THE WHITES MAY HAVE TAKEN IT FROM THE INDIANS, BUT THE JAPANESE ARE TAKING IT FROM THEM.

THE REAL PROBLEM IS THAT THEY ARE GETTING BLACK HOMES TOO, FROM WHITE PEOPLE WHO WILL SIMPLY TAKE THEIR PROFITS AND MOVE SOMEWHERE ELSE, BUT WHAT WILL YOU DO AND WHERE WILL YOU GO WHEN SOMEONE TELLS YOU IT'S TIME TO MOVE.

BLACK AMERICANS WILL BE AS HOMELESS, DISENFRANCHISED AND AS DESTITUTE AS THEY WERE DURING SLAVERY AND THE DAYS OF JIM CROW. While the whites take from the blacks, the Japanese who are taking from all of us realize that their lot is being made easier because the more the whites do to the black man the less they will have to deal with. In fact, because all Japanese life revolves around a father figure, they probably loath dysfunctional and disenfranchised black males. Those same Japanese who have a history of discrimination infer that blacks "ruin the atmosphere," alluding to the way whites move out when blacks move in. There are also overt discriminatory hiring policies and franchising opportunities by United States based Japanese companies as well as degrading references and images advanced against blacks, like pickaninny dolls with red lips that are sold in an attempt to degrade black Americans.

There are three million "village people" or burakumins who are already discriminated against in Japan and who are physically indistinguishable from them, so what chance does a black man have? THE JAPANESE, WHO HAVE THEIR OWN MINORITIES AT HOME WILL HAVE A NEW SLAVE ALREADY IN PLACE WHEN THEY TAKE OVER AMERICA.

THERE IS ONE OTHER THING HOWEVER. I BELIEVE THAT THE JAPANESE MALE HATES THE BLACK MAN FOR MANY OF THE SAME REASONS THAT THE WHITE MAN DOES. In addition to the usual social prejudices, I believe that Japanese males who are generally small in stature are also intimidated by myths about the black man's penis and, like the white male, Goodpussy is reassuring his male supremacy by making the black man and his organ disappear. WHITE MALES AND JAPANESE MALES HAVE SOME OF THE SAME PREJUDICES AND THE SAME INSECURITIES AND THAT IS CLEARLY WHY THE BLACK MAN HAS NOT BEEN ABLE TO MAKE IT AND WILL NOT MAKE IT.

In 1992 black men are still the last rung on the humanitarian ladder. Because of the violent and often anti-social actions of a few, almost all black men are condemned, those who know it as well as those who do not.

I am reminded of two movies which together help to mirror the black man's experience. Those two movies were "Trading Places," starring Eddie Murphy and Dan Akroid, and "Wolfen."

218

In Trading Places an experiment was conducted whereby two men, a white man from an upper level economic status, as a result of contrived misfortunes, was forced to switch places with a black man of low economic status, to see what the results would be. Predictably, the person of low economic status enjoyed the privilege of luxury while the man demoted to a life of deprivation and mistreatment exhibited the same negative, anti-social behavior he had so despised before his fall.

In the second movie, "Wolfen," wolves that had been displaced from their natural homes in the wild had inhabited the city, attacking and living on the weak and those who would do them harm. Viewed as wicked and evil, they viciously eradicated those who were threatening their own existence. The wolves simply wanted to live too.

The black man was savagely removed from his own native soil and transported to a land where he has not been well treated. In his own country he was a part of nature's delicate balance, but when dehumanized in America, he evolved as the wolf did. SURVIVAL OF THE FITTEST IS INDEED INSTINCTIVE; AND "THE BLACK MAN IS FIGHTING AGAINST THE ODDS TO SURVIVE." AND HE STILL IS BOTH THE VICTIM AND THE TARGET.

INSECURITY, LOW SELF-ESTEEM
AND VALIDATION

She was a beautiful woman. That is why you had to make her your wife. And when she slapped you for asking her where she had been all night and told you it was none of your business, you took that too. The price you paid for your new car, all that jewelry and your new wardrobe - that was pretty steep, too. Your wife spends even more than you do in spite of the fact that you can barely keep your heads above water with both salaries combined. And when your supervisor at work callously told those off color "nigger jokes," why did you laugh so hard? Sure, you probably wear the strong mask of self-confidence, but lurking somewhere deep down inside is insecurity, low self-esteem and a need for validation.

AS A BLACK MAN IN AMERICA, YOU MAY HAVE A REAL RIGHT TO BE INSECURE. You have had to fight three times as hard to get where you are and there are no guarantees that you will still be there tomorrow. Norman, 43, a high school basketball coach, was recently ridiculed publicly during a pep rally by a female principal who said "I really don't know why we are having a pep rally because we don't win any games anyway." Had Norman not been a strong black man who was secure in himself, he surely would have been devastated and possibly driven to do something he might be sorry for later.

TYPICALLY, IN AMERICA, BLACK MALES HAVE BEEN SO DISENFRANCHISED THAT FEELINGS OF INSECURITY AND LOW SELF-ESTEEM HAVE SILENTLY BECOME A WAY OF LIFE FOR MANY OF THEM. BECAUSE THEY ARE GENERALLY POWERLESS, THEY ARE VIEWED AS VALUELESS, AND A VALUELESS MAN IS A WORTH-LESS MAN. A WORTH-LESS MAN IS AN INSECURE MAN. Although he is unique in all the world, others have convinced him of his innate inferiority.

BECAUSE SOME BLACK MEN CANNOT SEEM TO GET AHEAD, THEY NOW BELIEVE THAT THEY ARE INCAPABLE OF ACHIEVEMENT. SOME BLACK MEN HAVE INDEED TOLD THEMSELVES THAT THEY

ARE LOSERS WHO WILL ALWAYS FAIL. Because they feel inadequate and overwhelmed, they no longer even bother to try and become satisfied letting their lives tragically slip away by doing nothing. Black men who have been discouraged or prohibited from doing anything become even more discouraged. They unwittingly become co-conspirators against themselves. THOSE WHO HAVE NOTHING TO DO OFTEN FEEL WORSE BECAUSE THERE IS NOTHING TO DO.

Others, of course, feeling the same helplessness and hopelessness, aggressively develop destructive feelings of self-hate. These negative feelings make them believe that their negative thoughts are actually valid. SELF-DEFEATING THOUGHTS ENCOURAGE SELF-DEFEATING EMOTIONS AND ACTIONS WHICH INTENSIFY SELF-DISAPPROVAL. Bob, an unemployed airline worker, tried everywhere he could to find work. After six months he convinced himself that things were hopeless. He isolated himself from his friends and family staying in bed for what seemed like days at a time barely eating and staring up at the ceiling. Finally, he angrily convinced himself that he was indeed helpless and decided instead to resentfully stand on a street corner with a sign which read, "I will work for food."

NOT BEING ABLE TO POINT TO ACCOMPLISHMENTS OR SUCCESSES, MANY BLACK MEN LOOK DOWN UPON THEMSELVES. BECAUSE THEY ARE CONVINCED OF THEIR WORTHLESSNESS, OTHERS ARE CONVINCED AS WELL, AND A VICIOUS CYCLE IS CREATED. Self-esteem is based on value, on our own assessment of ourselves as well as the assessment of others. LABELING BLACK MEN AS DANGEROUS, LAZY AND WORTHLESS HAS BECOME CRITICAL AND HAS DESTROYED MUCH OF THEIR SELF-ESTEEM.

Black men do not enjoy failure. In fact, many become furious at the suggestion that they gain some satisfaction from being rebellious or depicted as losers. Society's nagging and insults, in fact, often discourages movement, because it is only human nature to resist when you are pushed. MANY BLACK

MEN HAVE FELT BAD FOR SO LONG THAT THEY FIND IT
UNTHINKABLE THAT THEY WILL EVER FEEL GOOD AGAIN.
Because society has sabotaged black men so many times, they
no longer believe in themselves and feel that any effort they
might make is not worth it.

EVEN THE MOST FUNDAMENTAL ELEMENTS OF THE BLACK
MAN, HIS SKIN COLOR, HIS ETHNIC FEATURES AND EVEN THE WAY
HE COMMUNICATES HAVE BEEN USED AGAINST HIM TO LOWER HIS
SENSE OF SELF WORTH. His broad lips, coarse hair and dark
skin were alleged to be natural testaments to his innate
inferiority. Historically, many whites believed that blacks were
ugly and disfigured. They believed that the Negro's blackness
represented evil, filthiness, danger and repulsion, and their
whiteness purity, beauty, virtue and God. Different is just
that, however, just different and neither better nor worse.

And as far as the way blacks speak today, that is
historic too. Samuel, 58, a gardener, said that he felt pretty
low when Mrs. James, a wealthy black client, laughed at him
for saying, "Him be gone" and "I writes" while speaking about
his son Daniel, stationed in Saudi Arabia, during operation
Desert Storm. Mrs. James herself egotistically lacked the
knowledge that Samuel, like so many others, speaks what
linguists call "Plantation Creole." Plantation Creole is a
compromise between the King's English spoken by Europeans
and the native languages of tribesmen of Africa. Blacks in
slave quarters simply modified white aristocratic language.

Over 300 years ago slave traders brought the English
language to the West African coast. On the Congo River
alone, over 160 different languages were spoken. Pidgin
English, which was vital to communication, was used by slave
traders to simplify English so that they could communicate
with the African. Pidgin English was a compromise of English
and an African language called Gullah which has not changed
in over 300 years. For example, the African word for to carry
is "tote," and "watae" has become "o.k.," the world's most
frequently used word. So, again, if blacks were permitted to

know their history and to know who they are, then they could begin to have a healthy sense of accomplishment and self-worth. And although cruel jokes are frequently made about black features, I have yet to see notable affronts made about large pointed noses, straggly (limp) straight hair or (milky white) pale skin which are equally accessible to criticism or ridicule.

WE MUST BE REMINDED ALSO THAT THE BLACK MAN'S LOW SELF-ESTEEM HAS BEEN REINFORCED BY REJECTION BECAUSE OF HIS COLOR. REMEMBER, YOU CAN BE CONVINCED OF YOUR WORTHLESSNESS AND INFERIORITY BY OTHERS WHO CONVINCE YOU TO HAVE A NEGATIVE SELF-IMAGE. Whites (and other blacks), disapproving of some blacks, seem to have convinced many of them that they are indeed black and evil. Because blackness has always been linked directly with sin, the black man, who was always condemned, has sunk to a new level of self-condemnation. He subconsciously abhors the undeniable symbol he is destined to wear. COLOR HAS ALSO BEEN USED AS THE LINE OF DEMARCATION FREQUENTLY DETERMINING WHETHER A PERSON WAS FRIEND OR FOE.

Even black veterans who have won purple hearts and bronze medals return home to become alcoholics and drug abusers. . . Why? What did they find that so destroyed their self-esteem? Many are homeless and even a small thing like reaching into your pocket and not feeling a key, a house key, is self-defeating when you have nowhere to live. Looking back at the history of blacks in America, it is amazing that anyone could maintain their repressed position so long and still have not only a good self-concept but a powerful self-concept as well.

Blacks, however, should learn how to listen to their own inner voices so that they can begin to understand what the problem is as well as what the situation is for them. Why not turn the music down. . . or off, so you can hear something besides the constant beat of bass bottoms that drown out thoughts and help you deny your situation. The music blacks love to listen to so much may be the very same activity that keeps them from thinking, and understanding why their plight is so sad. Still, young black children, babies, are taught to shake their boodies before they are taught to read, if they are in fact ever taught to read at all. REAL POWER IS IN THEIR MINDS, NOT IN THEIR BEHINDS.

Black men who have low self-esteem invariably feel worthless. Feeling defeated and devastated, they suffer the horrible agony of inadequacy. Black men who have not made society's grade may as well have the word invalid stamped across their chests. They are defective and guilty while white men are automatically certified and innocent. The black male has to be proven innocent while the white male has to be proven guilty. MANY BLACK MEN WHO HAVE BEEN MARKED INVALID HAVE ALREADY THROWN THEMSELVES INTO A TRASH CAN SOMEWHERE. OTHERS WHO ARE TEMPORARILY CERTIFIED WITH "T-CERTIFICATES" DO NOT REALIZE THAT THE ONLY THING KEEPING THEM FROM THE SAME FATE IS PSEUDO-ESTEEM BECAUSE OF A JOB OR THE LITTLE MONEY THEY HAVE WHICH MOMENTARILY VALIDATES AND MAKES THEM ACCEPTABLE.

Again, black men who succumb to feelings of insecurity defeat themselves. Years of being brainwashed has worked. ALLEGATIONS ACCEPTED AS FACT HAVE CAUSED LOW SELF-ESTEEM AND INSECURITY TO SABOTAGE AND CRIPPLE MANY BLACK MEN'S WILL POWER. Feeling insecure and defective, they try to validate themselves by the only means they know, being physical. They assert themselves physically and sexually. They often thrive on material possessions including the number of women they have and the way they treat them. The only way they can feel good about themselves is to parade their accomplishments around in front of everyone. Not one person can be left believing that they are not successful or their whole image of themselves may collapse in ruins.

Stephen, 41, a warehouseman, boasted of buying his son Stephen, Jr. a $120 pair of Adidas tennis shoes, explaining that they were the only kind the 15-year-old would wear. My thoughts at the time were if he were my son he would either wear what I could afford, save his money and buy his own or go barefoot. Unknowingly, the elder Stephen was doing two things: He was attempting to validate himself by showing what a good parent he was to purchase such a wonderful gift, and he was trying to prove that he was successful enough to make the purchase in the first place. In fact, he really accomplished neither. What he succeeded in doing, however, was to reinforce some misconceptions in Stephen, Jr. about self-esteem. He was also helping to develop another criminal mind, because the moment Stephen, Jr. could no longer afford expensive gifts he would steal or sell drugs to satisfy his need. YOU CANNOT BUY REAL SECURITY OR SELF-ESTEEM, AND YOU CAN ONLY VALIDATE YOURSELF FROM WITHIN, NOT WITHOUT.

Again, to survive, the black man must know who he is. He can only get ahead by doing something and by trying to help himself. If black men want different results they must do things differently, because the only control they have is their own effort. Changing their behavior is the only thing that will make them feel better about themselves. BLACK MEN MUST ABOVE ALL ELSE REMEMBER THAT REAL POWER IS MENTAL. They must have enough mental power to persevere and cultivate their own sense of security and self-esteem. When you do have mental power, however, and you are trampled on, it hurts even more, and only those with strong hearts can keep coming back for more. With no mind, there is no hope. Real Goodpussy is being blessed with that mind.

BLACK FAMILIES, NO HUGS AND KISSES

If you are a black man or a black woman, when was the last time you gave your children a big hug or a kiss and told them that you love them? When was the last time you said it to anybody?

If you are a single man or woman, when was the last time you gave that special person in your life a big hug and a kiss, and told them that you love them? You know deep down in your heart how you really feel, but the words, or the gestures, never seem to come, even though you know it is important.

I believe that at least part of the answer to those questions may be historic. **BLACKS WHO WERE CONSIDERED LESS THAN HUMAN WERE NOT PERMITTED TO DISPLAY POSITIVE HUMAN EMOTIONS.** Slaves whose children were sold were often whipped if they cried. Again, fathers produced new laborers, not closely knit families with which to form loving bonds. If anything, it was better not to form attachments at all for loved ones who might be sold or killed by night fall. On larger plantations, even mothers did not have primary care of their young. That was the role of the mammy. BLACK PEOPLE, WHO WERE SUPPOSED TO BE ANIMALS WITHOUT SOULS OR HEARTS, SEEM TO HAVE BEEN BRAINWASHED INTO BELIEVING THAT THEY REALLY WERE NOT SENSITIVE, CARING HUMAN BEINGS.

Even shame probably played its role, as in instances of humiliation. Suppose, for example, that a father was stripped naked in front of his family and beaten, or that one of the young females was taken out at night and sexually abused by the master. The only real way to deal with such deep emotional issues was to deny or suppress them. The best way to cover up the shame was to pretend that nothing really happened, because the slave was powerless to do anything about it anyway. Their true feelings were perhaps so real, so passionate, that the only natural instinct would have been to kill.

TODAY BLACK PEOPLE STILL SEEM TO BE SUPPRESSING THEIR FEELINGS, EVEN FROM THEMSELVES, UNLESS THEY ARE IN SOME BAPTIST CHURCH OR AT A WAKE OR A FUNERAL. They seem to need a reason or an excuse before they can open up and let whatever is inside come out. This is truly tragic because black and brown people are as warm and as loving inside as the tropical climate that kindly nurtured them.

BLACK MEN, ESPECIALLY, SEEM TO BELIEVE IT IS A SIGN OF WEAKNESS AND VULNERABILITY TO SHOW THAT THEY CAN BE GENTLE AND LOVING. As black boys and young black men they were ashamed to openly express their real feelings, fearing that they would not still be considered one of the "fellas," and that they would be looked upon as a ninny or a sissy. Society had indeed shown them time after time that "a man who was weak really was beat." The black man's pride was his strength and his arrogance, and without that he was nothing. He had listened and learned well. He had a habit now, and he could not easily break it.

His father was a real man who had not broken the street code. The other black men he saw, they had not broken it either. Be a man, and be a serious black man, no matter what. (The best defense is a strong offense, so show no weakness.) AND SINCE THEIR FATHERS DID NOT TALK TO THEM OR SHOW THEM MUCH AFFECTION, THEY ARE NOT TALKING TO THEIR SONS OR SHOWING THEM MUCH AFFECTION, AND THEIR SONS WILL NOT TALK MUCH TO THEIR SONS OR SHOW THEM MUCH AFFECTION. IT IS A HUGLESS, KISSLESS, TALKLESS CYCLE THAT MUST BE BROKEN!

In many of the movies we see today, and most of us do watch television, rent videos, or go to movie theaters, we see some type of love scene where the hero, a white man, is kissing or holding a white woman, while black people hardly touch except to strike or stab each other. Naturally, there is a subliminal message here, and it is that the white male, who is the hero and who is human, gets the prize, the pretty girl, and he gets to feel those special feelings that only human beings can feel. The black man who is the loser and who is not human, only gets to watch.

Black men, black women and black children are consistently being negatively reinforced without even being aware of it. WHENEVER A BLACK MAN DOES REACH FOR THOSE GOOD THINGS THAT HE KNOWS ARE GOOD BECAUSE THE WHITE MAN HAS THEM (THE LUXURIES, THE GOOD LIFE, THE WHITE WOMAN OR EVEN HIS OWN HAPPY FAMILY), HE IS SLAPPED HARD ACROSS THE FACE AS A REMINDER THAT THOSE THINGS ARE NOT FOR HIM. It's like dangling a banana in front of a monkey. You know that he wants one, but when he reaches for it, you let him have it squarely in the face with a frying pan. Black people are not supposed to have feelings, and whenever those feelings do start to surface, here comes the frying pan.

The family is the primary socializing unit in any society, and in all societies there are four (4) family universals or functions in common. The family is responsible for "regulating" sex and reproduction. (So child bearing is managed through marriage and parenthood.) The family is also responsible for the care and rearing of children providing food, shelter, guidance and protection. It is responsible for economic cooperation as well, that is, deciding who works and how money is to be spent. Finally, the family is responsible for emotional support and companionship. It provides for intimate emotional needs and comfort.

UNLIKE MANY OTHER ANIMALS, A HUMAN BABY IS HELPLESS AT BIRTH AND MUST BE CARED FOR. It has no instincts. Everything is learned. It is the family that sustains the individual who helps to sustain his society. Saving the family is crucial to protecting ourselves. Protecting the family is crucial to saving ourselves. The family is the only thing that can save us. DESTROY THE FAMILY AND YOU DESTROY THE INDIVIDUAL AND HIS SOCIETY. The way to destroy a race is through the family.

Remember, Reverend J. M. Sturtevant wrote way back in 1863 that there was always a disconnected "lower stratum of the population that did not earn enough to support a family, and that many of their children would die." Is this not exactly what is happening to the black family? Are our children not in trouble because black families are falling apart? Is it not true that their sexuality is not regulated, that they are not adequately cared for, that they have no economic cooperation and that they gain no emotional support and companionship, all of which are provided for by the family?

YOUNG BLACKS WHO HAVE DYSFUNCTIONAL FAMILIES ARE VISIBLY LOST WHILE OTHERS WHO HAVE BEEN DISCONNECTED FROM THEIR CULTURE ARE IDENTIFYING WITH A WHITE CULTURE THAT DOES NOT WORK EITHER. If so many white people are confused and must see psychiatrists, then surely many blacks are mixed up too.

Again, the nuclear family is a recent white phenomenon that does not work. MOST CULTURES RELY ON

EXTENDED OR LARGER FAMILY GROUPS, INCLUDING GRANDMOTHERS AND GRANDFATHERS, BROTHERS AND WIVES, AUNTS AND UNCLES, NIECES AND NEPHEWS, IN-LAWS, EVERYBODY WHO IS RELATED. And they all take care of each other, doing their very best to make sure each other's needs are met.

Other cultures realize the real importance of the family in guiding their young and have "rights of passage." YOU DO NOT AUTOMATICALLY BECOME AN ADULT WHEN YOU TURN 21. Rights of passage are deliberate steps to guide you toward adulthood by helping you to face responsibility. You learn how to accept pain and adversity, and how to deal with hardship rather than fall apart, because naturally there will be problems in life.

MARRIAGE AND RAISING A FAMILY IS A RESPONSIBILITY THAT INDIVIDUALS SHOULD BE PREPARED FOR AND OTHER CULTURES RECOGNIZE THAT. How much can you possibly know without guidance. That is why African parents, for example, get involved. They want to make sure their child marries the right person, with good character from a good family. They want to know who she is, and even though it is much easier to get a divorce in Africa, they have almost none compared to the United States. African parents do not want their children with someone who will drive them crazy, a person who does not know who he or she is.

AND EVEN AFTER MARRIAGE THE BRIDE AND GROOM SPEND TIME WITH OLDER PEOPLE WHO TEACH THEM HOW TO BE RESPONSIBLE HUSBANDS AND WIVES, SO MARRIAGE AND FAMILY ARE A CONTINUOUS LEARNING PROCESS. In our western culture we are grown and on our own at 21, and once we are married we spend most of our time with a spouse who doesn't know any more than we do, a person who may not understand either sacrifice or loyalty. And that other person probably knows nothing about human nature either.

OUR CULTURE DOES NOT PREPARE US FOR PARENTHOOD OR FAMILYHOOD. It has somehow confused love with sex instead of unconditional giving. AND LOVE IS TOO OFTEN

MATERIALISTIC RATHER THAN FEELINGS BASED ON CARING AND
RESPECT.

Black people do love, however, and they love very
deeply. It is their nature. Because of their circumstances,
they have learned to love silently, but times and needs do
change. In the past, love was unspoken but everyone knew
that it was there. In these very complex and demanding times,
we all need every drop of love and support that we can get --
the words, the expressions, the gestures and more.

Fathers need to start talking to their sons and to their
daughters. Mothers need to start talking to their daughters
and to their sons. Brothers need to talk to sisters and sisters
need to talk to their brothers. In essence, the family needs to
start communicating again and taking care of each other. And
if there is no father in the home or no mother, whoever is
there is the family, and they must be there for each other.

Today both psychologists and psychoanalysts believe
that there is a troubled child in each of us. Supposedly we
have all suffered a feeling of being alone and abandoned
somewhere in our youth, and before we can go on with our
lives in a healthy way, we must first resolve this old, unfinished
business. That's why we must begin to reach out for our loved
ones, for our sake as well as theirs. WE MUST LEARN THAT
THERE IS NO SHAME IN SHOWING AND SHARING LOVE, WHETHER
IT IS THAT VERY PERSONAL LOVE THAT WE HAVE FOR THAT
SPECIAL PERSON IN OUR LIVES, OR THE LOVE WE HAVE FOR OUR
FAMILIES, OR THE FEELINGS WE HAVE IN OUR HEARTS FOR OUR
FELLOW HUMAN BEINGS IN GENERAL. Being able to love and to
show that love is Goodpussy.

BLACK ROLE MODELS

It has been over 150 years and we still haven't learned anything. We are constantly bombarded by statements about young black boys having no positive role models. And while that may generally be true, it is only the tip of the iceberg.

TODAY'S BLACK MALE IS TRYING TO DETERMINE HIS OWN DESTINY, WITH LITTLE HELP FROM AN UNFRIENDLY SOCIETY THAT SEES HIM AS A CURSE. No one has ever sat down with him, as one person to another, to explain things, to share things, to listen to him, to show him how things are done, or to help him understand the difference between right and wrong or good and bad. We argue with vehement conviction that everyone knows how to act, and that he surely knows the difference between right and wrong, or good and bad, but right and wrong for whom, or good and bad for whom?

232

Ann Rand, in her book, "The Art of Selfishness," says there is no such thing as a compromise, that there is only a stronger good over a lesser good, and that the former usually wins. As far as blacks and black boys are concerned, theirs is obviously the lesser good. If a dog urinates on your lawn is he doing wrong? Similarly, is a black boy who has never been told that it may be illegal or improper to urinate on your property wrong when he does so? Would you have either the dog or the boy arrested? Good, for both of them, may have been simply emptying their bladders, with no real knowledge that they might be violating your rights or damaging your thick green grass.

BLACKS, WHO ARE LABELED ANIMALS AND EXCLUDED FROM SOCIETY, ARE EXPECTED TO UNDERSTAND SOCIAL CODES OF BEHAVIOR, EVEN THOUGH SOCIALIZATION IS LEARNED BY BEING SOCIALIZED. If you don't want that same pet to urinate in your bed or on your living room carpet, you "house break" him, you train him. Young black boys who have not been "house broken" or socialized, are visibly resentful and living in a state of near rebellion because they are lost, and because no one is trying to show them the way. Some of them actually do not realize they are doing anything wrong -- like stealing cars or selling drugs -- because they believe that's just the way it is. There are others who know they are doing wrong, but they are angry because no one seems to be willing to listen, or to tell them how to do it the right way. It is all too easy for those of us who did have help to condemn someone else.

But who would we be and where would we be if someone had not been interested enough to guide us? WE HAVE ALL HELPED TO FORM A VERY LONG IMPERSONAL ROPE, AND IF WE DO NOT CAREFULLY TIE AND SECURE A KNOT AT THE END, WE WILL ALL SLIP OFF. Whites, who argue that blacks are inferior, are not helping them, while blacks, who argue that less fortunate blacks are inferior, are not helping them either.

YOUNG BLACK MEN, WHEN SOMEONE DOES TALK, ARE USUALLY TALKED AT, NOT TO OR WITH. THIS APPROACH MUST

CERTAINLY CHANGE IF WE EXPECT THEM TO LISTEN, BECAUSE THEY WILL NOT RESPECT US UNTIL WE BEGIN TO RESPECT THEM. Again, it is equally as important to remember that since they have been deprived of their history, they have no real knowledge of who they are, and that fact is undeniably not their fault.

Life -- a reasonable life -- is, hopefully, a series of experiences that we more easily learn by doing, receiving encouragement when we are successful and correction with care, patience and understanding when we make mistakes. It is a proven fact, for example, that if a person wants to learn to speak French, it is easier to learn by actually hearing the French language being spoken naturally, picking up bits and pieces more normally than just seeing French words and phrases written in a book.

Similarly, to effectively learn to use a computer, it would be nice to have more than just a manual. "YOU NEED HANDS-ON EXPERIENCE AND A TEACHER, PREFERABLY A GOOD TEACHER."

BLACK BOYS NEED GOOD TEACHERS, DEDICATED TEACHERS WHO WILL TEACH THEM HOW TO LIVE, AND THEY NEED HANDS-ON EXPERIENCE. Police officers with guns and itchy trigger fingers, judges with over crowded jail cells, school teachers with inflated egos, drug dealers with women and money and church ministers wearing gold and diamonds and long robes with colored stripes that look like racing jackets, should not be their teachers. They are all part of the problem.

How can ministers and other leaders tell young people not to be like a drug dealer, when they look at either one and cannot tell the difference. They are just in different businesses that's all, and many drug dealers do indeed see themselves as businessmen in the black community. But many ministers and legitimate businessmen commute to black neighborhoods. They do not live there. They are not really accessible while the drug dealer is. He lives in the community.

234

He is a part of it, all day, everyday. With all his opulance he becomes the role model.

And yet, I think one of the biggest mistakes we collectively make is focusing on the fact that young black males do not have positive black male role models to emulate. WHILE A POSITIVE BLACK MALE ROLE MODEL IS IMPORTANT, A POSITIVE BLACK FEMALE ROLE MODEL IS ALSO IMPORTANT FOR BLACK MALES. A man is only 50% of a relationship. His woman is the other 50%, and it is important to understand how they work, interact and fit together. A BLACK BOY NEEDS TO BE ABLE TO LEARN CODES OF GOOD BEHAVIOR BY WATCHING A MAN WITH A WOMAN AND A WOMAN WITH A MAN.

SIMILARLY, "BLACK GIRLS WHO WILL BECOME BLACK WOMEN NEED TO HAVE GOOD BLACK MALE ROLE MODELS AS WELL AS STRONG BLACK FEMALES TO EMULATE." We seem to have forgotten that black girls have their problems too. Because they are not murdering each other, stealing, and wholeheartedly selling drugs, they do not appear to be the ones in trouble, the ones who are a threat to society. Black girls and black women do hurt, however, and even though they are not an overt threat to society, or rather white society, they are at least 50% of the threat in black relationships, or to black society. IF BLACK WOMEN AND BLACK MEN DO NOT RECOGNIZE THE NECESSITY OF LEARNING TO LIVE TOGETHER, THEY WILL SUCCESSFULLY DESTROY EACH OTHER, WHILE WHITE AMERICA QUIETLY AND PATIENTLY WAITS.

WHITE AMERICA DOES NOT WANT US TO THINK OF EACH OTHER AS A TEAM, AS A PARTNERSHIP, AND THEY DON'T WANT TO REMIND THEMSELVES THAT WE ARE HUMAN TOO. In the movies and on television, white people are normal and decent, always the good force or the hero. They may have family problems, but they do have a family.

The black man, when he is on the screen, is generally the villain, or the buffoon, with no family or conscience. Some of our earlier screen models included characters like Farina, Buckwheat, Stepin Fetchit, and Amos and Andy, all wonderful but demeaned individuals, whose characters had grown out of the days when slaves made fools of themselves to entertain the master and his family. Things have not changed. Blacks are still entertaining the world on the screen - either singing and dancing or in sports with a football or basketball. BUT BLACK YOUNGSTERS NEED REAL ROLE MODELS WHO WILL HELP THEM TO SURVIVE IN A REAL WORLD. They need to understand that singing and playing ball are not enough and that making it to the top that way is a long shot, just like finding a million dollars on the ground in a paper bag.

BLACK BOYS NEED TO LEARN TO APPRECIATE THE ABILITY TO READ AND WRITE AND TO THINK FOR THEMSELVES AFTER LEARNING HOW TO THINK. They need to know that they can learn to count and become mathematicians or pharmacists or anything else that they want to be, but all they see are the same old slavery carry-overs entertaining everybody, including us. They need to learn to get the facts straight first, and the only way that can be done is by getting the facts from somebody who knows the facts. That can be the little old lady across the street or the janitor who cleans the school.

WHAT IS SO TRAGIC IS THAT MANY OF OUR BLACK LEADERS WHO CONSIDER THEMSELVES OUR ROLE MODELS ARE SOME OF THE BIGGEST SUCKERS AND A--HOLES OF ALL. They are the idiots and false prophets who have placed themselves on pedestals and sold us out. If they were as smart as they think, they would realize that they are only being used to mislead and distract the rest of us while America marches on.

BLACK MEN AND BLACK WOMEN SHOULD COME TOGETHER IN RESPECT AND HARMONY AS ONE. Together we are our most vital role models. What none of us needs anymore are images of angry, illiterate, brutal black men slapping helpless women and children around or pulling out their big black penises. That would be Goodpussy for Black Mankind.

236

EDUCATION, THE KEY TO SURVIVAL
(Brains Not Chains)

Education, or really being educated, is the key to just about everything, especially survival. KNOWING MORE THAN THE PERSON SITTING NEXT TO YOU DOES, UNDERSTANDING THE STOCK MARKET, BEING ABLE TO QUOTE THE BIBLE VERSE BY VERSE, OR EVEN HAVING A Ph.D. DOES NOT MEAN THAT YOU ARE EDUCATED. It simply implies that you can ingest information and not that you really understand very much or have any real knowledge at all. How educated is a computer whiz who can solve the most complicated problem but who needs help getting a candy bar out of a vending machine?

For almost two decades I have argued that our society trains rather than educates, and that training is limited

237

whereas being educated is limitless. EDUCATION IS REALLY KNOWING AND UNDERSTANDING AND BEING ABLE TO APPLY OR EFFECTIVELY TRANSFER THAT "REAL KNOWLEDGE" OR THAT "REAL LEARNING" TO OTHER SITUATIONS. KNOWLEDGE OF YOURSELF, OF COURSE, IS PRIMARY. You must know who you are before you can really know what anything else is or where it belongs. For example, driving a car does not mean that you are educated. All it means is that you have been trained to perform a function. SIMPLY STATED, TRAINING IS BEING TAUGHT HOW TO DO SOMETHING, WHEREAS EDUCATION IS A PROCESS BASED ON REAL UNDERSTANDING.

A sad fact is that in this country we do so many things wrong because we do them for the wrong reasons. And we do them for the wrong reasons because we are not educated enough to understand exactly what we are doing. For instance, one of the biggest mistakes that we make is electing leaders who cannot lead either themselves or us. We choose them for the wrong reasons (not for educated reasons that will benefit us). And simply by possessing their positions they become the authorities or the experts and we all get stuck with mistakes made by people who never really knew anything in the first place. And the cycle goes on as others like themselves get placed in key positions. Each religiously supports the other's re-election so that no one who really does know anything will ever get a chance to straighten things out. Again, because we are not educated and because we do no think for ourselves, we accept everything the authorities tell us, no matter how ridiculous it is.

BLACK PEOPLE, ESPECIALLY, NEED A REAL EDUCATION SO THAT WE CAN KNOW WHO WE ARE. Being trained to believe that you are inferior because you are different or that white people are just naturally superior because they are white means that you are definitely not educated. Historically, controlling the slave's mind, making him believe what was best for the white man was best for him, was one way to maintain a slave. The other way was physical, guarding him, punishing him and keeping him fenced in, and white males who are the great, great grandsons of slave-holding ancestors are still using some of the same methods on their 20th century slaves. DESTROY YOUR MIND, ERASE YOUR HISTORY AND YOUR CULTURE AND TEACH YOU WHAT THEY WANT YOU TO KNOW AND THEY'VE GOT YOU. Practicing their culture and believing that you are not supposed to be in authority of yourself just proves how well trained you are, and how educated you are not.

JUST AS BLACK PEOPLE IN GENERAL NEED TO BE EDUCATED, HOWEVER, BLACK BOYS, ONE OF OUR MOST VALUABLE ASSETS, ESPECIALLY NEED THIS PRIZE. "Why should I go to school?" they ask. "I'm not going to get a job anyway. Most of the black men I know went to school, and where did it get them?"

Questions, or rather statements like these clearly express what is in the minds of young men today. Why are these young black boys seemingly going backward rather than forward? Again, one of the obvious answers is education, or rather the lack of it. IN A SYSTEM THAT TRAINS RATHER THAN EDUCATES, BLACK BOYS MORE THAN ANY OTHER GROUP ARE LIKELY TO GROW UP IN A FAMILY WITHOUT A FATHER OR A MALE ROLE MODEL WHO WILL HELP TO EDUCATE THEM IN LIFE AND THE PROPER WAY TO LIVE. Once more, a female role model is important, but black boys need to see successful images of themselves as well. Black girls, of course, learn to be women by watching their mothers, hopefully good mothers.

EDUCATION IS ONE OF THE SINGLE MOST IMPORTANT FACTORS IN BECOMING SUCCESSFUL, AND ATTITUDE IS BASED ON KNOWLEDGE JUST AS SURELY AS ACHIEVEMENT IS. Are young black males today so stupid that they cannot understand how important it is to learn to read and write and count? I really don't think so. Besides, we already know that they know how to count, maybe not academically or formally, but they can surely count their own money, no matter how high the numbers go. And surviving on the streets of dangerous urban areas is as demanding as staying alive in a battle zone, surely requiring the ability to think, to project, to anticipate and to adapt. Which is more difficult, surviving in school where there is help, or out on the streets where you may be on your own? THESE YOUNG BLACK BOYS ARE SMART, AND THEY HAVE "MOTHER WIT," BUT WHAT THEY LACK IS A REAL EDUCATION.

Again, education is understanding, and a transfer of learning and knowledge, and black boys believe that they are doing just that for themselves, having been abandoned by the system. Recognizing their own incompatibility and their own low self-esteem, black boys are trying to validate themselves by proving that they can handle themselves on the outside physically rather than academically in a school somewhere. BLACK BOYS WHO HAVE LEARNED TO ADJUST TO THEIR ENVIRONMENT ON THE STREETS NEED TO BE PROPERLY EDUCATED SO THAT THEY CAN ADAPT TO LIFE. The system that exists for them now is as unnatural as eating mustard greens with a spoon.

BLACK BOYS IN AMERICA REALIZE THAT EDUCATION IS NOT FOR THEM, AT LEAST NOT EDUCATION AS WE KNOW IT. Why go to school to be taught calculus when society has already shown you daily that you will never be a geologist or an architect? Since this training does not apply to him, why should he waste his time? School is simply Eurocentric indoctrination for African American citizens. FURTHER, WHY SHOULD HE SIT IN CLASS ALL DAY LISTENING TO THINGS THAT HAVE ABSOLUTELY NOTHING TO DO WITH HIM? How interested would you be in hearing about somebody else's family tree day after day after day after day after day for years and years and years and years? Sure, white students are supposed to enjoy hearing about themselves, but are we? Would they want to hear about black people every day, all day for at least 12 of the first 17 years of their lives? BLACK BOYS NEED TO LEARN TO READ AND WRITE ABOUT THEMSELVES AND TO UNDERSTAND RELEVANT THINGS ABOUT "WHO THEY ARE."

And "who they are" is something that they should have known from their earliest days. We all need to know who we

240

are and a good place to begin is at the beginning. BLACK BOYS WHO ARE PRESSURED THE MOST SHOULD START TO DEVELOP A HEALTHY SENSE OF SELF FROM THE START. They need to be educated like little personalities with minds and not merely taught like little wooden Indians. Most of all they too should especially stop being given worthless wooden nickels.

Already they have been taught that even if they go to school, and when they make good grades, if they are lucky enough to find a summer job it will be sweeping floors or working in a fast-food restaurant, while a white boy will have a clean job that pays three times as much working for his uncle. . .That is the education that the black boy gets.

OUR EDUCATORS, WHO ARE MANDATED TO EDUCATE, ACTUALLY STRIVE TO ASSIMILATE. AND WHILE THERE IS BASICALLY NOTHING WRONG WITH ASSIMILATION, EDUCATION AND NOT ASSIMILATION SHOULD COME FIRST. When correct, education itself may foster assimilation. Another important point to be considered is that a young person today is exposed to much more than young people were 50 or even 10 years ago.

Bill is a 17 year old black male who is an "A-B" student. He intends to pursue a degree in pharmacy after completing high school. Bill lives with his mother Christine and a younger brother Aaron in a comfortable middle-class neighborhood. He works evenings as a delivery person for his neighbor's courier service, he has his own car, and he has been dating his girlfriend Jennifer, a college freshman, for the past two years. Bill is very serious about his future but becomes frustrated and angry when he talks about his teachers. Like many young people today he feels that educators are not educated. He believes that a profession that was once occupied by knowledgeable, responsible adults who were cultured, aware, who maintained discipline and who cared is now staffed by personnel whose aim is to train and not to educate. Because of these ill equipped "training teachers," there is chaos, confusion and abject failure. BLACK BOYS

CAPABLE OF LEARNING DO NOT APPRECIATE BEING TRAINED TO JUMP THROUGH SOMEONE ELSE'S HOOP.

Again, "those who do not know their history are doomed to repeat it," and black boys who are smart enough to know they are being treated differently and that something is missing, are reacting. Realizing that something just is not right, they reject authority today just as their ancestors did as slaves. EDUCATION, A REAL EDUCATION, DOES NOT BELONG TO BLACK BOYS TODAY JUST AS FREEDOM DOES NOT BELONG TO THEM, AND THEY KNOW IT. They see the whole "school experience" for what it is, an instrument of pacification -- theirs. And just where do those ideas come from? Where else, from many of their teachers of course, simply by watching them. Black boys today have about a 1 in 684 chance of becoming a doctor but a 1 in 45 chance of becoming a drug abuser. And there are more black males in jail than there are in college. When society discourages them from learning to read it is really discouraging them from learning to think or to succeed.

In today's schools it is hard to find black male teachers. WOMEN RUN THE SCHOOLS AND "THE SHOW" AND MOST OF THE MEN WHO ARE AROUND ARE USUALLY NOT HELD IN VERY HIGH ESTEEM. This is what young black males see and they want to have nothing to do with it. Most black male teachers are not respected by them. They are viewed as losers who are stuck in education with women because they are weaklings who could not do any better. Many times females themselves are thought to be frustrated old hens, whether they are married or not. At any rate, young black boys do not see either one of these role models as one of them. Sometimes those men who do rise from the ranks to become administrators do so not so much because of their great prowess as leaders, but because they have gone to the classes just like the women have, and they have received their M.A.'s and their Ph.D.'s, and because they are black men who will not rock the boat.

WELL, WEAK BLACK MALE ADMINISTRATORS BECOME THE SYSTEM TOO, WHILE BLACK BOYS SEE THAT STRONG, INDEPENDENT BLACK MEN WHO DO GIVE A DAMN, AND WHO DO UNDERSTAND, AND WHO DO CARE ABOUT THEM, GO ABSOLUTELY NOWHERE. And just how do they view these weak black male administrators? Believe it or not, as today's Uncle Toms who want to make things better for themselves by sucking up to "the boss." As far as they are concerned, these black teachers and administrators are just like the house servants from the old days who had been around white people so much they started thinking like them, or at least that's what they thought they were doing. They believe that these slippery, two-faced Uncle Toms are trying to teach them to be good little house niggers who will never own their own homes or be responsible for themselves.

Black boys feel that they are being sold out by corrupt "nigger traders," who want them to want what white people want, what is not for them anyway. "Be like white people, you know, speak like them, act like them, and you'll be alright." No way. UNCLE TOM IS NOT THE BLACK MAN THEY WANT RESURRECTED FOR THEIR ROLE MODEL.

There is yet another very serious reason for the failure of education and problems that black males are having. In the past, when education was valued, good families always wanted their sons to have opportunities and an education, so they made sacrifices to send them to college. These eager young men who wanted to make their families proud of them did well, and went into the best field that was open to them, education. They were strong young men who wanted to help others as they had been helped, and to give something back in some small way. These days things have changed however, and for many reasons strong black men are choosing other careers. Unfortunately, many of the black males going into education today were the same boys who actually were weak in grade school, soft men who really have taken the easy way out.

WEAK BLACK MALES (PUSILLANIMOUS MALES) WHO HAVE BECOME ADMINISTRATORS DO NOT WANT THOSE WHO ARE UNLIKE THEM (STRONG BLACK MEN WHO ARE REMINDERS OF THEIR WEAKNESS) AROUND THEM. A weak ineffective male is not a real man, and young black boys who are instinctively aggressive know that too. They also know that adults who are not meeting their responsibilities are pointing the finger at them, and while they may be causing some of the problems, they are not at the root of that problem.

IT IS THE PROCESS AND NOT THE PRODUCT THAT IS THE REAL PROBLEM. If you are using fresh fruit to bake an apple pie and the pie burns because you leave it in the oven too long, is it the apples' fault that the pie was ruined? Strong black boys need strong black males to keep them in check and no man at all is probably better than a weak man. In fact, even a white man, who is viewed as powerful, may be better than a weak black man. Even if he is a homosexual white male, he may be respected more because educators are still respected by whites who benefit from education, and because the decision to teach was his choice. The white male's "self-concept" is still intact. WITHOUT REAL MEN TO EDUCATE YOUNG BLACK MALES, THE CYCLE IS IRREVERSIBLE.

Also, the same "I'm in charge now" female attitude that they had seen outside the school had followed them inside too. Black males do not believe that these women who are trying to run things by being power brokers even know who they are or what they are doing. They have already made up their minds that these women are not going to order them around. "Push Mr. Jones around if you want to, he's a prick, anyway, but don't try it with me." Some women are causing problems everywhere and they are so busy carrying their pedestals around from place to place that they cannot even see it. (In fact, some of these same bossy women may be responsible for problems that these boys have as men later in life with women.)

244

It is estimated that only 6% of the classroom teachers in the United States are black males, and who knows what percent of that number are real men? There is a direct correlation between that number and young black boys' lack of achievement. AND ALL THE WHILE SOCIETY MUDDLES ALONG, WHILE EGOTISTICAL, SELF-SERVING TEACHERS AND ADMINISTRATORS MISDIRECT THEIR CHILDREN'S LIVES, APATHETICALLY AND HAPHAZARDLY HALF TRAINING RATHER THAN EDUCATING THEM.

The blame is not all the academicians however, because responsible parents have a responsibility to see to it that their children are treated responsibly. IN EFFECT, BAD TEACHERS AND BAD ADMINISTRATORS CAN DO NO MORE DAMAGE OR HARM THAN PARENTS ALLOW THEM TO DO. If the school systems are being properly run by qualified personnel, why are they falling apart? And if they are not being properly managed, what have you and your neighbors done lately to correct the problem? PARENTS OCCASIONALLY VISIT THE SCHOOLS, BUT OUR CHILDREN ARE OUR SCHOOLS, AND THEY KNOW BETTER THAN WE DO WHAT IS NOT RIGHT. Our children are tired of watching adults who do not care about them play games with their lives.

Speaking of games, as an artist and an art teacher in the New Orleans school system, I noticed that the same black students were systematically being placed in my art classes, in a home economics class next door and in other courses such as music, woodworking and special education. At the same time, a disproportionate number of my white students with influential or wealthy parents were being enrolled in honors and advanced classes. What I did not know at that time, however, was that this was a national trend and that black students were also more likely to be expelled or suspended. Realizing that not being enrolled in college preparatory courses was severely hampering my students' chances of being enrolled in college and succeeding, I immediately addressed the issue with my principal and the school board. As a result, there were scheduling changes and a black administrator was placed on the scheduling committee to make sure black boys and girls were given "real" classes too.

AND EVEN WHEN THE BLACK STUDENTS DO MAKE IT TO COLLEGE, THEIR CHANCES OF SUCCEEDING ARE STILL SLIMMER THAN MOST BECAUSE OF CURRENT TRENDS TO WIPE OUT HISTORICALLY BLACK COLLEGES AND UNIVERSITIES. While less than 17% of black college students attend black schools, black schools produce a majority of the black graduates. Black students in these schools see this as a sense of genuine concern about their futures. BLACK COLLEGES AND BLACK UNIVERSITIES HAVE ALWAYS BEEN INSPIRING FOR SERIOUS BLACK STUDENTS. But today, in the wake of desegregation efforts, these schools are being pressured more than ever. Whites want to either hang on to the white schools, or put white administrators, faculty members and business managers over the public black schools, ultimately turning them white and using whatever excuse they can find to discredit black administrators.

And a white administration generally means more white students, which means higher admission standards, which means higher tuition, which means fewer blacks attending and fewer blacks graduating, which ultimately means a smaller black professional workforce, and fewer blacks who can really make a difference or who are close enough to see what is really going on.

A national survey that was recently conducted has shown that black men and black women pay more for a new car when they buy one, in excess of $1,000 in the case of most black women, and I'm sure the same is true in housing and just about every thing else. It is no small wonder that no matter how hard they work, black Americans can never seem to get ahead, or even catch up. WITHOUT EDUCATED PROFESSIONALS IN KEY POSITIONS TO PROTECT OUR INTERESTS, WHITE AMERICA WILL USE YET ANOTHER STRATEGY TO WALK ALL OVER US AND TELL US THAT IT IS OUR FAULT.

WAY, WAY BACK WHEN, EVEN BEFORE THE CIVIL WAR, BLACKS, BOTH SLAVES AND FREE MEN, DREAMED OF AN EDUCATION. In addition to being free, learning to read and to write was the salvation they prayed for. In the north, free black children attended schools opened by black people when they could not attend public schools. Sometimes whites even admitted blacks to their private schools. Some states opened separate schools as more and more blacks migrated to their regions, but the schools were not large enough to hold all of the black youngsters who wanted to learn. (Is it not interesting that at least 40% of the black children today drop out of school and that at least 40% of the people in the United States never read books.) Southerners who hired tutors for their children had little interest in public education anyway, and passed laws prohibiting blacks from learning to read and write. But they learned anyway, being secretly taught by black teachers and white teachers alike, and in 1826 John Russwurm became the first black man to graduate from a college in America. AND BLACK BOYS AND BLACK GIRLS WHO DO NOT KNOW THAT THEIR AFRICAN AND AFRICAN-AMERICAN ANCESTORS VALUED EDUCATION SO HIGHLY, DO NOT WANT TO LEARN.

BECAUSE OF PROBLEMS LIKE CHRONIC UNDERACHIEVEMENT, APATHETIC ADMINISTRATORS, DISCIPLINE AND EVEN VIOLENCE, MANY TEACHERS, INCLUDING BLACK MEN AND BLACK WOMEN, HAVE ABANDONED THESE YOUNG BLACK BOYS. Believing that these young men are dangerous (which some of them may well be) many teachers either cannot or will not challenge them, and the female principal or the pusillanimous male who has come up through the ranks will not either, so that there are only a few responsible adults left to manage the schools and their many situations.

WITH LITTLE SUPPORT AND EVEN LESS RESPECT, TALENTED TEACHERS WHO WANT TO TEACH YOUNG BLACK CHILDREN ARE GETTING BURNED OUT AND ABANDONING EDUCATION. By the year 2000, 40% of the students in

247

elementary and secondary schools will be black and less than 5% of that number will be black male instructors, which translates into even fewer role models, gigantic identity problems and even more resentment and hostility.

Some dedicated black teachers do care, however, and they have not given up yet. Realizing that these boys and girls need to know who they are, they are trying to help them by telling them more about their ancestors as they sympathetically attempt to socialize and educate them.

A VIVID PARALLEL TO THE PLIGHT OF OUR SCHOOL SYSTEMS IS A PROUD, PRANCING ROOSTER IN THE BARN YARD. IF HE IS BUSILY STRUTTING AROUND BUT THE HENS AREN'T LAYING ANY EGGS, THE FARMER AT LEAST HAS ENOUGH SENSE TO CORRECT THE MATTER.

It is important, if not urgent, that concerned adults begin to step forward and influence the direction of education in this country. Obviously our system is broken and it desperately needs to be fixed, immediately. We must stop trusting and relying on a system that does not work to save our children, even if the alternative is to open our own schools and facilitate our own goals. Today schools still tend to be white oriented even though proportionately white students do not attend public schools. Japanese students make our kids look like imbeciles, as do Asian, European and even African boys and girls.

IF AMERICANS, ESPECIALLY BLACK AMERICANS, ARE TO SURVIVE, WE MUST STOP TAKING ANY MORE OF THOSE ROTTING "WOODEN NICKELS." Our kids are being outsmarted while they are busy thinking that they are the ones doing the outsmarting. They may be the ones who are shooting hooky from life, but the biggest sucker of all is us. OUR CHILDREN ARE GETTING LOST SIMPLY BECAUSE WE ARE NOT EDUCATING OURSELVES AND BECAUSE WE ARE NOT EDUCATING THEM.

CONCLUSION

What is Goodpussy and what makes black men tick? Hopefully these questions have been answered for you. But there was still another issue. Why are black relationships falling apart?

"In Search of Goodpussy" is the story of today's black man and his quest to live the all-American dream. The reality is that many blacks in America are living a horrible nightmare. After three and one-half centuries we are still the "others" and the "strangers." Many whites still have an aversion to our darker skin and our customs are still too different for them to accept. Our color continues to be a sign of our past and a barrier to our advancement. The "good guys" still wear white while the "bad guys" wear black.

As predicted in the 1800's, the black man is still standing basically in the same place. As predicted, he cannot feed his family and his children are dying, one way or another. Some have advanced but most have regressed. Many are homeless and destitute, our families (those that remain) are increasingly dysfunctional and our personal relationships are collapsing all around us. A large segment of the black community has indeed become "vicious and degraded." But poverty usually leads to misconduct. Whenever people experience continued severe depravation, you will find crime, disease, juvenile delinquency, drugs, illiteracy, destruction, filth, low self-esteem and hopelessness. These are natural consequences when large numbers of people are forced to do without. They become less civilized and often react with self-hate. The black man's environment is deliberately being engineered to destroy him. Black men are becoming an endangered species and their sons are not expected to live as long as they have. As President George M. Bush proudly announced during the war against Iraq, "America is on course."

249

Overall, black Americans still do not think. We still do not listen. We still hang out on Saturday nights. We still eat too much. We still buy expensive clothes and jewelry and we are still preoccupied with doing "the wild thing." We still live in slums and we still break things.

After three and one-half centuries we still do not know who we are and we still do not know why we are here or where we are going. Black men who get no respect are not able to maintain either themselves, their relationships or their families. We know, only too well, what the white man has done to keep us down, but how have we helped him to do so?

I believe that the answer to that question is historical, too. Let us suppose that, hypothetically, rather than following Dr. Martin Luther King, Jr., our parents had listened to the teachings of the honorable Malcolm X, instead.

But historically, black people have always revered their spiritual leader. The preacher was the epitome of learning and morality. Originally, the white man had ministered to the black man, but he was soon replaced by the black man chosen by the master, still preaching the same old message. So historically, black men became leaders by protecting the white man's interests. "Obey your masters and you will be rewarded later on, in heaven."..."Later on, in heaven."

In Sunday school the slave was told to be nice to "massa and missus"; don't be mean and work hard. Your masters and mistresses are God's overseers and if you disobey them God himself will punish you in the next world. Historically, believing in God was one of the things that had saved the slave, but the white man was using religion to brainwash him into being passive and submissive.

With all due respect to the late Dr. Martin Luther King, he was a minister, not a psychologist or an historian. He did his best with what he had. He simply did not have enough. He led us valiantly, but we still needed something else or we would not be as messed up as we are today. I believe that Dr. King imminently knew who we were, but he

250

did not have sufficient information to adequately consider the true nature of the Anglo Saxon, which is to enslave and to kill. He did not know who they were.

Dr. King, a benevolent Baptist minister who was the son of a Baptist minister, could not appreciate the Anglo Saxon gut resolve to keep everything for himself and leave nothing for the Negro. He also could not appreciate how one race could be so driven (unchristian like) to destroy another race. Beyond his middle class religious upbringing, his privileged education at Morehouse and his ordered life with God-fearing Christians, how much "real" living had Dr. King done? (I raise the question only to get at the truth, because I too came up in the church - the New Zion Baptist Church where Dr. King had helped to found the Southern Christian Leadership Conference - and not until I had lived in the real world did I begin to fully understand what life was all about.) Dr. King's ideas were based on honorable ideals, but not "gut" reality.

Dr. King and his followers were principally God fearing people who took pride in being law abiding. But laws are nothing more than rules made up by people in charge to keep everybody else in line. Being law abiding just means that you are good at following white people's rules. After all, how many laws (rules) have black people made? And if we do make up any how many white people will follow them? When black people do not like laws they are disobedient. When white people do not like laws they change them, especially when those law may help blacks.

Black people have always wanted freedom, but if we had gotten it when honest Abe Lincoln signed the Emancipation Proclamation in the 1860's, why were we going back for it again in the 1960's. History itself is proving that if you are given something called freedom and you have not fought to get it, it can be taken back whenever your benefactors change their minds. We had it in the 1860's and lost it in the 1880's. We had it in the 1960's and lost it in the

1980's. Is history repeating itself or is there some other reason why blacks seem to be in the same place? Or, as my wonderful grandmother would say, "It's just the same old soup warmed over again."

Courageous black slaves who were willing to stand up for their rights as human beings started a job that no one seems to be able to finish. White America's dream was for an all-white America, an ambitious goal many still hold dear. Our continued struggle, and our fight, if necessary, should have been for independence rather than an illusive concept called freedom. After all, even the whites had predicted a race war, seeing that as the only way the black man would ever be able to get fair treatment in America and be able to stand on his own.

Even when the colonists fought the British, after the Revolutionary War they signed the Declaration of Independence, not the Declaration of Freedom. And America has not gone back to England once to ask for independence again. So, they knew what was important.

Freedom is too vague and too nebulous. What exactly is freedom anyway but the ultimate perceptual distortion? Unfortunately, Dr. King's expectations were unrealistic. The only way the black man could **permanently** stop being pushed around was to shove back.

Ida B. Wells, a courageous black female journalist, had boldly done so much to advance the cause of the black race during the 1800's, that she was told she would be hanged if she ever went back to Memphis, Tennessee. It was she who had convinced hundreds of blacks to leave town so that they would not be murdered, an action which terrified the white business community. Ms. Wells wrote "For the Negro was famous then, as now, for spending his money on fine clothes, furniture, jewelry, and pianos and other musical instruments, to say nothing of good things to eat." It was also Ida B. Wells who had traced charges against hundreds of black men, women and children who had been lynched, discovering that most of them were indeed innocent of all charges against them. Ms. Wells, who carried a gun, said that "A Winchester rifle should have a place of honor in every home." Ms. Wells said, "When the white man...knows he runs as great a risk of biting the dust every time his Afro-American victim does, he will have greater respect for Afro-American life."

Malcolm X also supported our right to self-defense against racist terror. He argued that we were controlled by people who believed in segregation, discrimination, and racism. He said that "We do not judge you because you are white. We judge you because of what you do and what you practice." Malcolm X believed the day the white man turns the other cheek - you do. He believed that the principle of non-violence was against the first law of nature, self-preservation. Malcolm also said that the idea of non-violence was so ludicrous that it made everybody who was against the black man deliriously happy. He believed that the Negro would never be respected until he reacted as other normal human beings do.

That submission is virtuous is a definite fallacy. Remember, people do walk on door mats and if they don't the next person coming along will. Instead of turning the other cheek, we must begin to defend ourselves. Malcolm X also said that "America practices violence and wants us to be non-violent." He suggested that we be intelligent.

Currently, there is a move afoot for a national gun control policy. Historically, the white man has never wanted the black man armed -- not even during the American Revolution, the Civil War, World War I or even World War II. After all, a white soldier might step in front of a black man with a gun and become a casualty of "friendly fire," or a black pilot might accidently drop his bombs on a white platoon. It was alright for the white man to have a gun, but seldom the black man. Even with gun control legislation, criminals will still have weapons and white people will still have police protection or friends in government who will help them find loopholes. But how will you protect yourself and your family? If the police are racist and the government is racist, who will defend you? With gun control laws you may be the only fool standing there empty-handed, waiting for help to show up. Besides, white people do not need guns in their neighborhoods, but you may well need one in yours. Remember, if the white man said something was good, it was probably just the opposite.

What we need is independence, including the ability to independently defend ourselves and independently protect our property. In fact, protecting ourselves and our families should be at the top of our list, along side education, learning to think for ourselves. We need the same thing white men need. Sure, they would give us so called freedom, but never independence. Whenever black men become too prosperous or too ambitious, or whenever competition seems imminent, the white man always resorts to violence to keep the black man in his place. Today, they have even tricked and manipulated us into using violence against ourselves.

Black men understood that they needed to determine their own priorities and shape their own destiny. They needed to be able to take aggressive, affirmative responsibility for themselves. White men have always believed that "any tendency of one member of the system to assert themselves against the masters threatened the whole," and they would never permit that. Again, independence and not freedom is the key. That is why even today Asian Americans, Hispanics, Europeans, and every other race has been able to do what the black man in America has not.

That old Negro hymn goes:
Free at last
Free at last
Thank God almighty,
I'm free at last.

254

Today it should be:

Independent at last
Independent at last
Thank God almighty
I'm independent at last.

In the 1960's we had two choices, Dr. Martin Luther King, Jr., a Baptist minister and Malcolm X, a radical Black Muslim. Our parents were still basically intellectually unsophisticated, moral country people rather than secular people who were open to change. Of course, they would naturally follow tradition and listen to their speaker, their leader, their minister who was an honored, trusted and respected friend.

Malcolm X, the Black Muslim, represented the same thing for them that they had been to the whites. He was the "stranger," the "other," and Malcolm X was saying fight back, something they had been brainwashed all their lives not to do. Malcolm was also saying let's do something drastic now, while the black man's docile nature was anything but reactionary.

But the Reverend Martin Luther King, Jr. uttered four words that sealed the course of history, and with them the black man's fate. Dr. King said, "I have a dream" and good black Christians familiar with Sunday School lessons and bible school lessons remembered Joseph with his coat of many colors, his ability to interpret dreams and his gift of prophecy. These "country people" literally took that to mean that he actually had a dream, that Martin Luther King had the gift too. In 1990 the inscription on Dr. King's monument in New Orleans had to be changed because it also read, "I had a dream." Dr. King also said, "I have seen the promised land," and black people stopped what they were doing and started looking for it, too, over the next hill, and the next hill and the next hill. Remember, too, that the hereafter (promised land)

255

was what blacks had been brainwashed to believe since the beginning. Forget about now. Wait for tomorrow.

But let's suppose we had gone the other way. What might have been different? Well, Dr. King stressed freedom while Malcolm X was a proponent of independence. Unlike Dr. King, Malcolm did not grow up around good church folk. He had grown up around white people. He had been a pimp, a drug dealer and an ex-convict. Malcolm had lived the "real side" of life and he knew who white people were. Suppose we had listened to him and fought for our independence rather than accept "hand-outs" under the guise of freedom. Secure people do not need hand-outs and independent people do not need to ask for freedom. The whites who had expected us to do what they would do under the same set of circumstances had predicted a race war. They knew themselves better than we did. There was no war, so obviously they would have done things differently.

If the blacks following Martin Luther King, Jr. were not going to do anything, and the Black Muslims would not do anything because they were religious rather than political, then white America's worse nightmare would never happen, no race war. Militant blacks belonged to the Black Muslims, so Malcolm X said that Elijah Muhammad had an understanding with the federal government not to interfere with the Black Muslim Movement. If anything had happened to the Muslims, the volatile blacks in the movement would have switched over to the Civil Rights Movement and walked all over Martin Luther King, Jr. and non-violence.

But let's suppose that Malcolm's dream for independence had become our dream. We are only 12%. of the population so we can never be equal - to 88%. Equality is another cruel perceptual distortion blacks have blindly bought into as well. But if we were independent we could at least have our own 12%, which we do not have today. Spending our three hundred billion dollars a year on ourselves would make us independent. Independence, and not freedom could make us equal, at least in terms of personal security. Independence could give us freedom. If we had our own, we would not have to wait for them to give us anything, or not to give it to us. But independence would mean competition and breaking up white America's monopoly of our three hundred billion annual dollars. America already owes the black man over 350 years in back pay plus damages for pain and suffering. When and where do we collect?

We could have our own books, our own private schools if necessary, and our own banks. We would have 12% of the real wealth, 12% of the jobs, 12% of the real estate and 12% of the elected officials representing us. We would know who we are and we would support each other because we would have confidence in each other. Black men would no longer be the "vicious and degraded" class and those old perceptual distortions would disappear.

Being successful and independent we would have healthy self-esteem. Because we would feel good about ourselves (having our own), relationships between black men and black women would be working out rather than falling apart. Because our relationships would be healthy, black families would not be dysfunctional (at least no more so than any other race). Because our families would be fulfilling their four universals, our children, their children and their children's children could be as happy and as healthy as any other children are.

> What I am saying is that pursuing freedom rather than independence is one of the main reasons why black relationships are in trouble.

But why have black people taken the wrong fork in the road? Besides being the reason why we are where we are today, what are the other implications? Again, that's simple, too.

> If I always do
> What I always did
> I'll always get
> What I always got.

If black people want different results it's time to start doing things differently. There can be no meaningful progress without conflict. It is time to face the truth, deliberately, aggressively and intelligently. But where did we go wrong and how do we begin to change the mistakes of the past?

The answer came to me in a revelation that was probably one chance in ten billion. I had fallen asleep trying to understand what I had overlooked in my thinking about Martin Luther King, Jr. and his views, and Malcolm X and his views. I knew that Martin Luther King, Jr. was a theologian, but there was something that was still missing, and I couldn't quite put my finger on it.

When I woke up at 6:00 a.m. my television was on, and sitting in a chair, as if speaking directly to me, was a philosophy instructor talking about Aristotelian philosophy. According to Aristotle, progress is made by taking something that is confused and general, and moving to specific and precise knowledge. When the man on the screen said that a minister was a theologian but that a theologian was not a philosopher, I knew that was it. I had found the answer. In explaining the difference between theology and philosophy he said that theology is based on revealed knowledge (as in the Bible) while philosophy is based on facts that exists in the present domain. Philosophy takes general knowledge and asks questions (specifies) while theology or religion simply accepts something that has already been said. Philosophy investigates. It looks for answers. Religion does not. It accepts answers.

Our whole black focus is rooted in theology (listening to our ministers) rather than philosophy (looking for answers).

Martin Luther King, Jr., a minister, had a dream, but he had no comprehensive plan because he was not a philosopher. Malcolm X had a comprehensive plan, but he was not a Christian. While every successful culture is based on philosophy or an ideology, African-American culture alone is not. Instead of trying to find real answers for ourselves, we are still being force-fed somebody else's ideas, and that somebody else often doesn't really know any more than we do.

Protestant ministers may be learned men, but they are theologians, not philosophers. A lawyer is a learned man, but you would not allow him to operate on you if you needed surgery. A minister is more like a general practitioner. Religion is the subject he trained for and specializes in.

Aggressive young black males do not go to school. They do not go to church either. Is it possible that today's black church, like the Catholic church, is no longer getting the right message out? Why is there no more progressive, creative, relevant contemporary thinking - since they helped to get us registered to vote? Is today's black church comfortable resting on its laurels, and its reputation? Nothing but three hundred plus years of being free on the other side gets to be just a little bit tired sometimes.

Black people need to take their heads out of the sand and stop hiding behind their bibles. How much longer are we going to wait for the Lord to deliver and for the Lord to provide? Once a week, every Sunday, black men and women - boys and girls go back to church for more "do nothing" brainwashing. They sing old Negro meters like "I'm Going Home" and "Swing Low Sweet Chariot." But what about here and now? If new ideas were science the black man in America would still be living in the Dark Ages waiting for someone to turn on the light, or sitting on his front porch waiting for something to happen.

Martin Luther King, Jr. got all the answers (revealed knowledge) and gave his answers to us (revealed knowledge). That was all we needed to know. Now all we have to do is wait. We made Dr. King our hero - our savior (unfairly placing all the responsibility on his shoulders, but what about our own shoulders?) Everybody started imitating him, accepting his ideas as the only answer, and we stopped searching for others. The puzzle was already solved. (Incidentally, the white man made Dr. King our hero too. Why?)

And how have our leaders helped us? What have they taught us or prepared us for? Sure, they may be doing just fine, but what about the rest of us? Malcolm X said that hand picked leaders should not say look how much progress we are making, but look how much progress I am making. What have black leaders done for you lately?

Today black people must truly understand that it is not their assigned destiny to be the world's misfits. Do we really believe in our hearts that God meant for us to live the way we do? In 1760, Samuel Hopkins, a Newport minister wrote of the Negro that "we have been used to look on them in a mean, contemptible light: and our education has filled us with strong prejudices against them, and led us to consider them, not as our brethren, or in any degree on a level with us; but as quite another species of animals, made only to serve us and our children; and as happy in bondage as in any other state." Is that how we see ourselves, too?

Today's black man must develop a comprehensive plan that is compatible with today's realities - with realistic expectations. Most black leaders are neither intellectuals, scholars nor philosophers. They have no answers and do not know how to find them or solve problems. We must find intelligent, thinking leaders who are determined, dedicated and uncompromising in their resolve to serve as leaders who are not sitting around tables calmly discussing important issues, but strong men who are willing to jump up and down on top of the table, yelling to the top of their lungs if necessary, to be heard. The old soft-shoe song and dance hasn't gotten the rest of us anywhere. We want different results. We need

260

men who will do things differently. Sure, today's leaders may ride in limousines and eat expensive lunches, but the rest of us are locked outside under the house. He cannot be one of us trying to be one of them. And we cannot win by playing their games. The old way of doing things, The Civil Rights Movement, with its emphasis on integration, actually underminded and discouraged black self-reliance.

Our leaders should be sincere, compassionate intellectuals who have come up through the ranks - wise, caring men who know what life is really about. Average men who come up through the ranks become the average person who represents us. He is not our best and only our best will do. Every member of the Congressional Black Caucus should be a militant (crazed fool) for black people's rights, driven and committed to seeing us lose not one more inch. First there was **slavery**. Then there was **segregation**. Now there is **separation**. Our leaders must be our voices, our eyes and our ears, protecting us from the horrors of the **three S's.**

Recently, during the political campaign for President of the United States, it struck me as being curious that some white candidates kept trying to out-do each other in declaring themselves the most conservative. Being a man of words, I wondered if there might be something I might be missing. Naturally, I went directly to the dictionary. For myself and for most black people I don't believe that we really gave it too much thought. It was no big deal. A conservative person was someone who was moderate while a liberal was a politician who was more progressive.

According to the Random House Dictionary of the English Language, conservation really means "the act of conserving: preservation from loss, injury, decay and waste." So white conservatives are promising their white constituents that they will preserve them from loss, injury, decay or waste. What precisely does that mean for black families or for black relationships? Who will protect us?

Both Martin Luther King, Jr. and Malcolm X did brilliant jobs, searching for the truth the best way they knew how. We did not do our job.

We Stopped Thinking.

We lazily accepted what these two great men had painfully discovered.

We Stopped Doing.

As a race of people we are suffering from learned helplessness, having convinced ourselves that there is no way out. Many of us have been down so long we can't even think about getting up. Yes, life has given us lemons, and many of them, but it's time to take those lemons and make lemonade. As is our nature, we were governed by a fine ideal, but our agenda was inappropriate and it's time for change. We still have no philosophy and no collective ideology. The time is long overdue, and for a comprehensive plan as well. Goodpussy (the American Dream) is not for blacks or any other minority. We must formulate our own dream. Black people do not even know that they do not know. And that is why after 373 years black America is still

"In Search of Goodpussy."

The black man's condition is part of an elaborate plan to control him. Because he is being deliberately held back, both his relationships and his life are in imminent danger. It is a true to life spy-thriller complete with intrigue, conspiracy and secret pass words. "In Search of Goodpussy" breaks that three and one half century old code so that the black man, the black woman and the black child may safely and successfully move on, no longer repeating the mistakes of the past.

EPILOGUE

And now, what about me? Well, I have a confession to make. I'm the man on the cover. For most of my life I have had it my way - the cars, the women, the excitement - I've had it all. The confession I now make is that unknown to most of my friends and associates, I have been so alone for so long that each day of my life was a struggle to stay alive. I have spent countless hundreds of days hoping that it would all be over with because I found myself having no purpose in life, with nothing to live for. If you didn't believe the old saying that "You can't judge a book by looking at the cover," then take another look at the cover of this book. That man on the cover, me, has been in excruciating pain for most of his life. The title of my book addresses itself to my own mission in life as well and anyone else's. Because of my own unbearable pain, however, I knew that I must find a way to throw myself a life raft before I threw myself overboard. Even though I was surrounded by people, I often found myself alone and confused. I literally had thousands of friends and associates but few understood or could truly appreciate my unique perspective. Birds of a feather may flock together, but the flock I belonged to (being black) was going around in circles and driving me crazy. I knew that I marched to the beat of a different drum but I did not know why. "In Search of Goodpussy" has helped me to begin to understand who I am, what my problems were and why.

For much of my life I thought that my life was good, as lives go. I grew up in a working-class, black neighborhood with my mother and father, my two brothers and a younger sister. Even as a boy of 12 years of age I was already getting Goodpussy. For my birthday I received that shiny new red and white deluxe bicycle with white wall tires and chrome fenders that I had drooled over in copies of Boy's Life Magazine in the school library, even though the bicycle was five times more expensive than an ordinary bicycle. Other jealous boys had beaten me up while trying to steal it, and on another occasion classmates in elementary school had literally torn a silk jacket that I was wearing to shreds, simply because they didn't have one.

As a child, I was a cute little boy, fair skinned and quiet, and my mother was active in the school, so I suppose my teachers saw me as an ideal student. The very thing, however, that was getting me spoiled was also causing me problems as my classmates ridiculed me, denouncing me as a white negro. I didn't know it then, but I realize today that advantages bring with them disadvantages as well. Being cute as a boy, a young man, or even as an adult will gain you many advantages but cause you to lose many others. At any rate, during the summer my brothers, my sister and I spent leisurely days in the country on a lovely lane in Baton Rouge with my godparents having picnics and taking short trips. It was truly a great time to be a little boy.

As a teenager I attended a small exclusive high school with dedicated teachers and a reputation for excellence. And having a high I.Q. was one of the admission requirements. During the previous summer, my father had told me that it was time that I learned to work, and as a result, I had gotten an all-American job delivering newspapers in the evenings. By the age of 16 I had hit a Goodpussy Double Header. I had that shiny car that was even nicer than the cars my teachers were driving, and my girlfriend was one of the brightest and prettiest girls in the junior class. Armed with neck ties and arms full of books, my buddies and I were the academic elite going off to annihilate ignorance.

It was in high school that I had gotten my first taste of Plato, Socrates, Aristotelian philosophy and the Greek philosophy of a healthy body and a healthy mind. My instructors were scholars and philosophers who had sparked my desire to find answers. These included two brilliant brothers, the Blanchards, who were scientists, and my principal, Dr. Mack J. Spears, who became the first black

264

member and president of the public school system in New Orleans. He had later chuckled about telling my mother-in-law to be that I was a brilliant young man, and that I would have an exciting future. My minister, Reverend A. L. Davis, Jr., a personal friend of Dr. Martin Luther King, Jr., was a staunch civil rights leader who became New Orleans' first black city councilman. Uncle Jack, as we affectionately called him, had spent many hours as well, talking to me and explaining things to me. My high school assistant principal, Dr. Everett Williams is currently Superintendent of Schools in New Orleans while my seventh grade teacher, Jim Singleton is currently serving his fourth term as a city councilman.

Eminent sociologist, professor Emertus, Dr. Daniel H. Thompson, as well as surgeon and civil rights pioneer Dr. William Adams were role models and mentors, and countless other like themselves. They all helped me to know how important knowledge is and how important thinking is.

College life was just as kind to me, still more Goodpussy. I had gotten a shiny new customized Ford while attending Dillard University, a small prestigious black private college. My girlfriends and my future wife were some of the most attractive women on campus. I myself was revered as an artist, a thinker, and a rebel. My friends were all the important people, the smart, the popular, the beautiful and the well-to-do, like Fats Domino's daughter, Antoinette, who might drive a new Eldorado to school one day and a new Lincoln the next day. She wasn't allowed to drive the Rolls.

During my senior year I had gotten yet more of the American dream, more Goodpussy, a new Cutlass convertible. And when I drove into the brake tag station a mere 20 years old, the grown attendants had all actually stopped serving older adults to come and take a look at my car. America loves cars, remember, and women, and I knew just about all the campus beauties in New Orleans and then some.

By the age of 22 I was probably the youngest black male in New Orleans with his very own customized Corvette, and by 24 my wife and son and I owned another American dream, our own home near the lake.

Soon divorced, I was on my own with an unbroken line of women making their way to my door. At one point my neighbors had playfully joked about putting a traffic signal on my front lawn and buying my house to protect the neighborhood children. If women were the key to happiness, then I must surely have been delirious in paradise.

By the time I met my second wife, I was moving toward yet another shiny new Corvette and by the time we were married we had his and hers dream cars, resort property and still more Goodpussy, a gorgeous replica 1935 Auburn Boattail Speedster. (Incidentally, the Franklin Mint is now reproducing scale models of that famous car, the fantasy of rich playboys in the 1930's.) There were only two "baby Deusenbergs" in New Orleans and one of them was mine. Our wedding was one of the most elegant seen that year, and all the right people were there. Once again, everything was the best with beautiful women everywhere, many of them former girl friends of mine. This may all seem just too unreal to be true, but it was, and my second wife was one of the nicest and most coveted blonde-headed, green-eyed Catholic Creole women in New Orleans, a kind and gentle young woman who also happened to be listed in the national directory of "Outstanding Young Women of America."

Socially, I had planned elaborate parties, exotic trips, and community service projects for different organizations. I was director of some of this city's most elegant night spots, and I met and dated thousands of interesting and attractive women. In fact, there were times when I had been seeing as many as 40 women at one time using codes and calendars to keep track of who I had seen, who I had talked to on the telephone, and who was up next.

In 1982 I was divorced from my second wife and my life fell apart for the second time. The first time had been after my first marriage. I loved my wife but had somehow lost her without really knowing why, the real reason. For seven years we had been best friends and now she, too, was gone.

Believing that I had somehow been touched by the hand of providence, more Goodpussy, I eventually met and fell in love with a glamorous blonde-headed, blue-eyed white female who was even more striking and just as wonderful as my last wife had been. Their birth dates were even the same. We, too, loved each other very much, but broke up because after seven years I had never spoken to or even seen her father, and even our holidays had to be divided. During that time, however, I had also maintained several other very important relationships for years that were equally as hopeless. What I didn't understand at that time, however, was how really afraid I was of being alone.

To the outside world I lived a charmed life, but for myself I knew that something just wasn't right. Of course I seemed to have it all. I did all the things most people can only fantasize about, high speed racing on the interstate at 130 miles an hour, formal candle-lit dinners with exotic women, private night flights in jazzed-up airplanes, elegant parties on luxurious yachts, countless parties with superstars - I did it all. Women loved me while men envied me. Of course some women and some men hated me too. If I met 100 women, I could be with 90 of them out of that 100. The other 10 I just wrote off as bad timing, poor opportunity, or devotion to a husband or a boy friend. Married, single, young or old, it really didn't matter. Even as a youngster in school, I had had crushes on two of my teachers. As a boy I thought that they were two of the most perfect women I had ever seen. As a grown man I still lived another of my dreams by making love to both of the women I had so idolized.

Because I have tried so hard to understand myself, I now understand why I did may of those things. One of the reasons was that I really did believe that it was my reward for being me. After all, I wasn't forcing anyone to do anything. I was a great son, a good person, old people loved me, young people idolized me, surely I had deserved all of this special treatment or I wouldn't be getting it. All those women who had tenderly surrendered themselves to me really just wanted to show me how dear I was to them.

As the moral person I believed myself to be, there were just certain things that I would not do. One of those things was to move to southern California and become a Gigolo. A wealthy love interest of mine had tried unconvincingly to talk me into leaving town to perform favors for some of her bored but well-to-do girl friends in Los Angeles. In return, I was to be guaranteed all the money I wanted, the car I wanted, and the living accommodations I wanted. Because I liked doing things my way and because I knew that that was one of the things that would break my mother's heart, I declined the offer. I enjoyed the game because it was my game.

If I watched television I saw women I had dated. At public functions there were always hundreds of people that I knew. I had even been in a movie, in my Auburn, supposedly being myself, a New Orleans playboy. In fact, one night at a dance, someone had called out my name and the woman standing in front of me turned, saying, "So you're the infamous Don Spears." Even at the elegant Saenger Theater on world famous Canal Street, I had been acknowledged. During the sold-out performance of a popular traveling play, a friend and I had been called upon stage, thanked for our support and given "the mike." Everywhere I turned there was Goodpussy, and from the outside looking in, my life had to be worth its weight in platinum.

But what was it really like? Certainly there were good times, but there were bad times as well. There were serious times, too. For instance, when the police thought that a jealous lover would attempt to kill me, they would check for a sniper before allowing me to take care of my own business, and I carried a gun everywhere I went - to the bakery, to the bathroom, and even to bed. I have seen women I know "set up" friends who were later found executed and stuffed in the trunks of expensive cars. When I said that I have probably seen more than you have, I meant just that.

But what about me? What about my life? Why? Only now can I say that there were many reasons why I did whatever I did. For one thing, even with all the women, the attention, and all the excitement, I have been alone for most of my life. I have grown to understand that I was reaching out for many women because I was afraid of being abandoned and left alone again. There was the wounded child in me, too, who had never resolved his own loneliness. For much of my life I had been seduced by the thrill of being placed on the pedestal, but found myself holding the stem and kneeling in the dust.

Generally, when I was with a women, my lovemaking was sincere, not so much because of the women but because I was having a Frontal Relationship with making love. Myself, and others like me, have occasionally found ourselves in different beds often wondering why we were there, and sometimes even wondering where we were. Women, even good women, love you and want to be there for you even though they sometimes know you will never be theirs. On several occasions married women have been on the brink of nervous breakdowns because we could not have a life together. I thought that I understood their pain because I truly was a caring man who just could not commit to one woman, no matter how much I loved her. And society didn't help me because it told me that my behavior was perfectly normal. But mixed messages will do just that, mix you up, as I had been for some time. Starting way back when, as a small boy, I began packing some "lonely baggage" that had been following me all through life. I did not realize that my father's drinking (he was a strong railroad man and a veteran) and his lack of openness, as well as my family's lack of affection were adversely affecting me, as were those solitary days of throwing papers and isolating myself to write. I had become the "Lone

269

Ranger," a bad son of a bitch. And people did whatever I wanted them to do, at least that's what I thought.

Society, culture and growing up black in America were the real villians. Like most black people, (both men and women) I did not know who I was or where I was really going. I thought I did, more than the rest. But I was playing follow the leader just like everybody else. I did not realize that a racist society was unscrupulously guiding my destiny and restricting my options, including the ability to have a meaningful relationship. Not until "In Search of Goodpussy" was I able to find the truth by putting "2+2" together. I was a product of my environment, and an external force was controlling me and pulling my strings, too. Like most black men, I did what I did because I thought I knew what I was doing. I thought I was in control. I know better now.

For much of my life I really was not personally aware of racism. In fact, I barely knew that I was black. Living a rather privileged kind of life, I got what I wanted, did what I wanted and had who I wanted. Not unitl my life took a downward spiral after 2 divorces, and being unemployed twice for long periods at a time, did I know what it was like not to have what I wanted and to be powerless. I realize now that knowing who I was (no matter what happened, and no matter what anybody else thought) was what was still driving me to succeed.

Like Malcolm X, I too am a scholar who has lived the real side of life. And that is why I have been able to painfully discover my own truth. A one-sided point of view will give you a one-sided distorted answer. You must live life to know life and I too had to live it to be able to understand it, to appreciate it and to know it. Like Eddie Murphy and Dan Akroid, I had to trade places. And like the wolves I had to fight to survive. Before "In Search of Goodpussy" I had been to paradise many, many times, but I had never been to me.

What I really wanted was someone to hold me, to love me, and to let me know that I was special and that they

270

wouldn't leave me. I didn't need another conquest for Don Juan. I needed a simple loving relationship, the kind many of my married friends had, children, grocery shopping on Saturdays, church on Sundays, someone special to call from the office to talk about little problems or happy thoughts. But the master (white) plan said that these things were not meant for me or any other black man.

I'm tired of being alone in my home. I'm tired of being alone in my car. I'm tired of being alone, period. I simply want what everybody else wants, what I started out with years ago when I got married for the first time, a good person who loved me and whom I loved, working and loving for our mutual well-being and happiness. What I want is love, devotion, support and respect with a dash of kindness, compassion and understanding added, from that very special lady in my life. And at the same time I am looking for a woman, the right woman, to spoil with love and devote the rest of my life to.

No, as of yet, I still haven't found it, but with God's help and just a bit more patience, I'm hopeful.

Thanks, and
Have A Great Goodpussy Day

Love God, Believe in Yourself, Adapt

271

CPSIA information can be obtained
at www.ICGtesting.com
Printed in the USA
BVHW072007100123
655899BV00003B/150